I0147693

The JOY *of* SOLITUDE

How to Reconnect with Yourself in an Overconnected World

Robert J. Coplan

SIMON & SCHUSTER

New York Amsterdam/Antwerp London
Toronto Sydney/Melbourne New Delhi

Simon and Schuster
1230 Avenue of the Americas
New York, NY 10020

First Simon & Schuster hardcover edition November 2025

Interior design by Wendy Blum

Manufactured in the United States of America

10 9 8 7 6 5 4 3 2 1

Library of Congress Cataloging-in-Publication Data is available.

ISBN 978-1-6680-5342-3
ISBN 978-1-6682-1922-5 (Int/Can Exp)
ISBN 978-1-6680-5341-6 (ebook)

Contents

Chapter 1

I Am Alone

Introducing Solitude

It turns out, all I needed to know about solitude I could have learned in kindergarten.

When I was a graduate student training as a developmental psychologist, my thesis research focused on the different ways that young children play at school. Consequently, I spent countless hours observing the day-to-day activities at preschools and kindergartens. I would show up each morning, armed with my clipboard and stopwatch, and spend the day sitting on one of those tiny child-sized chairs in the corner of the classroom, trying to be as unobtrusive as possible. Sometimes children would come up and ask what I was doing there or invite me to play. But after a while, everyone got used to me being there, and I just kind of disappeared into the background decor.

You can learn a lot about children just by watching. Most previous research about young children's social behaviors focused on how kids learned to get along well with others, which is a primary task of growing up. And, of course, getting along well with others remains a critical task for adults too. Historically, developmental psychologists have also been really concerned about the implications of children *not* getting along well with others. So, when they sat and observed young children together at school, they paid a lot of attention to episodes of conflict and aggression. This is not at all surprising, because these types of events are noisy and disrupt the classroom for everyone. And in the case of aggression, someone can get hurt. That is also why we pay so much attention to these same sorts of episodes among adults.

But I was interested in something different. I wanted to learn more about how children got along with *themselves*. For me, there was something fascinating about those children who played alone despite being around so many other potential playmates. So, I watched, and then I watched some more. Of course, every child is different. But after a while, some patterns began to emerge. I noticed that I could often classify the various children who tended to spend a lot of time alone at school into different specific types.

Some of these children seemed to be quite content to play quietly alone, building with blocks, drawing pictures, or doing other solo activities. When other children approached to invite them to play together, they often said yes. But when those social opportunities played themselves out, these children would happily return to their solitary activities.

Another type of child I noticed appeared more uneasy when alone. They would spend a lot of their time watching their classmates play but refrain from joining in. They certainly seemed interested in what other kids were doing and gravitated toward opportunities to make a social connection. However, the closer they got to the action, the more their growing discomfort seemed to push them back. So, they hovered on the edges of social circles, rarely moving past the periphery.

Yet other children who played alone were more boisterous. They tended to be somewhat socially clumsy and, as a result, were frequently rebuffed in their efforts to play with others. These children appeared frustrated when they ended up having to play by themselves. They did not want to be alone, and you could see it on their faces.

I also took note of the most outgoing children, who flitted around the room, constantly seeking social stimulation and engagement. In the rare moments when these children found themselves alone, it was clear that this was not a place they wanted to be. They quickly moved on to the next social thing.

At the time when I was conducting this research, I thought I already knew a lot about solitude. Today, I can look back and understand that not only did I not know a lot, but I had no idea how much I didn't know. It was all there right in front of me, though. The kindergarten classroom was the perfect microcosm for understanding the hidden complexities of solitude. These children were models of the many different relationships we can form with solitude. Maybe if I had looked harder, if I had opened myself up more to what these children might be thinking ("I wish someone would play with me" versus "What color should I paint this tree?") and feeling (sad versus content), I would have understood that these children's different experiences of being alone were key to understanding the complex and even paradoxical links between solitude and well-being.

I guess this would be a better story if, during one of those observation sessions, I had experienced a sudden revelation about the inner workings of solitude. But alas, that is not what happened. Nevertheless, it was those many hours spent just watching children play that first sparked my interest in the idea that solitude is more complicated than we might think. I didn't get my moment of true scientific revelation until almost thirty years later. But that is a story for later.

We Are All Alone

Solitude is a part of the human experience. According to the American Time Use Survey, at age fifteen, Americans spend an average of more than three hours per day alone. In our twenties and thirties, time spent in solitude rises to about four and a half hours per day. As we age, each passing year brings more time alone, and by age seventy, we average more than seven hours a day in solitude. Solitude is an experience we are all deeply familiar with. It is a fundamental aspect of everyday life. So, it is somewhat surprising that we know so little about it. And perhaps it is for that very reason that so many misconceptions, myths, and downright fallacies about solitude persist.

Solitude tends to evoke a wide range of reactions. In part, this is because each of us experiences it differently. As a result, we all form our own unique relationship with solitude. Relationships are tricky to predict and understand because they have what are sometimes referred to as *emergent properties*. This means that the full nature of a relationship is more than the sum of its parts, or the individual characteristics of the people involved in the relationship. Have you ever tried to play matchmaker with two of your friends? You might know both of these people quite well and feel certain that they will hit it off. But when the time comes, the date is a disaster, and your friends end up asking how you could have possibly thought they would be a good match. There is no need to feel bad. Relationships take on their own unique properties and are often unpredictable, even if you know almost everything there is to know about the two people involved.

Similarly, there are emergent properties at play in our unique relationships with our own company. For some people, this relationship is nourishing and intimate, and solitude makes them feel good; for others, this relationship is frustrating and exhausting, and solitude tends to make them feel angry; for others still, this relationship can be unnerving and ambivalent, and solitude often makes them feel anxious; and so on. But just like other relationships, our relationship with solitude can have both good and bad aspects, and if we really want our relationship with solitude to be healthy, we have to be willing to work at it.

One of the pervasive problems with solitude is that although it is often a regular part of our day, we don't pay much attention to it, and as a result, we neglect how important it is to our well-being. A friend of mine told me a story about an interesting conversation he had with the person seated next to him at a wedding. (You never know whom you will be sitting with at a wedding.) His tablemate was a physical therapist who specialized in the pelvic area and was passionate about his work. He mentioned that although serious problems in that area of the body eventually get dealt with, most people probably have some type of minor dysfunction that is negatively affecting them in ways they don't realize. He went on to say that this was likely because, although the pelvis is a critical part of our body in terms of our health and wellness, it can feel taboo to discuss: people just don't generally like to talk about pee, poo, and sex. His main lament was that if people just paid a bit more attention to their pelvis, and made even some minor adjustments, their lives would noticeably improve.

This strikes me as a good metaphor for what I think is going on with solitude—and it gets at the crux of this book. Most people probably don't think that much about solitude. We sometimes read about solitude in the news or come across the topic scrolling through social media. But these are usually extreme examples, stories highlighting the dangers of the growing loneliness epidemic or the trials of a solo adventurer who spent months alone in the wilderness. But I have learned that we need to pay more attention to solitude, our relationship to it, and how it impacts our health and wellness. Because just like our pelvis area, many of us probably have some type of minor dysfunction in our relationship with solitude, and it turns out that even small tweaks are likely to lead to noticeable improvements. In short, we need to talk more about solitude.

A classic and prescient quote about solitude comes from Blaise Pascal, a seventeenth-century French mathematician, inventor, and philosopher, who wrote, "All of humanity's problems stem from man's inability to sit quietly in a room alone." How about we give this a try.

Go find a quiet place and sit by yourself, alone with your thoughts, for fifteen minutes. No sleeping, no technology, no distractions: just you and the inside of your head. Set an alarm to alert you when fifteen minutes is up, but don't check the time remaining. Stop reading now and go do that, and then come back and pick up right here where you left off.

Fifteen Minutes Later

How did it go? Be honest. Did you cheat? Did you make it through the entire fifteen minutes? Did you check your phone? Did you fall asleep? Some people find this experience peaceful and relaxing, are surprised by how quickly the time passes, and feel refreshed when the alarm goes off. For others, it is just okay, and they were mostly bored. For yet others, sitting alone and unoccupied is unsettling; they just cannot seem to get out of their own head. And for many people, this exercise is excruciating and stressful. They count down the seconds until they can at last be released, if they even make it that far. So, every reader of this book might have been sitting alone, but each had their own uniquely personal experience of solitude.

What you just undertook was the basis for one of my favorite research studies about solitude. In 2014, the University of Virginia professor Timothy Wilson and other psychology researchers conducted a series of experiments in which they asked college students to sit on a chair, alone with their thoughts, in a small room with the door closed for fifteen minutes. Afterward, the students answered a series of questions about how they felt during this time. There were several variations to the structure of the experiment and to the context. For example, in some cases, the students completed their solitary time in a lab room at the university, and in other cases, students did this at home.

When I asked Wilson to tell me more about this study, he disclosed that his colleagues and students were split over what they thought would happen. Wilson himself believed that participants would generally enjoy this scenario, based on his own personal affinity for solitude. He admitted to being pretty surprised by the results: overall, and across all the studies and scenarios, students reported a strong dislike for this experience. They also recounted being very bored. Among the students who participated from home, about one-third confessed that they had cheated and failed to last the full fifteen minutes (so do not feel too bad if you didn't make it through the exercise yourself).

In one variation of the experiment, all the student participants had the chance beforehand to try out what it feels like to get a painful electric shock.* They were then given the same instructions to go sit alone with their thoughts in a lab room for fifteen minutes. But these participants were also told that they could receive the electric shock again by pressing a red button in the room. Amazingly, the majority of participants in the lab found the experience of sitting alone doing nothing so aversive that they chose instead to fill the time by self-administering a painful electric shock. Think about that for a minute: most people would rather inflict pain upon themselves than just sit alone for fifteen minutes with nothing to do but think.

As an aside, most of the participants gave themselves one or two shocks. But one male participant apparently self-administered 190(!) shocks to himself in a fifteen-minute period. I will not speculate here as to why he might have chosen to do that . . .†

Of course, this experiment was not just about solitude per se; it was also about being alone with one's thoughts. In this way, I would suggest that this experiment likely tells us more about college students' ability to cope (or not cope) with boredom and being cut off from

* This was done so that if they self-administered a shock later, it was not likely because of curiosity.

† . . . although it did make me think of Bill Murray's cameo in the dentist scene of the movie version of *Little Shop of Horrors* . . . just saying . . .

their smartphones than it tells us about typical experiences of solitude. However, a few years later in 2018, the same results were found in a much more diverse sample of several thousand participants across eleven countries. So, I think we can conclude that people generally do not like sitting alone with their thoughts. As we will discuss, solitude has a long-standing poor reputation, and studies like these reinforce it. These findings also underscore a major challenge in "selling" the potential benefits of solitude: some people just have an immediate negative reaction to being alone and cannot even imagine how it might be personally helpful. For them, almost any solitude feels like too much. Yet there are also people who crave solitude, and for them, it often feels like they are not getting enough time alone.

With that in mind, take a moment and answer this question:

Overall, the amount of time I get to spend alone each week is:

(a) definitely not enough

(b) somewhat less than I would like to

(c) just about right

(d) somewhat more than I would like to

(e) definitely too much

Did you choose "just about right"? If so, consider yourself part of a lucky minority. Over the years, I have asked this question to thousands of people, and fewer than one in three people select this response. The results of the other responses are distributed relatively evenly across the other options, with slightly more people typically choosing "somewhat more than I would like to" or "definitely too much" than "somewhat less than I would like to" or "definitely not enough." This means that more than two-thirds of people are *dissatisfied* with how much time they spend alone, either seeking to avoid feelings of loneliness and isolation (too much solitude) or craving the comforts of more "me time" (not enough solitude).

Of course, how much time you spend alone is only one component of your relationship with solitude. There's also the question of how you *feel* when you are alone (are you bored? anxious? calm? focused?); what you *do* when you are alone (do you meditate? pursue hobbies? get stuff done? scroll through social media?); and the *reasons* you are alone (are you trying to avoid stressful social situations? trying to recharge your battery after a busy and "people-y" day at work?). But no matter how you define or evaluate it, most people are dissatisfied with their relationship with solitude. The good news is it turns out we can do something about that.

The Promise(s) of (This Book on) Solitude

It has never been more important to understand the costs and benefits of solitude. Another finding from the American Time Use Survey is that the average amount of time spent alone across adults in the United States gradually increased from 2003 to 2019. This was before the COVID-19 pandemic, during which time alone increased much more dramatically around the world. More than four hundred years ago, the philosopher Francis Bacon famously wrote, "Knowledge is power." In this book, I will draw upon what I know from more than thirty years of studying solitude to empower you to establish and cultivate a healthy relationship with solitude. Regardless of whether you get too much alone time, not enough alone time, or just the right amount, this book is going to explain how you can get more out of solitude and why. Drawing from the most recent research in psychology, neuroscience, cultural anthropology, and evolutionary biology, but also combined with real-world experiences and what is trending on social media, I will help you unlock the potential of spending time alone as a positive force for your mental health and well-being.

In the first part of the book, we will take a deep dive into the science and psychology of solitude. We will learn about the *duality* of solitude and how and why it can be both harmful and helpful for our health and well-being. And along the way, we will answer all sorts of questions, ranging from "Is it solitude if I am with my pet?" to "Why does not getting to play catch with others sometimes feel like physical pain?" to "Why does walking alone in a forest make me feel calmer?"

In the second part of the book, we will apply this newly acquired knowledge about the complexities of solitude to help you optimize experiences of being alone across various domains in your life. This section is sort of like a user's guide for solitude, and we will address questions ranging from "How does solitude spark creativity?" to "Are married people really happier than singles?" to "How do I find the right balance in my life between time alone and time with others?"

So read on, and let's explore together when, why, how, and for whom solitude will be helpful versus hurtful. Because sometimes, it may be important for us to be left alone.

Chapter 2

I Think I'm Alone Now

What Solitude Is (and Is Not)

Tarot cards have become trendy again in the past few years, with a particular surge of interest and attention appearing on social media during the COVID-19 pandemic. Tarot cards were first documented in the mid-fifteenth century in northern Italy, where they were used to play a variety of card games. By the 1700s, tarot cards had spread throughout Europe, and their use evolved to include divination. The Hermit is the ninth Major Arcana card in traditional tarot decks. A typical depiction of the Hermit is an old man standing alone on a mountain peak, holding a staff in one hand and a lantern in the other. According to the Tarot Guide website, the Hermit represents opposite aspects of solitude depending upon whether it is drawn in the upright or reversed position. The upright Hermit represents spiritual enlightenment, self-reflection, inner guidance, and solitude. In contrast, the reversed Hermit indicates loneliness, isolation, withdrawal, and paranoia.

I think the creators of the Hermit tarot card could have written an excellent book about solitude. This description almost perfectly encapsulates the complexities of solitude and appropriately highlights its underlying duality. As it is stipulated, the Hermit can bring both joy and sorrow, depending upon how it is drawn. It has taken some time, but I think we are finally starting to work out why some people, metaphorically speaking, more often draw the Hermit tarot card in the upright position versus the reversed position. And importantly, we now have some pretty good ideas about how to help stack the deck so that the odds of pulling the upright Hermit are more in our favor.

As part of my job as a university professor, I regularly teach a course called The Psychology of Solitude. Each year, I ask the students in this class to do the fifteen-minute "sit alone with your thoughts" exercise as homework. When we talk about what it was like for them, a passionate discussion always ensues and serves as a great illustration of how solitude can mean so many different things to different people. For me, this is one of the things that makes it so interesting.

I also ask my students to complete the following sentence by filling in the blank with the first word or words that pop into their mind:

Solitude is _____.

What came to mind for you? Over the years I have asked this question to thousands of people of all ages. I never cease to be amazed by how many *different* types of answers I get back. Everything from solitude is "alone," "by yourself," and "separation"; to solitude is "bliss," "peaceful," and "awesome"; to solitude is "lonely," "sad," and "bleak." Not at all surprisingly, the general public does not agree on exactly what solitude is or what it entails.

But, of course, these days, if you really want to know how people feel about something, you need to check Twitter (now known as X). So, I did. In collaboration with my PhD student at the time, Will Hipson, and some colleagues who specialize in analyzing "big data," we set out to explore how Twitter users talked about solitude. To do this, our research team created a giant database of all the tweets that contained the words "solitude," "loneliness,"* or "alone" during a one-year period from mid-2018 to mid-2019. This resulted in a pool of almost twenty million tweets.† I was particularly interested in whether people differed in the way they talked about solitude versus loneliness. To answer this question, my very smart colleagues created a program that analyzed and compared the content of the other words that were included in each of the tweets that contained these target words.

We found that tweets that included the words "solitude" and "loneliness" were equally likely to also mention the word "alone." This was not particularly surprising. However, tweets with the word "loneliness" were also more likely to include words associated with negative emotions. For example, the most common words to co-occur in these tweets included "sad," "scared," "bored," "depressed," "hurt," and "broke." In contrast, tweets about "solitude" were more likely to include more positive words, with the most common co-occurrences including "enjoy," "peace," "quiet," "nature," "bliss," "spiritual," "recharge," and "Superman."‡

Of course, Twitter users are not all that representative of the wider population, but it is interesting to see how these words and concepts are used by this specific subset of individuals. I would be curious to see if we would find the same results if we used a different social media platform, like TikTok or Instagram, or analyzed text from some of the discussions on Reddit. For now, we can say that Twitter users do not consider solitude and loneliness to be equivalent. This is a good start: although the terms "loneliness" and "solitude" are often used interchangeably, they are not the same thing!

---

* All variations of these terms, such as "solitary" or "lonely," were also included.

† This data was collected before the onset of the COVID-19 pandemic. I assume that the usage of these words was even more frequent during the height of lockdowns and other social distancing measures.

‡ Aficionados of the superhero genre will note that this last one probably had something to do with Superman's hidden retreat, the Fortress of Solitude.

Loneliness has been much explored and discussed of late, particularly in the context of our experiences during the COVID-19 pandemic. The philosopher Paul Johannes Tillich provided an often quoted distinction between loneliness and solitude in his 1963 book, *The Eternal Now*: "[Language] has created the word 'loneliness' to express the pain of being alone. And it has created the word 'solitude' to express the glory of being alone." But it is the historian David Vincent who provided my favorite definition of loneliness, labeling it "failed solitude." Loneliness is most often the result of social isolation: spending too much time alone not by our own choice. In this way, loneliness creates a wanting. If you are lonely, you desire more—and deeper—social connection because there is a discrepancy between your social needs and your actual social experiences. To be clear, loneliness deserves our attention. Chronic feelings of loneliness can lead to serious mental health problems, such as depression, and it can even negatively impact our physical health. But loneliness is *not* solitude. We can feel lonely even in a roomful of people, be it a work event with colleagues or at a party surrounded by friends. Teenagers might feel lonely and disconnected while sitting at the family dinner table. In this way, loneliness does not presuppose solitude. And on the flip side, we can be completely alone but not feel lonely at all. This is most often the case if we've chosen to spend time in solitude. So, solitude does not presuppose loneliness.

But even if we know that solitude is not loneliness, that still does not give us a clear definition of what solitude is. Upon first instinct, it seems like solitude should be a straightforward concept to define. I certainly thought this was the case at the outset of my career.

Here are several hypothetical situations. In which case or cases would you consider yourself to be in solitude?

(a) Alone in a room with the door closed

(b) Sitting by yourself on a crowded commuter train

(c) Walking your dog in the woods

(d) Strolling and browsing the exhibits at a popular art gallery

(e) Video chatting with three friends on your smartphone

(f) All of the above

Which one(s) did you pick? It turns out that according to researchers who study solitude, the correct answer is actually *all of them.* Each of these scenarios has been used by researchers as an example of solitude. As you can see, even those of us who study this topic for a living do not actually agree on how to define and describe what exactly constitutes solitude.

So, What Is Solitude?

If you look up the word "solitude" in the dictionary, you will find definitions such as "the quality or state of being alone or remote from society" (*Merriam-Webster*) and "the situation of being alone without other people" (*Cambridge*). These dictionary definitions highlight a predominant theme in conceptualizations of solitude as a *physical separation* from others (think: "alone on a deserted isle"). From this perspective, someone who is standing in an open field with no one else around is demonstrably alone. This makes intuitive sense and, at first glance, seems like a pretty straightforward definition. But first glances can be deceiving. Things start to blur as you take a closer look. For example, how far apart do you actually have to be from others for it to be considered solitude? Should it be as far as the eye can see or the ear can hear? Are you still alone if you can make out some indistinct human forms in the distance? Is there a particular distance threshold from others that, once surpassed, renders you officially alone? Or does distance matter less than a physical barrier that creates a separation, such as a teenager in their bedroom with the door closed? As it turns out, there is no actual agreed-upon criterion for the minimum physical distance separated from others required for someone to be classified as in solitude.

To further complicate matters, this is only considering one's physical distance from other *people*. Do other living things count? Are you alone if you are snuggled up on the couch with your dog or cat? If this issue is to be considered, how far up or down the evolutionary ladder do we have to go for your nonhuman companion to make you "not alone"? Are you alone if you are with your parrot? Fish? Chia Pet? Resist the urge to roll your eyes—this is a serious question! There are real reasons we might be interested in whether someone is truly alone if they are with different types of pets. Research shows that pets can indeed serve a social function. After reviewing studies of pet ownership conducted during the COVID-19 pandemic, German researchers concluded that having a dog or cat made both children and adults feel less lonely.

Regardless, this suggests that physical distance should not be the only criterion for determining solitude. Indeed, as the philosopher Friedrich Nietzsche (allegedly) said, "My solitude does not depend on the presence or absence of people" (and maybe also pets). What else can we consider to help us clarify the definition? Let's borrow an idea from William Shakespeare, who famously wrote that "all the world's a stage."

More than fifty years ago, the sociologist Erving Goffman proposed using the theater stage as a metaphor to help us understand how we think about ourselves when we are in social situations. He suggested that as we go about our day in the presence of other people, we are "onstage," and the rest of the world is our audience. This is an intriguing idea. Imagine yourself on an actual stage in an auditorium full of people. When we are onstage, we are in the spotlight and must consider how others see us, what they might think of us, what they might say, and how they might act. In this situation, we are very, and sometimes painfully, aware of everything we do because it is being watched and evaluated by an audience filled with potential critics. This constant pressure to self-monitor our performance can make us feel under the gun and lead to exhaustion.

Now, imagine you have finished your performance, the audience has left, and you step offstage. This is solitude. When we are offstage, we can be ourselves completely. No one is observing or evaluating us, and there's no one we must engage with, respond to, or perform for. In this way, solitude is simply freedom from social demands, freedom to be our true selves, freedom to just . . . be.

This leads to the conceptualization of solitude as a *perceived separation* from others. In this way, solitude is less a state of being and more like a state of mind. From this perspective, solitude can be found when walking the streets of a foreign city or reading alone at a table in a crowded coffee shop. This approach also adds a very subjective and personal dimension to solitude. Some may consider themselves alone while browsing the shelves of a local bookstore, but others may be acutely aware of the presence of others and feel too self-conscious to pull out and peruse a book dealing with a particularly sensitive topic. But even if you are in the former camp, the shop owner might inadvertently shatter your cocoon of perceived solitude at any moment with an offer to help you find something.

This example highlights another core element of solitude: its fragility and potentially fleeting nature. The philosopher and author Philip Koch defined solitude as being disengaged from other people, but he lamented that true solitude was never truly achievable because the world is ultimately inescapable. Koch raised these ideas in the early 1990s, and with the benefit of hindsight, we can see that they were prophetic. Even then, Koch called into question whether we can truly be alone if we are always on the verge of being interrupted. Sound familiar?

This is a common theme in the age of smartphones and social media. Indeed, when it comes to defining solitude, technology complicates everything. It is now possible (and quite common) to be physically alone but virtually interacting with others—or at least on the verge of doing so. This can be a double-edged sword.

For example, during his teenage years, my son spent countless hours alone in his bedroom playing video games. But this was something quite different from the stereotypical isolated, brooding, basement-dwelling teenage gamer of previous generations. Although my son was indeed by himself in his room, between his smartphone and his headset, he was in almost constant contact with his friends. What emanated through his closed door did not sound like someone alone at all. Instead, I heard a steady stream of screams, whoops, laughs, and shared glee. In this case, would anyone really want to make the argument that he was sitting in solitude?

Indeed, many have opined that technology will mean the end of solitude. How can we ever truly be offstage if our phone or other devices are waiting in the wings and can interrupt us at any moment? And things are likely to only get more complex. The most recent advances in artificial intelligence now force us to consider the (previously unthinkable) question: Are you alone if you are interacting with AI? We'll table this for now and return to it later.

In the meantime, let's go back and consider two other dictionary definitions of solitude: "a state or situation in which you are alone usually because you want to be" (*Britannica Dictionary*) and "the state of being alone, especially when you find this pleasant" (*Oxford Learner's Dictionaries*). These definitions highlight the crucial component of autonomy. When it comes to solitude, having a choice matters . . . a lot. As we saw earlier, social isolation, which most often represents unwanted time alone, leads to loneliness, depression, and ill-being. But when you *choose* solitude, you are opening the door for a unique set of opportunities and potentialities that cannot be found in the constant company of others.

I am not sure that this makes for the best definition of solitude, but it is certainly a critical contributor to our experiences of being alone—and its implications for our well-being. So where does this leave us in terms of providing a clear definition of solitude? The most honest answer I can give you is that things still remain a bit fuzzy. Many researchers and theorists are transitioning to a more functional definition of solitude, settling on something like: "not interacting with others, either in person or virtually." I would still argue that it is more nuanced than that.

All the way back to the ancient Greek philosopher Plato, it has been argued that beauty is transient in nature and open to interpretation. This notion has since been expressed in various forms by many others, including Shakespeare ("Beauty is bought by judgement of the eye") and Benjamin Franklin ("Beauty, like supreme dominion, is but supported by opinion"). It was perhaps most elegantly articulated by the author Margaret Wolfe Hungerford in her 1878 book, *Molly Bawn*, as "Beauty is in the eye of the beholder." In many ways, I think we can say the same thing about solitude.

The Paradoxes of Solitude

The pantheons of Greek and Roman mythology do not include a specific god of solitude.* If we were to name one, though, a good candidate might be Hephaestus, the ancient Greek god of fire, the forge, and crafts. Hephaestus was said to lack the physical perfection of other gods. As a result, he was ostracized and ultimately cast out from Olympus. He spent most of his time alone in his workshop, where he honed his artistry and created an array of unmatched armor and weaponry,

* In Japanese mythology, a likely choice would be Amenominakanushi, who was first a deity who manifested when heaven and earth came into existence and is often described as "single," "solitary," or the "deity who emerged in solitude."

including the shield of Achilles, along with a multitude of exquisite statues and other works of fine art. This mythology may be one of the first depictions of the archetype of the solitary artist, a common solitude trope that endures to this day.

But if it were up to me, the ancient Roman god Janus would be considered the honorary god of solitude. Janus was the god of beginnings and endings, presided over doorways and passageways, and is associated with transitions, like the new year.* Janus was often depicted with a double-faced head and is the source of the expression "Janus-faced," which refers to being hypocritical, duplicitous, or two-faced. Dualism is a fundamental concept in religion, mythology, and folklore: God versus the devil, yin versus yang, life versus death, good versus evil, and so on. As we saw with the Hermit tarot card, this duality also seems to be at the core of human experiences of solitude.

Embedded in this dualism, solitude evokes actual paradoxes, managing to simultaneously reflect two opposite things. Perhaps the most glaring paradox about solitude is that it routinely serves as both a reward and a punishment. For example, solitude is often given as a gift to others, like a spa day for an exhausted and stressed-out parent. And many of us reward ourselves with time alone. This "me time" might take the form of a long walk, a hot bath, curling up with a book, bingeing a favorite show, or watching endless cute cat videos on TikTok. Whatever activity you choose, solitude can function as a well-earned payoff.

I heard some of the most poignant illustrations of this not long ago, when I was a guest on a live radio show. Listeners were prompted to call in and tell me and my hosts about a time when solitude was "good during challenging times." One caller told us about her experiences working as a first responder during the early part of the COVID-19 pandemic. The cumulative strains of her job later led her to be diagnosed with

* Fun fact: This is why the month of January was named after him.

post-traumatic stress disorder. She characterized herself as always having been an extravert, but during her treatment and recovery, she found it very difficult to be around people. For her, spending time alone was a present she could offer herself, a calming place to catch her breath and reset. I was particularly moved by her description of solitude "being like gold" to her.

Toward the end of the hour-long show, a mother of three young children called in to tell us her story. After her own mother succumbed to cancer, this caller described the excruciating challenge of mourning her loss while caring for three little ones, who, of course, could not understand what she was going through. She talked about how she had to "fake it all day long." Looking for a way to cope, she took up running. Each day, she would lace up her jogging shoes and wait for her husband to come home from work. As soon as he came in the door, she would literally run out it. She confided that she usually spent the first half hour of her solitary runs crying but that this catharsis was incredibly healing. She cherished the gift of having "full permission to feel everything [she] was feeling." By the end of each run, she felt grateful for all the good things she had in her life. As these compelling narratives illustrate, solitude can sometimes evolve from a pleasant "bonus" to an absolute essential need for our mental health and well-being.

On the flip side, solitude also routinely functions as a form of punishment. In this respect, solitude represents something to be avoided. For example, when a young child misbehaves or does not follow instructions, many parents will place the child in a time-out. Most often used with younger children, this procedure usually involves having the unruly child sit quietly alone for some period of time. This disciplinary technique has proven to be quite effective in reducing problem behaviors and is widely advocated as an alternative to spanking and other forms of physical punishment.

Doesn't it seem a bit odd that the punishment we sometimes dole out to our children, namely spending quiet time alone, is the same reward we give to ourselves as adults? It is also the case that some children don't mind just hanging out in their rooms, even if they aren't allowed to do anything, which would kind of defeat the purpose of the punishment to begin with.* When my own kids were young, I used a variation of the traditional time-out that did not include social isolation but instead consisted of sitting on the stairs.

A more extreme form of enforced solitude is also one of the harshest punishments in the penal system. Imprisoned inmates are reprimanded for additional misbehaviors with episodes of solitary confinement. This procedure (also euphemistically referred to as "restrictive housing") involves isolating inmates in a small cell, often for days at a time. This has been a common practice in US prisons for more than two hundred years. However, there is a growing recent consensus about the problems that solitary confinement presents in terms of human rights, legality, and mental health. Many US states now have laws in place that limit the use of solitary confinement for extended periods of time. In December 2023, the New York City Council voted to ban the use of solitary confinement in city jails altogether. Personally, this strikes me as a positive development. As we will see later, prolonged social isolation can have damaging effects on both the mind and the body, reinforcing the notion that solitary confinement should be considered a cruel (although unfortunately still not unusual) form of punishment.

A second paradoxical aspect of solitude is that it is widely considered to be both normative and deviant. On the one hand, solitude is a common, ordinary, and universally shared human experience. A young child playing alone in the sandbox during recess at school does not

* To be fair, I think the "punishment" part of a time-out has as much to do with being bored as being alone. I think we can assume that children probably find sitting alone doing nothing about as enjoyable as the participants in the Wilson study who chose to self-administer electric shocks!

draw any undue attention from teachers or other students. An elderly gentleman sitting alone on a park bench and feeding the pigeons does not provoke a second glance from most passersby. Yet, someone eating alone at a table in a fancy restaurant still draws some stares, and a person choosing to live by themselves in an isolated cabin in the woods is likely to be seen as a loner or a hermit—or at least a bit quirky.

A frequent collaborator of mine is Julie Bowker, a psychology researcher at the State University of New York at Buffalo. In a series of studies, we set out to more formally explore under what conditions and to what degree people tend to believe that solitude is "normal." One way we did this was to ask more than two thousand adolescents and young adults how much it was "okay" versus "wrong" for someone who likes to spend time alone to do so. Overall, more than 80 percent of people responded that it was "perfectly okay," with another 15 percent saying that it was "sort of okay." So, it seems pretty clear that in general, choosing to spend time in solitude is not viewed as particularly deviant.

But it is also fair to say that some forms of solitude are viewed as more "normal" than others. For example, the US-based researchers Rebecca Ratner and Rebecca Hamilton explored people's attitudes about participating in different types of activities while alone versus with others. Across a series of five studies, their results showed that adults were much less likely to engage in a solo *hedonic* activity (something fun), such as seeing a movie in a theater or eating at a newly opened restaurant, compared with a more *utilitarian* activity (something practical), such as going food shopping or taking a walk for exercise. Reasons for this had to do with people's self-conscious concerns that if they went bowling alone (another example of a hedonic activity), they would be perceived by others as a "loser" and not having any friends.

At the extreme end of this paradoxical continuum, solitude can also be considered a significant indication of deviance. Spending time alone has long been viewed and studied as both a cause and a consequence of psychopathology. The *Diagnostic and Statistical Manual of Mental Disorders* (more commonly known as the *DSM*), published by the American Psychiatric Association, and the *International Classification of Diseases* (aka the *ICD*), published by the World Health Organization, are authoritative handbooks that define, classify, and provide criteria for diagnosing mental health disorders for health care professionals around the world. In the first edition of the *DSM*, published in 1952, people who spent too much time alone and had difficulties relating effectively to others could be classified as suffering from either a psychotic disorder, such as schizophrenia; a psychoneurotic disorder, such as anxiety; or a personality disorder, such as a schizoid personality. Although this has changed to a certain extent in subsequent editions, even today, various aspects of solitude, such as self-isolation, chronic avoidance of social situations, and disturbances in social relationships, are still considered part of the diagnostic criteria for many clinical disorders, including major depression, social anxiety disorder, avoidant personality disorder, and schizophrenia.

Extreme social withdrawal is also the defining characteristic of hikikomori, a clinical syndrome whereby adolescents and young adults seclude themselves, often in their bedroom at their parents' house, for weeks, months, or even years at a time. The term *hikikomori* is derived from the combination of two Japanese words, *hiku*, which means "to pull back," and *komoru*, which means "to seclude oneself." It was originally identified as a culture-bound phenomenon that was exclusive to Japan. Data from the World Mental Health Japan Survey (conducted between 2013 and 2015) indicated that just over 2 percent of the population suffered from acute hikikomori during their lifetime.*

Cases of hikikomori have now also been documented in several other countries around the world, including the United States. However,

---

* Defined as staying in their house for more than six months, not going to work or school, and having little communication with others.

there is continued debate as to the exact criteria for conceptualizing and diagnosing it. A primary dispute is whether hikikomori should be considered a "new" clinical disorder versus whether it could be accounted for using a combination of already existing disorders, such as social anxiety disorder, schizoid personality disorder, or major depression disorder. Regardless, this phenomenon provides a clear and apparent exemplar of how solitude can represent a deviant behavior that reflects a serious mental health disorder.

I can think of several other paradoxical aspects of solitude, and I am sure there are more: experiences of solitude can also both help (think: "absence makes the heart grow fonder") and hurt our relationships with others; solitude is something that is purported to be beneficial (as we will see), but it also can be aversive and even painful (like spinach, for some people). If we tied up all these smaller paradoxes into a knot representing one big and complex contradictory enigma, it would be that solitude can be both "bad" and "good." This is not a new idea. As we will see in the forthcoming chapters, there is a long history of solitude being portrayed as both a boon and a curse. This duality of solitude has been described across many domains, and we will explore examples not only from psychology but also from philosophy, religion, mythology, literature, and popular culture.

Let's finish this chapter with a final conceptualization of solitude that is a bit more metaphysical in its approach. The American psychology researchers Christopher Long and James Averill drew an intriguing analogy between solitude and time. They asserted that although events are experienced in time, time itself is not an experience. In this same regard, they made the argument that we experience events in solitude, but solitude itself is not an experience. This strikes me as a very thought-provoking idea. But I am not sure I completely agree.

As I suspect is the case for many others, I do sometimes feel as though I experience time. I can think of instances in my life when time has seemed to speed by, slow down, or even almost stop. This may or may not be what it means to actually "experience time," but regardless, I would still assert that episodes of solitude have felt very different to me on different occasions. I can think of some instances when solitude has seemed like a vast, empty expanse. Yet, at other times, solitude seems to be somehow full, sometimes of opportunities, sometimes of warmth and coziness, and sometimes even of connections, with myself, with others, and with the world around me. I think just like time, we can all experience solitude in a wide range of unique and deeply personal ways.

Chapter 3

Why Solitude Gets a Bad Rap

I've Got a Theory

When I was a graduate student studying developmental psychology at the University of Waterloo, I had the privilege of being supervised by Kenneth Rubin, a renowned expert in the study of children's peer relationships. Ken is an academic force of nature, and I will admit to being a bit intimidated by him at the outset. Just a few weeks after I had started my program, Ken asked me to coauthor a chapter he had been invited to contribute to an academic volume. I knew right away that this was an incredible opportunity for me. And, of course, I desperately wanted to impress Ken and show him he had chosen wisely by accepting me from among all the applications he received from prospective graduate students.

He assigned me the task of preparing a first draft of a particular section of the chapter. To this day, I have never worked harder on any piece of writing. After a few weeks, I was ready to give Ken my draft for feedback. This was in the early 1990s, so I printed out my document using my handy dot matrix printer, stapled the corner, and nervously placed it in Ken's mailbox in the psychology department. Then I waited.

A few angst-ridden days later, Ken returned the document to my mailbox. With some trepidation, I steeled myself and began flipping through the stapled pages. My heart sank. The pages were so covered with red ink that I could barely make out my original (admittedly low-resolution) print. Entire paragraphs were crossed out, the margins were littered with comments, and most of my text had been overwritten.

Imposter syndrome is common among graduate students. You go from being near or at the top of your class in college to being in a cohort consisting entirely of top students from across the country. It is a classic case of the big fish in a little pond discovering that they are not so big after all when they suddenly find themselves in larger waters. When I saw all that red ink, I distinctly remember thinking, *Oh well, it was nice being in graduate school for a few weeks . . . I absolutely knew this would happen. I clearly do not belong here . . . Ken has realized that this was all a terrible mistake and that I had somehow slipped through the cracks during the admission process. The next time he sees me he will ask me to leave the program and go back home to my little pond.*

In the 1920s, the American psychologist Walter Cannon coined the phrase "fight or flight" to describe the ways that humans instinctively react to stress. That day, I chose flight. Yup, my very mature and sophisticated strategy to try to prevent Ken from kicking me out of the graduate program was basically to hide from Ken, and everyone else, for as long as I possibly could. As a short-term solution, it kind of worked. For over a week, I stayed away from Ken's office and went to our lab area, where student office space was located, only in the evenings. I even avoided my friends and lab mates, as I was much too embarrassed by my perceived failure to even consider talking to anyone about it.

I am sure you will not be surprised to hear that as a long-term solution, this strategy was entirely ineffective. My time spent in solitude that week was fraught with worry, and my rumination only served to worsen my feelings of self-doubt, inadequacy, and outright failure. And, of course, despite my best efforts, I was not even successful in avoiding Ken. One morning while rushing to make it to a class on time, I flew around the corner of one of the psychology building's mazelike corridors and ran right into him.

Since Cannon first described the fight-or-flight human responses to stress, two others have been added to his list. Faced with the immediate threat of colliding with the very person I was desperately trying to avoid, I responded with the third option: freeze. I just stood there, dumbfounded, for what felt like an eternity. Then, since escape was impossible, and there was absolutely no way I was going to "fight" Ken, I switched to the most recently added fourth option: fawn (or, in my case, grovel). In a desperate last-ditch attempt to avoid getting booted out of my graduate program, I started profusely apologizing to Ken for my poor work and stammering that if he would just give me another chance, I would work so much harder to do better. Ken listened to my outburst with a wry smile on his face. When I finally stopped blathering for a moment to catch my breath, he looked me straight in the eye and said, "You did good. I edit because I care, and I edit a lot when I am working with something that is worth working on. Keep at it."

As my mentor, Ken taught me countless invaluable lessons not only about psychology but also about life. That day, I learned the importance of accepting constructive criticism and using it to make improvements to your work—and to yourself. I also learned something important about solitude. Using solitude as an escape from social situations you are seeking to avoid does not solve anything. In fact, it usually only serves to make things worse.

I thought about Ken as I began writing this chapter because much of his research focuses on how children learn to get along well with others. Going all the way back to Sigmund Freud, psychologists have stressed the critical role that adults play in children's lives. But those aren't the only relationships that matter. A primary drive of Ken's illustrious career was to raise awareness about how it is also important for children's healthy development to spend time with other kids. A common extension of the notion that interacting with friends promotes children's positive development is that *missing out* on these social interactions can be problematic for their well-being. Why would children miss out on opportunities for social engagement? As the argument goes, it is because they are spending too much time alone. Ergo, solitude is bad for children's well-being.

This was certainly a major theme of my academic socialization as a graduate student in Ken's lab. But now that I am academically all grown up, a central focus of my career is raising awareness about the important and unique positive role that solitude serves in children's healthy development and adults' well-being. I guess in some ways, this makes me a defiant student who rebelled against my academic parent.

Solitude Is "Bad" Because Being with Others Is "Good"

Within the field of psychology, the notion that solitude can be problematic goes back a long way. In fact, one of the earliest recorded psychology experiments thoroughly dissed solitude. In 1898, Norman Triplett of Indiana University asked children to participate in a competition that involved spinning a fishing reel to make a flag attached to the line race around a track. The goal was to have the flag complete the circuit as quickly as possible. In some cases, children completed the task alone; in others, they were paired with other children. Overall, children's race times were slower when they competed alone than when paired with others performing the same task. Thus, even at the turn of the last century, it was clear that we do things better together and worse alone.

Outside the domain of psychology, the general notion that solitude is "bad" can be traced back to biblical times: "Then the LORD God said,

'It is not good that the man should be alone' " (Genesis 2:18). That is pretty much as clear as it gets. But if it does not make the point strongly enough, there are other passages in the Bible that also intimate that being with others is better than being alone, including:

> God settles the solitary in a home. (Psalm 68:6)

> Two are better than one, because they have a good reward for their toil. For if they fall, one will lift up his fellow. But woe to him who is alone when he falls and has not another to lift him up! Again, if two lie together, they keep warm, but how can one keep warm alone? (Ecclesiastes 4:9–11)

In the interest of transparency, I should disclose that there are also passages in the Bible that refer to more positive aspects of solitude. Most of these describe retreating to solitude as a context for prayer, such as "Very early in the morning, while it was still dark, Jesus got up, left the house and went off to a solitary place, where he prayed" (Mark 1:35). Nonetheless, I think it is fair to say the seeds that grew into solitude's "bad rap" were planted a very long time ago. Since then, evolutionary psychologists, social psychologists, developmental psychologists, and others have all put forth theories that highlight the negative aspects of solitude. Although they differ somewhat in their specifics, these theories are all grounded in the same general premise: since we get so much good stuff out of social interactions, relationships, and communities, therefore, by extension, solitude must be bad.

Humans evolved to be together. In his book *Politics*, written in the fourth century BCE, the Greek philosopher Aristotle famously wrote, "Man is by nature a social animal." If we are truly social animals, then the time we spend away from others (i.e., solitude) works against our basic human nature and is thus inherently adverse. This idea is consistent with the evolutionary perspective on solitude. Broadly speaking, evolutionary approaches examine the adaptive qualities of human traits and behaviors. An adaptive trait is something that grants a subset of organisms who share this characteristic any kind of advantage that promotes their survival. Surviving longer, in turn, generally provides these specific organisms with greater opportunities to mate and pass on this trait to subsequent generations.

A classic example illustrates how giraffes evolved longer necks. Individual giraffes who happened to be born with a gene that results in a slightly longer neck had an advantage over their shorter-necked brethren in procuring food: they could reach higher up trees to eat more leaves. More food generally means a better chance of survival. So, over time, this led to more offspring sired by giraffes with longer necks, until this characteristic eventually became the norm in the species.

By way of an example with humans, let's consider the potential adaptive nature of shyness. Shyness is a personality trait characterized by feelings of unease and self-consciousness in social situations. Individuals who are shy also tend to be more sensitive to perceived threats in their environment. With that in mind, let's imagine a very shy and anxious caveman. Sitting in his cave one day, the cautious caveman feels his stomach grumbling from hunger. After putting it off as long as he can, he slowly inches toward the edge of his cave to go searching for food. Suddenly, he is startled by the sound of a bush rustling in the wind and quickly retreats to the safety of his cave. A while later, his hunger intensifying, he tries again. But a shadow of something flying above passes over him as he approaches the threshold of the cave, and so again, he withdraws. After several additional unsuccessful attempts to leave the cave for similar reasons, the shy caveman gradually becomes increasingly weak and lightheaded from hunger. Eventually, he starves to death, dying before having any children.

Now imagine a bold and impulsive caveman in the same situation.

When the exuberant caveman feels the pangs of hunger, he immediately leaps up, grabs his trusty "food-killing" spear, and strides confidently out of his cave . . . where he is promptly devoured by a saber-toothed tiger crouched nearby. He also dies before having any children.

From this oversimplified fable, we would surmise that being somewhere near the middle of the shy-bold continuum would be most adaptive for the human species. But it's important to remember that the adaptive or maladaptive qualities of traits and behaviors for the survival of different species very much depend on their "fit" with the characteristics and demands of their environment. That is, under different circumstances, both boldness and shyness may be more advantageous.

For example, in contexts where resources are scarcer, our more bold and assertive ancient ancestors would likely be more successful in competing for food and mates than their shy and submissive counterparts. There is actually some evidence in support of this idea from research with "shy" and "bold" animals. The US-based researcher Stephen Suomi and his colleagues examined the effects of overcrowding in a troop of rhesus monkeys. Under normal living conditions, relatively little violent conflict was observed among the monkeys. In this context, monkeys previously identified as "shy" or "bold" (yes, there are shy and bold monkeys) shared the same relatively low incidence of injuries. When monkeys were confined in an overcrowded environment, unsurprisingly, the overall amount of violent conflict increased. Under these circumstances, it was the shy monkeys who suffered the most injuries. In other words, the under-resourced environment strongly favored bolder monkeys.

Going back to our fable, we could further surmise that the shy caveman would be more adept at avoiding predators. We would also expect the tendency to "look before you leap" to be more valuable in higher-risk environments. There is research in animals that supports this assertion as well. The Canadian biologist Grant Brown and his colleagues found that shy rainbow trout (yes, there are shy and bold fish) were more successful at evading prey in a high-risk environment[*] compared with their bolder piscine counterparts.

Humans evolved and continue to live in complex, unpredictable, and rapidly changing environments. It appears that different degrees of shyness and boldness persist in offering different advantages and disadvantages in these different contexts. From this perspective, at the species level, the best chance for survival and proliferation for humans is the maintenance of a distribution of individuals that includes a wide range of shyness and boldness. This helps explain why, thousands of years after our fabled cavemen succumbed to their respective dooms, we still see such variations among people in terms of shyness and boldness (and also why there are still shy and bold fish, dogs, mice, monkeys, and so forth).

What about the trait of "seeking solitude"? For our earliest human ancestors, choosing between solitude and spending time with others was likely a matter of life and death. At that time, social connections were more than just desirable and enjoyable; they were essential to survival.[†] Humans who lived in groups were afforded innumerable well-documented evolutionary advantages. At the most basic level, the presence of others provided additional protection against predators: as it is said, there is safety in numbers. Social groups also offered opportunities for cooperative hunting, sharing food and other resources, and division of labor. And, of course, living in a community also meant greater proximity to a larger pool of potential mating partners. Humans who chose to live alone would not be afforded these clear evolutionary advantages.

I would also make the further claim that even among our ancestors

---

* In this case, the presence of pumpkinseed fish, which are a natural predator of trout.

† As we will see in the next chapter, there is evidence to suggest that this may still be true today, although perhaps for somewhat different reasons.

who lived together, choosing to spend more time than others in solitude would be frowned upon. In the earliest human communities, there were constant threats to survival, including starvation, predators, and even attacks from other human groups. People were completely dependent upon one another to meet their continued existence. In this context, choosing to spend time alone meant you were not pulling your weight in the group and therefore damaging the collective as a whole.

Of course, the nature of our environment has changed dramatically since the days of our earliest human ancestors. I think a case could be made that from an evolutionary perspective, solitude is less maladaptive, particularly in terms of the specific outcome metric of "survival." For example, consider an urban dweller who lives alone and has procured a job that allows them to work from home. If they shop online and have groceries and other necessities delivered, they could easily spend almost all their time in solitude, even living in the midst of an overpopulated megalopolis.* This is actually not a new idea. It has long been suggested that modern cities are designed to make millions of people feel as though they are alone. As the German sociologist Georg Simmel wrote in his 1903 essay, "The Metropolis and Mental Life," "One never feels as lonely and as deserted as in this metropolitan crush of persons."

Nonetheless, environment still matters. In Western societies, individualism, independence, and choice are generally highly valued. This is thought to be one of the main reasons choosing to spend time alone is often viewed as a normative behavior in these parts of the world. However, in Eastern cultures, for instance, which tend to more highly value group orientation and contributing to the collective, choosing to spend time alone evokes a different response. The University of

* I think for most people, although they might be able to "survive" living the life of an urban hermit, they would certainly not "thrive."

Pennsylvania psychologist Xinyin Chen* conducted a series of studies on the implications of preferring solitude among children and adolescents in mainland China. He consistently found that choosing to spend time alone was viewed as selfish and deviant, because in this cultural context, one should not prioritize one's own needs above those of the collective.

According to the psychology researchers Roy Baumeister and Mark Leary, the evolutionary drive for our species to form social connections continues to manifest in modern humans as an inborn desire to establish relationships and communities. They labeled this phenomenon as the *need to belong*. In the more than thirty years since this theory was proposed, there has been considerable research to support the importance of social connections for our well-being, mental health, and physical health. In a 2022 essay summarizing this work, Baumeister, Leary, and their colleagues succinctly wrote, "A very brief synthesis of the bulk of the work that has been done on belonging might read: belonging is good. The absence of belonging? Well, that is bad." This brings us back to the heart of the matter at hand. If we spend too much time alone (even if by choice), we may not meet this basic human need and could suffer negative consequences, such as feelings of distress, sadness, and loneliness. And as we will discuss in much more detail in the next chapter: loneliness sucks.

Happier together. Think back to the exercise at the outset of this book and the experience of spending fifteen minutes alone with your thoughts. As we have seen, although many people really hate this, others are more neutral about it, and still others would consider it bliss. Yet, although individuals' responses to solitude vary widely, there is pretty clear evidence that the moments we spend with others seem better, on average, than the moments we spend alone. For example, in a series

---

* With whom I shared an office when we were in graduate school together.

of studies, the University of Rochester researcher Harry Reis and his colleagues found that instances of fun are experienced as *more* fun if other people are present. This was particularly true when the other people present were good friends or family members, but it was also true with strangers. Even engaging with previously unfamiliar people tends to make us feel better.

For me, the most striking evidence of this effect was demonstrated in 2014 by the psychology researchers Nicholas Epley and Juliana Schroeder. They conducted a series of experiments manipulating people's social experiences on commuter trains and public buses in Chicago. North American social norms and assumptions about talking to strangers in these contexts are pretty overt and straightforward. When you get on a bus or train, you do not typically expect to interact with other passengers, even when you are sitting right next to them. However, if your seatmate does try to strike up a conversation with you, engaging in some small talk would not be considered a cultural taboo. As an aside, such customs vary considerably around the world. Scandinavians tend to particularly value privacy and personal space, so attempts at small talk with a stranger in Norway will likely evoke a cold stare. In contrast, Brazilians are likely to strike up a conversation with just about anyone, anywhere.

In their research, Epley and Schroeder wanted to explore whether talking to strangers would make us feel better, even in a context where it (somewhat) violated social norms. In a series of studies, research assistants approached passengers waiting alone to board either a commuter train or a public bus and invited them to participate in their experiment. One random subgroup of participants was given instructions to "keep to themselves and enjoy their solitude" during their bus/train ride. A second subgroup was told to "initiate a conversation with a new person on the bus/train and try to make a connection." Before starting their trip, passengers were also asked to predict what they thought their experience sitting alone or initiating a conversation with a stranger would be like. How did they think it would make them feel? Perhaps not surprisingly, given the aforementioned social norms in this context, passengers expected more positive experiences during their commute while sitting alone compared to speaking to a stranger.

After completing their journey, participants in both groups reported how they *actually* felt during their train or bus commute. The results were unequivocal—and exactly opposite of what participants expected. Passengers who initiated a conversation with a stranger reported having more positive experiences than those who sat alone and kept to themselves. Similar results were found in subsequent experiments involving people taking a taxi home from the airport, where they were instructed to either speak to the cabdriver or sit in silence, as well as with people sitting in a waiting area for an appointment, where they were instructed to either speak to another person in the waiting room or sit in silence.

So, across multiple contexts where people would typically expect to spend time "alone in a crowd," they felt better after initiating social contact with a stranger. And importantly, this was despite their (mistaken!) assumption that they would enjoy the experience more if they kept to themselves. Also of note, these results held even after accounting for participants' personality characteristics. In short, no matter how people scored in terms of traits like introversion, neuroticism, or agreeableness, overall, people who engaged with others felt better than those who sat alone. Taken together, these findings provide robust evidence that, despite our expectations, making a social connection, even with a stranger, boosts our mood. It is not hard to extrapolate from this that if we are truly happier together, spending too much time alone will make us sad (or at least, less happy).

However, just because being with others tends to make us feel better, this does not mean that we do not also need time alone. Social prescriptions are not one-size-fits-all. As we will discuss later, too much socializing can also be draining, particularly for people who tend to be more introverted. There also appear to be some limits in terms of dosage here. The Tilburg University researchers Olga Stavrova and Dongning Ren explored the benefits of social contact on health and longevity using data from the European Social Survey, which included more than 350,000 participants from thirty-seven countries. They found that more frequent social contact was associated with better health and longer life, but only up to a point. Once social contact reached moderate levels, the researchers found it had diminishing returns. Moreover, there were even some indications that at the highest levels, too much socializing might even be bad for us. So, it is not the case that more and more socializing is always better. Eating too much chocolate will eventually make you feel sick.

With a little help from my (childhood) friends. The history of developmental psychology is also full of warnings about the dangers of solitude in childhood. In the 1890s, the philosopher and psychologist William James famously wrote that "the great source of terror in infancy is solitude." Freud considered solitude to be a universal human fear and believed that excessive time alone during childhood would cause psychological pain and suffering. From this perspective, a potential cause of trauma in very young children was the loss experienced from being separated from their mother and other objects of primary affection. Although Freud's theories no longer dominate the psychological landscape, this negative stigma about solitude endures.

In contemporary psychology, the main reasons solitude is considered damaging for children mirror the previous evolutionary and social psychological theorems: namely that solitude is bad because being around others is good. In the case of children, this approach tends to focus on all the "good" children get from hanging out with other kids. This leads us to believe that "missing out" on this good stuff by spending too much time in solitude is damaging.

Peers are the general purveyors of social mores, tenets, and customs. If we did not spend time with our peers, we would not know how to dress, how to talk, what music to listen to, what shows to watch, or what video games to play. Peers are also excellent sources of support, intimacy, and fun. A primary task of childhood is learning to get along well with others, and the peer group is a unique context where children acquire, develop, and implement the critical interpersonal skills that will allow them to accomplish this task. It is with our friends that we best learn social skills, like how to cooperate and resolve conflicts, in ways that are different from interacting with parents, siblings, and teachers. It is with other children that we also learn emotional skills, like keeping our temper and resisting impulses, as well as communicative skills, like expressing our likes, dislikes, wants, and new ideas. And the stakes here are high. Children who do not learn to get along well with others tend to grow up to be adults who do not get along well with others.

Like any other ability, the mastery of interpersonal skills requires practice, practice, practice. Thus, as the argument goes, children who spend less time practicing, which in this case refers to interacting with peers, will likely lag behind when it comes to acquiring and mastering these skills. Over time, this skills deficit is likely to become cumulative and continue to worsen. It is like missing the first three weeks of math class.

As they get older, children who are hindered by this growing gap in interpersonal skills will find it more difficult to engage positively with their classmates, teammates, and other potential friend groups. As a result, when they do interact with others, these comparatively unskilled children are more likely to end up rejected and victimized. Unfortunately, chronic negative social experiences can cause significant long-term harm to mental health and well-being. Again, you can trace the arrow here directly to solitude: children should not spend too much time alone because it will damage their relationships with others as they grow into adults.

The Swiss developmental psychologist Jean Piaget emphasized the importance of peers in helping children see things from different perspectives. According to Piaget, young children suffer from *egocentrism*, meaning they see things only from their own perspective (although I suspect we all know a few adults who continue to display this tendency). Overcoming these self-centered biases is a major cognitive task of early childhood. The peer group is an ideal context for challenging such egocentric views.

Routine social experiences in the classroom and on the playground expose children to a wide range of diverse views, abilities, beliefs, and characteristics. For example, because of his egocentrism, a young boy who absolutely loves Hawaiian pizza might assume that everyone feels the same way he does. However, he will quickly be disavowed of this notion after showing off his pineapple-laden pizza at lunchtime in kindergarten.* Such exchanges help to highlight for children the immense variety of likes, dislikes, and alternative opinions that populate their social realms. Over time, this repeated exposure helps eat away at the rigid walls of egocentrism and promote children's abilities to understand diverse views and take on others' perspectives.

The sociologist George Herbert Mead argued that peers were essential for the development of self-identity, self-esteem, and self-perceptions. I have always found his arguments here particularly interesting because so much has been written about solitude as a positive context for exploration of the self and identity, particularly in adolescence. Mead believed that young children's concept of self was heavily influenced by their perceptions of how they were seen by others, especially by important others, such as family, teachers, and friends. He called this the *looking-glass self*, a metaphor for the notion that

* Fun fact: The creation of the first Hawaiian pizza is attributed to Sam Panopoulos, who immigrated to Canada from Greece in the 1950s. In 1962, he served the first pizza with pineapple on it at his Canadian restaurant, Satellite.

children come to see themselves "reflected" in how others speak and behave toward them and then internalize these views as their own.

Of course, parents, family, teachers, and others contribute to this process. But for Mead, peers played an especially important and unique role. Whether it be in a childcare center, preschool playroom, kindergarten classroom, organized extracurricular activity, or local playground, young children spend more than 50 percent of their waking hours in the company of other kids. Entrance into these groups of peers provides young children with multiple sources of immediate and frequent feedback. Children are suddenly able to compare themselves with others who are similar to them but also clearly different in important and meaningful ways. This shapes their developing sense of self and helps them figure out where they "fit" within this broader social community.

And there is no question that this feedback carries significant weight. I can vouch for that from my personal experience. When I was eleven years old, my mother bought me a new pair of corduroy pants. My eleven-year-old self was not particularly concerned about my manner of dress or, if I am being honest, my appearance in general. So when these pants made their way to the top of the pile in my clothes drawer, I did not think twice about wearing them to school. It turned out that this particular pair of corduroy pants made audible and distinctive *whiff-whiff* noises when I walked. This phenomenon was immediately brought to my attention by my classmates, and I spent the rest of the day being the butt of nasty jokes and other forms of torment. When I got home after school, I yelled at my (poor, unsuspecting) mother for ruining my life, and I vowed that under no circumstances would I ever wear those pants again. I was prepared to suffer any punishment that my mother might have cared to dish out, as nothing she could have done to me would have compared to what I had endured that day at school. Like countless other children, I had reached the stage when the views of my friends almost always outweighed the views of my parents.

No matter how you slice it, it seems pretty clear that humans are "social animals." There are clear benefits, at all stages of life, to spending time around others. As you may have guessed, however, the picture isn't quite as simple as "solitude is bad because we're better off together." But before we get into a deep discussion of all the benefits of solitude, which have been shortchanged for too long, we need to consider another set of arguments that take this tack more directly. In this case, though, the focus is on why too much solitude, particularly at the extremes, is *really* bad.

Chapter 4

Not Only the Lonely

Confronting the Very Worst of Solitude

At the outset of the previous chapter, I wrote about one of the many occasions when I felt like an imposter in graduate school. I also remember the exact moment when I first knew that I belonged there; it was the same moment I realized I had been granted the extraordinarily rare privilege of finding a career path that offered me opportunities for purpose, challenge, engagement, and even joy.

During the time I was a graduate student, my mentor, Ken Rubin, started a research collaboration with the University of Maryland researcher Nathan Fox. This was no ordinary partnership. Ken and Nathan were at the absolute top of their respective fields, Ken in the study of social development and peer relations, and Nathan in the areas of neuroscience and the developing brain. This was the academic psychology equivalent of a collab between Taylor Swift and Beyoncé.

One of their first joint studies attempted to establish links between children's shy and sociable behaviors and patterns of electrical impulses measured in the brain using electroencephalograms (EEGs). This work was based on a relatively new theory at the time, which described links between how our brains process instances of mild stress and our emotional responses. For example, this theory suggested that amplified electrical activation in the right frontal lobe, the region of the brain thought to process punishment, would correspond with more negative emotional responses. Alternatively, a greater response in the left frontal lobe, a part of the brain associated with experiences of reward, would be associated with more positive emotional reactions.

Some initial support for these ideas had been found in studies of infants and adults. But Nathan and Ken expanded these ideas and, for the first time, applied them as a way of trying to help understand the underpinnings and origins of children's shy and social behaviors. They hypothesized that shy children would display a distinct pattern of elevated EEG activity in the punishment-oriented right frontal lobe.* In contrast, they expected more sociable children to demonstrate this amplified response in the reward-focused left frontal lobe area.

Their groundbreaking study involved months of meticulous data collection. Young children between the ages of four and five years were brought into the lab in groups of four. Prior to the experiment, none of the children had met. These quartets of youngsters participated in a series of scenarios designed to mimic common social situations experienced at school. These included play sessions, where children were free to play as they chose in a room with age-appropriate toys; a ticket-sorting task, where children had to distribute tickets of different colors into various piles; and a show-and-tell exercise, where each child was asked to stand up and talk about their last birthday party.

The sessions were video recorded through a one-way mirror. This allowed us to generate a detailed record of instances of shy and sociable behaviors during the various segments. For example, we calculated how frequently each child played with other children versus being

* This pattern was expected in response to not only social "stresses" (such as meeting a new person) but also just "in general." The idea here is that shy children's nervous systems are always a little bit "activated" in this way, as if they are expecting something scary to jump out from around the corner.

off by themselves. We recorded the amount of time each child spent speaking across the sessions. We also noted and tracked overt signs of anxiousness, like averting eye contact, a hunched over body posture, or fingernail biting. Each child was also individually tested with EEG equipment. Because they were so young, this was done using an age-appropriate protocol that involved children pretending to put on a space suit and board a rocket ship for a voyage to Mars. (The "space helmet" was actually lined with EEG electrodes.)

Finally, after all the data was collected and meticulously coded, we were ready to see if the results worked out as Nathan and Ken had predicted. As the lab's resident statistical expert at the time, I was entrusted with conducting the data analysis. I vividly recall sitting in front of our lab computer (a state-of-the-art IBM 386) and carefully typing in the relevant commands, with Ken and Nathan impatiently pacing back and forth behind me. The weight of the group's anticipation was palpable in the room. Just before I hit the final critical keystroke, I reminded myself that I was in the presence of two very important and very serious scientists and that this was a very important and very serious moment. No matter the result, I was determined to match my demeanor to the magnitude and formality of the occasion.

Then, with that firm resolve, I tapped the return key, and the final numbers popped up on the screen. The results were exactly as Ken and Nathan had predicted. Children who were more sociable and outgoing during the free play, ticket-sorting, and show-and-tell sessions displayed an EEG pattern highlighted by greater activation in the left frontal lobe area of their brain. In contrast, children who were more shy and socially withdrawn demonstrated a greater activation in the right frontal lobe. Holy crap . . . This was huge!

On the inside, I was doing cartwheels and hollering like a well-lubricated spectator at a professional wrestling match. On the outside, I turned slowly and prepared to stoically comment that this was a promising result. It was then that I saw Ken and Nathan raucously high-fiving each other, dancing like maniacs around the room, and whooping at the top of their lungs. In that moment, I was enveloped in feelings of shared joy, acceptance, and belongingness. It was awesome. I had found my people.

It is somewhat ironic that Nathan was present for such a foundational moment of social connection and community for me. I note this because that uplifting personal social experience is in such stark contrast to the reason I thought of Nathan as I started writing this chapter. Not long after these events, Nathan cofounded the Bucharest Early Intervention Project, which was born out of the horrific historical events that destroyed the lives of thousands of helpless Romanian children. I wanted to open with a warm and fuzzy story, because this chapter deals with some very dark content, including the findings of that project.

This was a hard chapter to write—and it's likely not much fun to read—but to fully understand solitude, we must reckon with its darkest aspects. We need to discuss social isolation, because it is the most extreme form of enforced solitude. We need to discuss ostracism, because it is a common human experience and the reason so many people suffer unwanted solitude. And we need to talk about loneliness, because it is the most common result of unwanted solitude, and it comes at a terrible human cost. So, please be advised, this chapter describes unconscionable cases of abuse, neglect, and human suffering.

The Tragic Consequences of Extreme Social Isolation

For obvious ethical reasons, it is not possible to study the impact of extreme social isolation on child development or adult well-being by experimenting on human subjects. Instead, this type of research has historically been conducted with mice or rats. These studies typically involve placing the animal in solitary confinement for extended periods of time and observing the effects.

Dozens of studies have shown that extreme social isolation causes some pretty bad stuff, including cognitive deficiencies, impoverished brain development, health problems such as morbid obesity and type 2 diabetes, and even increased mortality. Further, when infant rats and mice are placed in isolation at an early age, they grow up with serious and enduring impairments, particularly in terms of how they interact socially, even if they are placed back into their normal social environments later. The results are unequivocal: social animals—like humans—are seriously and often irreversibly harmed by extreme isolation (especially in childhood).

Such experiments certainly raise questions about the ethical treatment of mice and rats. And, of course, no reasonable person would ever contemplate using such procedures with people. However, sadly, sometimes history intervenes, and children are made victims of unspeakable crimes. These tragedies have shown us that the profound negative effects of extreme social isolation are just as devastating in humans as experiments on rodents would have us expect.

There have been several documented historical cases of "feral" children who were forced to spend extended periods of their early developing years with little or no human contact. Although difficult to contemplate, these examples give us the most direct evidence of the specific detrimental effects of extreme social isolation on the human brain and body. Understanding these impacts not only underscores the critical and irrefutable need for social connection but also establishes boundaries and warning areas in considering the benefits of solitude. In short, knowing more about the dangers of solitude at the extremes helps us to safely and effectively explore the positive aspects of time alone under the more normal range of our typical experiences.

Perhaps the most well-known historical example of a feral child was a boy discovered by a group of hunters in a forest near Aveyron, France, in the late 1790s. About ten years old when he was found, the child had apparently been living alone in the forest for several years without human contact. He was taken into the care of the physician Jean Marc Gaspard Itard, who named him Victor (although he was colloquially known as the Wild Boy of Aveyron). When he was first brought to Itard's attention, Victor was able to produce vocalizations that sounded like speech, but he did not voice real words.

Itard developed new educational techniques to teach Victor and tried to integrate him into society.* Despite some progress, Victor's cognitive, linguistic, and social skills remained quite limited. It has been speculated that Victor displayed signs of autism and other neurodevelopmental issues, which may have been why his parents abandoned him at an earlier age. This highlights one of the major challenges in drawing conclusions from these types of "real-world" examples. It is simply not possible to discern which parts and how much of Victor's enduring difficulties were a direct result of his extreme social isolation or may have been present regardless.

Another infamous case from more recent history was Genie (née Susan Wiley), who was subjected to unfathomable abuse by her deranged father. Genie essentially spent her entire childhood locked in her room, tied naked to a potty chair. If she made any noise at all, her father beat her. She was never spoken to. Genie was discovered by child services in 1970 at the age of thirteen. Her father was charged with child abuse and later shot himself.

Genie was made a legal ward of the court, and a team of pediatricians, psychologists, and linguists was assembled to oversee her rehabilitation. Although Genie progressed in some areas, her language

* The educational techniques pioneered by Itard in his work with Victor greatly influenced Maria Montessori and helped form the foundation of the classic Montessori method still practiced in schools around the world today.

abilities improved only up to a limited point, and she struggled to communicate with others. The cases of Victor and Genie were viewed as initial evidence of the now widely accepted notion that there is a "critical period" for brain development related to language in childhood. Simply stated, if infants are not exposed to and taught language by a certain deadline in childhood, they will never be able to learn it the same way afterward.

As was the case with Victor, however, there are circumstances that make it challenging to draw clear conclusions; it is simply not possible to know how much of Genie's lasting difficulties were due to social isolation and how much were a result of the horrific physical and psychological abuse she suffered at the hands of her father. Moreover, these are both case studies of individual children, which makes it unclear how much we can generalize to the broader population at large. However, unfortunately, there are other examples that have occurred on a larger scale.

In the 1970s and 1980s, thousands of infants experienced extreme social isolation in state-run Romanian orphanages, under squalid, barbaric, and inhumane conditions. In the aftermath of the 1989 revolution to overthrow the dictator Nicolae Ceaușescu, the true extent of the horrors these institutionalized children experienced came to light. In 1999, the Bucharest Early Intervention Project was initiated by a team of American pediatricians, neuroscientists, and psychiatrists led by Nathan Fox, Charles Nelson, and Charley Zeanah. The stated goal of this program was to "examine the effects of early institutionalization on brain and behavior development, and to examine the impact of high-quality foster care as an intervention for children who have been placed in institutions."

Many of the children were able to be placed in foster care. The researchers tracked their progress over time, completing follow-up assessments as the children grew into adolescence. Today, after following a subset of these children for more than twenty years (the study remains ongoing), several conclusions are evident. The somewhat good news is that placing children in high-quality foster care was broadly effective in improving developmental outcomes. These children demonstrated marked improvements in a number of domains, including their cognitive, language, and social skills. This was particularly true for children who were placed in foster care before the age of two years. However, sadly, some of the long-term effects of this social deprivation and profound neglect, including deficits in cognitive abilities and persistent behavior problems, appear to be more irreversible.

The profound and devastating effects of social deprivation are tragic and heart-wrenching. It is important to emphasize that being subjected to enforced isolation over prolonged periods of time is different from solitude. But even in a much less extreme form, being actively excluded and ostracized by others carries some significant negative consequences.

Ostracism Hurts like a Kick in the Cyberballs

I have always found attending academic conferences to be a lot like going back to high school. There are cliques and crowds, and most people are just trying to figure out where, and with whom, they belong. You also have to get up in front of the class and talk about your homework. In high school, your social status might be conveyed by how you dress, how you wear your hair, and whom you sit with at lunchtime in the cafeteria. At conferences, who you are is on full display for all to see. Everyone wears an ID badge bearing their vital stats: name, university affiliation, and academic position. I am sure the intention here is to promote social connection, networking, and interpersonal exchange. But this practice also serves to place an even greater emphasis on status, which can make things intimidating, particularly for early career scholars.

When I attended my very first conference, I was as green as they come and admittedly bewildered by the entire situation. There were thousands of people there, and the program listed dozens of simultaneously occurring sessions. There was a seemingly infinite array of symposia, discussion panels, debates, and poster sessions to choose from in each time slot. It was a lot to take in. On the first day, I sheepishly joined the crowd filing into a huge auditorium to attend the opening ceremony and keynote address. I squeezed into a seat, reeling a bit from the crush of people, and took a moment to take in my surroundings. And there, on my left, seated right next to me, was one of my academic heroes. This was someone whose work I had followed and admired for years. He had truly been an inspiration to me.

I took a deep breath and reminded myself that meeting people was one of the main points of conferences like this. Then I tapped him on the shoulder and introduced myself. In a quavering voice, I told him that his earlier research on children's friendships was one of the main reasons I became a developmental psychologist and that it was a true honor to meet him. He paused for a moment, glanced down at my ID badge, and presumably registered me as an academic "nobody." I say that because he curtly responded, "I don't do that work anymore," turned away, and started talking to someone presumably more important who was seated on his other side. I was crushed. I recoiled as though I had been punched in the chest. I also vowed that if I was ever "famous" enough in academic circles that a young person approached me in a similar way, I would always take the time to chat and connect with them.

Ostracism is the experience of being ignored, rejected, or excluded by others. It is, unfortunately, something everyone has—or will—experience at some point in their life. We have already talked a little about physical ostracism, which is when someone is forcibly isolated from others. This type of ostracism most often occurs when solitude is applied as a form of punishment. Some examples include parents disciplining an unruly toddler (time-outs), communities actively displaying their displeasure with a nonconforming member (shunning), additional reprisal for an imprisoned criminal offender (solitary confinement), or nations deposing a ruler (exile).

However, ostracism also comes in other forms. My deflating experience at the conference was an example of *social ostracism*, which refers to being ignored or excluded while in the physical presence of others. This could include being given the silent treatment by someone, a frequently deployed tactic on schoolyards and playgrounds everywhere. For adults, the modern and technology-enhanced version of this is *phubbing*.

Phubbing is a portmanteau of "phone" and "snubbing," defined by the *Cambridge Dictionary* as "the act of ignoring someone you are with and giving attention to your mobile phone instead." The term originated in 2012 as the result of a campaign by an Australian dictionary to create a new word to describe this phenomenon. Its use around the world has continued to spread steadily, and it has now also become the focus of psychological study. For example, growing research, including a study by the University of Kent psychologists Varoth Chotpitayasunondh and Karen Douglas, suggests that phubbing is a significant cause of frustration and conflict within romantic couples. It has a direct negative impact on relationship satisfaction and damages well-being. Perhaps not surprisingly, phubbing is also an increasingly common parental behavior that has been shown to have detrimental effects on several aspects of children's development. For example, the Shanghai Jiao Tong University researcher Pengcheng Wang and colleagues found that parental phubbing led to increased loneliness six months later among adolescents.

Phubbing may be a novel technology-fueled incarnation of social ostracism, but the underlying phenomenon is hardly new. A lot of what we know about the psychology of social ostracism over the last twenty years comes from research conducted using a computer program called Cyberball. Cyberball was developed by the Purdue University researcher Kipling Williams as a controlled and ethical laboratory procedure for examining the effects of being excluded and ignored. In a typical application of this program, participants log in to an online experiment and, as a cover story, are told that they will first play a short game designed to hone their visualization skills before they move on to the main experiment. In actuality, the short game itself is the primary focus of the experiment.

During the Cyberball activity, participants play a virtual game of catch, typically with two or three other players who are represented by animated icons. Participants are informed that the other players are "real people" who have logged in to the experiment remotely. This is another deception; in actuality, the other players are programmable computer-generated characters. Thus, the experimenters can strictly control how often the real person in the game is thrown the ball. The game usually lasts about five minutes. To simulate the experience of ostracism, the other characters are programmed to pass the ball to the participant once or twice at the outset of the game and then to ignore them the remaining time.

Imagine yourself as the subject of this experiment. You start playing a simple little computer game, pressing a keyboard key to toss and catch a virtual ball to avatars of other players. Then, out of nowhere, they just stop passing the ball to you. How do you think you would feel? Would this really be anything more than a minor annoyance at worst? Would you be invested enough in this experience for it to actually upset you?

It turns out the answer to the last question is likely yes. Even Williams was surprised by how much of an impact the Cyberball experience had on participants. In a 2006 essay describing the origins of the Cyberball paradigm, Williams wrote, "The results astounded us. Although participants were playing a game with a disk or ball that did not actually exist and with fictitious others whom they did not know and whom they did not expect to meet, they actually cared about the extent to which they were included."

Indeed, participants did more than care. In the first set of studies trying out this new paradigm, Williams found that not being thrown the virtual ball in this "meaningless" exercise had strong negative effects on participants' subsequent mood, self-esteem, and feelings of belonging. It also substantially raised their levels of distress. Simply stated, being left out of a five-minute virtual pitch-and-catch game with strangers made people feel like crap.

Since the initial study, tens of thousands of participants have been virtually ostracized while playing Cyberball under a wide range of conditions and circumstances. The results are robust and quite remarkable. Across age, gender, countries, and continents, being ostracized makes us feel terrible. Amazingly, this is the case even when participants are told they are playing with a computer as opposed to real people!

There is also some evidence to suggest that being rejected and excluded *physically* hurts us. The University of California, Los Angeles, researcher Naomi Eisenberger used functional magnetic resonance imaging (fMRI) to observe blood flow in the brains of people who experienced ostracism while playing Cyberball. She found increased activation in the dorsal anterior cingulate cortex, an area of the brain that registers the experience of physical pain. More recently, the Hong Kong researcher Kai-Tak Poon found that participants *watching someone else* experience ostracism during Cyberball reported feeling physical pain themselves. To be clear, the overall level of physical pain reported by those observing Cyberball participants being excluded would certainly be characterized as mild. But it is nevertheless the case that even witnessing social ostracism seems to hurt us.

Finally, there is another, more recently studied type of ostracism unique to your phone, known as *cyberostracism*. This occurs in the realm of electronic media when some manner of response or reaction is expected but not received. This includes such phenomena as being "left on read" (you have sent a message and can see that the recipient of the message has viewed it but has not yet replied) and being "ghosted" (when someone cuts off all forms of communication without explanation). However, although it occurs out there in the ether, cyberostracism, like Cyberball, has real-world impacts on our well-being.

In a study led by one of my former PhD students, Bowen Xiao, along with the Canadian researchers Jennifer Shapka and Natasha Parent, we adapted the ideas behind the Cyberball protocol to look at cyberostracism. The goal of our study was to explore what happens when university students receive different amounts of positive feedback on social media. First, participants were asked to create a personal profile with an avatar and a short self-description. They were then added to a social media group that included eleven other members. Participants were able to view one another's avatars, read their descriptions, and respond with a "like." Each profile had a like counter that increased with each click, and participants received a pop-up notification when their profile was liked by someone else.

Although each participant was told at the outset of the study that they were interacting with other students, the other avatars were fictions created as part of the experiment. Participants were then randomly placed into conditions where they received either few (1 or 2), some (4 or 5), or many (9 or 10) likes during the three-minute session. Even from this brief experience, we found that participants who received fewer likes later reported more negative emotions, lower self-esteem, and even reduced feelings of a meaningful existence. Ladies and gentlemen . . . the awesome power of social media!

The ongoing rapid growth of technology—and particularly social media—has made it fertile and exciting ground for research on social dynamics, but it is important to note that ostracism often occurs in "real-world" settings too, where its effects are just as pronounced. Among adults, one such environment is the workplace. Workplace ostracism includes a wide range of negative experiences, from refusal to return greetings, to the silent treatment (apparently not just the exclusive purview of children on the playground), to coordinated and overt efforts to exclude and harm employees. Unfortunately, such experiences remain all too common. Studies in the United States routinely find that more than 70 percent of employees report that they had been ostracized by their supervisors or coworkers. As we have seen, these experiences come at a cost. The University of South Alabama researcher Matt Howard and his colleagues reviewed ninety-three studies that explored the impact of workplace ostracism. They found that such experiences negatively influenced outcomes across several domains. For example, employees who experienced ostracism in the workplace were more likely to suffer from poorer job performance, greater stress, and emotional exhaustion, as well as mental health problems like depression. Workplace ostracism was also a predictor of the desire to leave one's job and actual job turnover. So, unsurprisingly, being ignored and excluded at work is incredibly damaging to our mental health and well-being.

To sum up, there are many ways that experiences of ostracism make us feel bad. But sadly, we still need to consider one of the most common short-term and long-lasting effects of enforced solitude: social isolation and ostracism make us feel *lonely*. As I mentioned earlier, loneliness sucks. It is not only bad for our mental health and well-being, but there is increasing evidence that loneliness takes a heavy toll on our physical health as well.

So Lonely . . . I Could Die

In the chorus of his 1956 chart-topping monster hit "Heartbreak Hotel," Elvis Presley croons that he is feeling so lonely that he might die. The song was written by Mae Boren Axton and Tommy Durden, but its origins are the stuff of music history legend. Various versions of this sordid tale all center around the songwriters supposedly reading a newspaper article in the *Miami Herald* describing a desolate man who committed suicide by throwing himself out a hotel window, leaving a suicide note emblazoned with the words "I walked a lonely street."

More than sixty years later, an exposé published in *Rolling Stone* magazine debunked this story as an urban myth. Instead, the article claimed that the line "I walked a lonely street" was actually part of an unpublished memoir written by a man who was killed while robbing a liquor store. Regardless, I think it is safe to say that Axton, Durden, and even Elvis himself did not have any idea how prophetic these words would be with regard to future epidemiological research on the devastating long-term impacts of social isolation and loneliness.

Loneliness is what we feel when the quality and quantity of our social life does not meet our personal wants and expectations. It is a *discrepancy* between our social desires and our social reality. In this way, loneliness is a dissatisfaction with a particular sphere of our life. It can manifest as an aching and longing that permeates all aspects of our daily existence. And as I have written already several times in this book, loneliness really sucks.

As discussed in the previous chapter, humans have retained an inborn need to belong, thought to reflect the evolutionarily adaptive necessity of social communities. From this perspective, loneliness is the inevitable result of what happens when this need is thwarted. According to the late social neuroscientist John Cacioppo, who was considered the world's leading expert in this area, loneliness served an evolutionarily adaptive function: the pain of loneliness was an alarm bell that was difficult to ignore, prompting us to renew social connections that were essential to our survival.

Today, however, loneliness itself has evolved into a global epidemic impacting people of all ages. The psychology researcher Louise Hawkley and her colleagues used data from the US General Social Survey in 2014 and 2018 to compare levels of loneliness across age groups. She found a U-shaped curve, with the highest levels of loneliness among young adults (below thirty years of age) and the very old (above eighty years of age). Of note, she found evidence for broad universal predictors of loneliness across all age groups, including lower household income, living alone,* being widowed or separated/divorced, poorer self-rated health, and, not surprisingly, less frequent social contact.

Historical rates of loneliness have been rising for decades and were only made worse by the COVID-19 pandemic. Although there is some indication of improvement as experiences of lockdowns and social distancing measures fade further into history, chronic loneliness remains prevalent around the world. According to a Meta-Gallup survey conducted across 140 countries in 2020–2023, nearly a quarter of all adult respondents reported currently feeling fairly or very lonely. That percentage represents more than a billion people in terms of the world's population. Interestingly, the young adults (aged nineteen to twenty-nine) in this survey reported the highest level of loneliness, even more so than adults aged sixty-five years and older. This finding contrasts with historical research suggesting that loneliness has often been highest in old age, and it certainly suggests that the pandemic took a particular toll on the social lives of young people.

Loneliness is insidious. It taints how we view ourselves and others, seeping into our everyday moments like a spreading infection. For example, across a series of studies, the Tilburg University researcher Olga Stavrova had participants report who they were with and how they were feeling at multiple random intervals across several days.

* Much more on the growing global trend of living alone and its potential implications in a later chapter.

Participants high in loneliness reported more negative emotions and lower well-being overall. Stavrova also found evidence to suggest that, in some cases, being around other people *amplified* the negative impact of loneliness on well-being. So, when we are already feeling lonely, sometimes being around others actually makes us feel even worse.

This is part of what makes loneliness so sinister. Humans evolved to be socially connected, to live in communities, to be with others. As we saw in the last chapter, even short interactions with total strangers tend to make us feel happier. But chronic loneliness somehow disrupts these emotional benefits, sabotaging the emotional boost we get even from the simplest social contact.

But loneliness is even more diabolical than that. In a series of studies, the University of Maryland psychology researcher Edward Lemay and his colleagues found that loneliness creates a negative bias in how people view their relationships with important others. Regardless of the *actual* quality of these relationships,* people who were lonelier perceived their romantic partners, family members, and friends as caring less about their needs, as well as less empathetic, responsive, and supportive. Thus, devastatingly, by poisoning the lens through which we view our closest friends and family, loneliness erodes our relationships with the very people in our lives who are most likely to make us feel less lonely.

It has been widely established, and increasingly reported in the news and on social media, that loneliness takes a significant toll on our mental health and well-being. Across hundreds of studies, loneliness is related to a wide range of serious negative outcomes, including poorer life satisfaction, less happiness, and lower self-worth, as well as increased rates of depression, anxiety, and suicide. But we are also now starting to understand that loneliness also puts a significant strain on our *physical* health.

* As assessed based on reports from the other members of these relationships, other informants, and objective observations of interactions with these individuals.

There is growing evidence that enduring loneliness over time increases the risk of a wide range of physical health problems, including dementia, heart disease, type 2 diabetes, and stroke. A 2023 advisory from the US Office of the Surgeon General asserts that chronic loneliness and social isolation increase the risk of premature death by more than 25 percent. By this metric, loneliness is worse for you than drinking six alcoholic drinks a day or about as unhealthy as smoking fifteen cigarettes a day!

In 2018, the United Kingdom appointed a minister of loneliness following the release of a report from a committee commissioned to investigate ways to reduce loneliness. In 2021, Japan followed suit and appointed its own minister of loneliness, with a goal of reducing rates of social isolation, loneliness, and suicide, all of which increased during the COVID-19 pandemic. Most recently, in 2023, the World Health Organization launched a new Commission on Social Connection, with stated goals of addressing loneliness as a pressing health threat, promoting social connection as a priority, and accelerating the scaling up of solutions in countries of all incomes.

The major takeaway here is that ostracism makes us suffer, whether it comes in the form of forced physical isolation, social exclusion from a game of catch, or not receiving enough likes on a social media post. But as we reach the end of this chapter, I feel it is critical to emphasize again that ostracism is a primary cause of *unwanted* solitude, which often leads to loneliness and its suite of associated ills. However, loneliness and solitude are not the same thing. I would never want anyone to interpret my passion for solitude as in any way diminishing the profound negative consequences of ostracism and social isolation. Elvis had it right nearly seventy years ago, and we must continue to raise awareness and combat the epidemic of loneliness sweeping across the globe. But, and importantly, this should not prevent us from also embracing and empowering the positive aspects of solitude as a means of fostering happiness, mental health, and well-being.

Chapter 5

Well Enough Alone?

I've Got a Theory

Growing up, my siblings and I all took piano lessons. My parents had both come from musical families and felt strongly that this was something they wanted to pass on to us. The family "rules" were that you had to start piano lessons young, usually around age four, and had to continue at least until you turned thirteen. This policy was implemented for my two older sisters and was still in full effect when it came to me. My little brother, however, as youngest siblings often do, benefited from the rest of us slowly wearing down my parents' resolve, and he got to stop lessons at age ten.

We were all taught strictly classical music. Lessons were every Thursday afternoon with Sister Gabriellina, a kindly nun with the patience of Job, who had developed her own methods for teaching young children piano. She tried to make everything fun, inventing games that served to stretch and strengthen fingers ("Pretend to squeeze a lemon . . . tight, tight, tight . . . now let it go!") and placing stickers on each page of my piano books when a song was well learned. Her tiny frame exuded an exuberance and genuine joy for music. She was truly wonderful.

And I hated it. I hated it all, but I particularly hated having to practice every day. I hated scales, arpeggios, and other finger exercises—even when they were disguised as games. I hated learning the pieces. I hated playing them. My parents had to force me to practice—with threats of punishment—and I railed against this unfairness. Oh, the injustice! Why should I be coerced into practicing this thing I despised every day? But my parents persevered, and I counted down the years, months, and days until I would finally be freed from this tyranny. As soon as I turned thirteen, I quit taking piano lessons.

This is not one of those stories with a moral about the wisdom of listening to your parents, although I now admit that, in retrospect, I am glad that my parents forced me to take piano lessons when I was young. Instead, this is an example of the psychology of human motivations, which, simply put, helps us to better understand why we do the things we do.

From this perspective, it is easy to explain why I stopped taking piano lessons at my very first opportunity. My motivations for taking these lessons in the first place were *extrinsic*. Extrinsic motivations lead people to do things for all the wrong reasons. If we are extrinsically motivated to do something, it typically means we're driven by a desire to either earn a reward or avoid a punishment. This could mean staying in a job you really do not like because you need the money or, like me, practicing piano every day to avoid being disciplined by your parents. One thing about behaviors that are driven by extrinsic motivations is that they do not tend to be self-sustaining; when that external source of reward or punishment is removed, people do not tend to continue the behavior.

After I stopped taking lessons, I did not play piano at all for several months. But then something interesting happened. One day, I heard "Your Song" by Elton John on the radio and thought, *Maybe I could play that*. So I sat down at the piano and tried to figure it out. This led me to want to learn to play more of the songs I heard on the radio. And just like that, things were different. I liked these songs and genuinely wanted to be able to play them. With my portable AM/FM radio plugged in next to the piano, I would wait for a particular song to come on and then try to play along as best as I could. This was quite fun, and over time, I got better and better at quickly figuring out the chords for my favorite songs.

As I improved and endeavored to learn more complex songs, I ran into a problem. My fingers simply could not move fast enough or stretch far enough to play the right notes in the right rhythms. At that point, a little light bulb went off in my head. I realized that this was exactly why Sister Gabriellina had made me play scales, arpeggios, and other finger exercises every day. But suddenly, I *wanted* to do this. Suddenly, practicing was the pathway to accomplishing something I was passionate about.

I suspect the irony was not lost on my parents. They went from having to utter threats to get me to practice to having to yell at me to stop playing the piano so much because it was late at night and they wanted to go to sleep. From a psychological perspective, what had happened was that I had developed an *intrinsic* motivation for playing piano. Intrinsic motivations are more likely to lead people to do things for all the "right" reasons. These motivations are driven by interest, meaning, and enjoyment. In short, intrinsic motivations are when you do something for you.

I believe that understanding how motivational theory applies to solitude can go a long way toward unlocking the benefits of spending time alone. In the end, it almost always comes down to *why* you are doing it. Consider a few examples of why people spend time alone. Some people might spend time alone because they recently moved to a new city and have not yet made any social connections. Others might be by themselves more often because they just retired and have been severed from the social networks that they took for granted at work every day. Yet others might retreat to solitude because they find being around other people stressful and anxiety provoking.

Under circumstances like these, individuals' motivations for solitude are not likely to be intrinsic in nature. The first two cases illustrate social isolation, whereby external circumstances result in *unwanted* solitude. As we have seen, being forced into solitude most often leads to bad things. However, the third case, which relates to social anxiety, is a bit more nuanced. This person may genuinely want to engage with others, but that desire is thwarted by their social unease and self-consciousness. In this way, they are "choosing" solitude for extrinsically motivated reasons: to avoid the "punishment" of having to endure social situations that make them feel stressed. And as a result, their time alone will often feel empty and unfulfilling.

Now let's consider people who are spending time alone because they enjoy knitting, taking a solitary stroll in a nearby park, or cozying up with a book, a blanket, and a steaming mug of hot chocolate in their favorite reading nook. What about people who seek time alone to make a meal plan, generate lists of Christmas gifts for loved ones, or just daydream? Or people who need to recharge their batteries after a busy day of work meetings, parenting, or other responsibilities? It is more likely that these individuals are experiencing intrinsic motivations for solitude. For them, time alone likely feels full and fulfilling, and they are primed and ready to soak up all the best stuff that solitude has to offer.*

Solitude Is Good! Passion Versus Proof

Although solitude has long had a bad reputation, passionate pleas extolling the "good" of solitude can be traced back just as far. Epictetus

---

* Of note, these are not exclusive distinctions. For example, some socially anxious individuals also enjoy some of their time alone, particularly when they are engaged in enjoyable and meaningful solitary activities.

was an ancient Greek philosopher who lived in the latter part of the first century AD. He belonged to the philosophical school of Stoicism, which espoused the basic premise that virtue is the essential path to achieving a well-lived life. In *Discourses*, a four-volume compilation of his philosophical writings, Epictetus included a brief essay on solitude (book 3, chapter 13).

In this piece, Epictetus advises that we all should strive to be able to be our "own companion." He argues that honing our ability to "talk with ourselves" can free us from feeling the wants of others. This would then allow us to more thoughtfully consider our place in the world, how we affect others, and what effects others have on us. It is only through this type of solitary introspection, Epictetus believed, that we can identify the things that hurt us and then determine how to cure or remove this pain.

I would say that Epictetus was pretty much right on the money when it came to solitude. In an essay written more than two thousand years ago, he essentially offers the same basic advice that I am writing about here in my book. We should all work to develop our *capacity* for solitude. Not only will doing so serve us in our relationship with ourselves, but as we will see, it will also serve us in our relationships with others. I guess I am lucky that not many people read ancient Koine Greek.*

There have been many subsequent essays in which philosophers, poets, authors, artists, and, later, psychologists, passionately championed the more positive aspects of solitude. In an essay written in the late 1500s, the French philosopher Michel de Montaigne opined that individuals should strive for experiences of solitude not only as a respite from societal pressures but also to free themselves from dogma, conventional ways of thinking, and the power of the group. In his famous 1854

* Confession that I am burying in a footnote: There are several excellent English translations of *Discourses* available.

book *Walden; or, Life in the Woods*, the American naturalist, author, and philosopher Henry David Thoreau reflected on the values of solitude in promoting self-reliance, meaningfulness, and self-discovery: "I went to the woods because I wished to live deliberately . . . I wanted to live deep and suck out all the marrow of life."

In 2003, the American psychologists Christopher Long and James Averill published the essay "Solitude: An Exploration of Benefits of Being Alone." This treatise summarized the state of the art of what we knew about positive aspects of solitude at the time. In it, the authors systematically describe several potential benefits of solitude, including creativity, self-exploration, spirituality, and, somewhat paradoxically, intimacy, the suggestion being that solitude can make us feel more connected to others.

The first time I read about these ideas, I knew deep down in my bones that they were "true." I also assumed that there was a long history of extensive research that provided clear and irrefutable evidence to support these claims. It turns out, not so much. Although solitude has been studied by psychologists for a long time, it has proven to be quite difficult to directly demonstrate how and why time alone can have positive impacts on well-being. This surprised me and, in part, fueled my drive to better understand the benefits of solitude.

What was missing at that time was a clear explanation of the *active ingredients* of solitude. For example, a common previous argument for the benefits of solitude, as articulated by Long and Averill in their essay, drew evidence from studies demonstrating that spending time in natural environments is good for us. Now, to be clear, being in nature is very good for us! Exposure to green spaces and other natural environments has been shown to make us feel calmer, happier, and less anxious. It has also been shown to aid our memory and restore our capacity for attention. However, what had been less clearly established is whether you need to be *alone* in nature to experience these gains. Would we see the same benefits taking a stroll alone in the woods compared with a walk with a friend or friends? We will tackle these questions shortly.

Similarly, the benefits of meditation and mindfulness have been cited as evidence of the positive aspects of solitude. Again, there is considerable scientific support for the assertion that meditation and mindfulness promote mental and physical health. Mindfulness, for example, has been shown to reduce symptoms of anxiety and depression, improve sleep quality, and even help cope with pain. However, as with being in nature, it is not at all clear that you need to be alone to realize the benefits of mindfulness practices. A skilled mindfulness practitioner should be able to enact mindful practices regardless of their social setting. Further, it has been argued that group meditation has its own unique pluses, including providing a sense of connection, meaning, and community.

I have studied solitude for a long time, and for many years it was very much a niche area in psychology. There were many times when, ironically, I felt like I was very much alone in this pursuit. But over the last several years, there has been an explosion of interest in the scientific study of solitude around the globe. This has led us to understand more clearly how, why, when, and for whom solitude can be good. And finally, some ingenious scientific studies have not only offered compelling explanations of the active ingredients of solitude, but they've also provided some of the first direct evidence of the concrete benefits of spending time alone.

Solitude Is the Land of the Free

I continued to play piano throughout my teenage years and got involved in several bands. Like many young people before me and since, part of me dreamed of making music my career. After starting university, I became increasingly interested in psychology, and I started contemplating what my life would be like if I pursued that avenue instead. Soon, the metaphorical fork in the road appeared directly before me. What path should I take? To the left, a future filled with music, writing songs, making records, and touring the world performing for legions of adoring fans. To the right, the ivied halls of academia: graduate school, then teaching, research, and the pursuit of scholarship.

I finished my undergraduate degree in April and received my offer of admission to start graduate school the following September. I had only a few months to decide. So, with the spontaneous resolve only a twenty-one-year-old could muster, I hopped in my car and headed out on the road to see what life would be like as an itinerant musician. I spent the next four months on a solo driving trip through the southern US states, bouncing from city to town, trying to support myself with whatever gigs I stumbled upon. I played for tips in piano bars and provided mood music in hotel lobbies, restaurants, and department stores. One night, I filled in at the last minute for the piano player in a bluegrass band, and we played our sets on a stage situated behind chicken wire in the rowdiest country bar I had ever seen. I even took on a brief stint as the organist for a minor league AAA baseball team in Jacksonville, Florida, playing the national anthem at the start of the game and "Take Me Out to the Ball Game" during the seventh inning stretch, and trying to rouse the crowd to cheer in between.

Although playing music can definitely be a social experience, I spent most of my time during my four-month odyssey by myself. I experienced all kinds of solitude: driving on the open road, sitting in a small room in a boardinghouse, walking the streets in a city where no one knew me, and feeling like a piece of furniture playing piano in the corner of a noisy restaurant, where I was considered nothing more than background noise. Of course, there were times when I felt lonely. But for perhaps the first time in my life, I opened myself up to the freedoms of solitude and soaked them all in.

This was a formative experience for me, and it allowed for the heartfelt self-exploration that can only happen when we give ourselves opportunities to be alone. It also gave me the space to contemplate my future and decide what I wanted to do and, ultimately, who I wanted to be. In the end, I gravitated to the idea that I could be a psychologist who plays music on the side, but not so much the other way around. Thirty-odd years later, I am still doing both.

The former defense minister of Israel Moshe Dayan once said that "freedom is the oxygen of the soul." If I had to sum up the underlying explanations as to why solitude can be beneficial in one word, I think "freedom" would be a good choice. In the essay I described earlier, Long and Averill also used the metaphor of freedom to describe how solitude confers its benefits upon us. Solitude provides both freedom *from* and freedom *to*. Freedom from the pressures and constraints of others, and freedom to do as we please. And just like the broader concept of freedom, the "freedom from" and "freedom to" offered by solitude also come with their own rewards.

Freedom From: Relax and Restore

When earlier describing different conceptualizations of solitude, I offered the sociologist Erving Goffman's metaphor of being "offstage." Being offstage means that you are no longer under the spotlight and no longer subject to the attention of others. This means you no longer have to modulate thoughts, feelings, and actions within the usual personal, social, and societal norms and constraints. Taking this a step further, being offstage can be understood as freedom from *social input*. We are bombarded by input in the physical presence of others, and this is only intensified by the technologies that can keep us virtually socially connected 24-7.

Imagine yourself driving on a highway in a car with all the windows cracked slightly open. The noise and pressure are likely overwhelming at first, as the air forces itself through the thin slits into the compact space of the car. But after a while, an adjustment usually takes place, and although they are still there, the constant currents of air become more like background noise and no longer grab your direct attention. Think of this as the social input people get when they are around others.

Of course, how much attention is paid to—and the immediate impact of—this social background noise and pressure is different for different types of people. For example, as we will explore in more detail later, people who experience social anxiety tend to be hyper-attuned to these continuous gusts of social pressure. In contrast, extreme extraverts are most comfortable under comparatively higher levels of social immersion. That is why some students need complete silence and no distractions to be able to concentrate on their homework, whereas others work best with the TV on in the background or while immersed in the social din of a crowded coffee shop.

Now think about what happens when all the windows in the car are suddenly closed. In an instant, the pressure just stops, and it is noticeably silent. For some, this can be a bit jarring, as we often don't realize just how loud the noise of the wind swirling through the car has been this entire time. But for many of us, including me, this is the feeling that solitude can bring: a (sometimes sudden) stop to the social pressures and noises that we did not even realize were buzzing all around us. When I make the transition from a social to a solitary space, I seem to almost automatically take a deep breath. It is like a heavy backpack, one carried so long that I almost forgot it was there, has been lifted off my shoulders. This is what I mean by "freedom from."

Deactivating your emotions. There are several theories that help to explain why "freedom from" tends to make us relax. In terms of how we feel, solitude appears to take the edge off our more intense emotions. Overall, being in the presence of and interacting with others tend to evoke more high-energy emotional responses. Psychologists describe these more intense emotions as being higher in *arousal*. For many, being around others typically elicits high-arousal positive emotions, like elation and excitement. But for others, social situations are also likely to trigger high-arousal negative emotions, like anxiety or anger.

In contrast, when we are alone, we are more likely to experience low-arousal positive emotions, such as calmness and contentment, but also low-arousal negative emotions, like boredom or sadness. So, when the metaphorical car windows close and we are removed from social stimulation, our emotions essentially take a deep cleansing breath and sort of flatten out.

The UK-based psychology researchers Thuy-vy Nguyen and Netta Weinstein labeled this phenomenon the *deactivation effect* of solitude. They found support for this theory across a series of studies where they asked adults to report at several random times each day how they were feeling and whom they were with. Overall, time spent alone was found to reduce feelings of anger and other high-arousal negative emotions, while also increasing feelings of calmness and other low-arousal positive emotions. In one of these studies, Nguyen and Weinstein instructed participants to spend fifteen minutes alone each day for a week. The "calming effect" of this solitude was still evident even a week later.

This latter finding has some potentially important implications for how people can harness the positive power of solitude. Even a relatively minor time investment in solitude, as little as fifteen minutes a day, appears to pay some emotional dividends. So you don't need to spend two hours each day meditating or walking alone in the woods (although some may enjoy doing just that) in order to realize the benefits of solitude.

Importantly, the deactivation effect theory does not stipulate that we generally feel more positive or negative when we are alone, just that solitude tends to make our emotions less intense. This can help us relax by smoothing out our emotional jagged edges and heightening feelings of calmness and serenity. But as we have seen, being alone can also make us feel sad and lonely. It turns out that which results we get often depends on our motivations for spending time alone. More on this in a bit.

Paying "soft" attention to nature. One place where people often seek "freedom from" is in nature. For me, being alone in nature is like dipping a tortilla chip in the salsa bowl. By itself, the corn chip is tasty, but the salsa adds a whole new level of deliciousness. Like solitude, exposure to green spaces and other natural environments has been shown to make us feel calmer. It lowers our blood pressure and reduces cortisol, a hormone that is released in response to stress. Being in nature also increases feelings of contentment and happiness by stimulating endorphins and dopamine, neurotransmitters released by the brain that promote feelings of pleasure and well-being.

One explanation for this is known as the *biophilia hypothesis*, which posits that humans have an innate capacity for connection with nature because of our long evolutionary history living in natural environments. The idea that humans have a deep and inborn connection to all forms of life can be traced all the way back to the writings of Aristotle. This theory remains very influential and has been cited as a reason for people's desire to live close to oceans, mountains, and parks. It also offers a compelling explanation for the enduring popularity of zoos, the strong attachments we often form with pets, and even the joy and satisfaction many of us get from gardening.

The relaxing effect of nature appears to be so ingrained and robust among humans that we do not actually need to be *in* nature to experience it. The Japanese researcher Hyunju Jo and his colleagues conducted a review of several studies examining the impact on people's emotions of viewing images of nature while indoors. They found that just looking at pictures or videos of beaches, trees, and mountains leads to more relaxed emotional and body responses. In contrast, images of urban and other built-up landscapes were more likely to evoke negative emotional responses and body tension. Similar effects have even been reported as a result of merely asking people to imagine themselves in a hypothetical natural environment.

So, we have solid reasons to believe that being alone in nature can be a particularly potent relaxant and a pretty good idea of why this is the case. But beyond its calming effects, we are also starting to understand how and why solitude helps us to *restore*. This is the idea that time alone can recharge our batteries, a primary claim made by introverts worldwide and one that we will sink our teeth into in great detail in chapter 7. For now, it is enough to note that time alone does more than just provide a respite from the drain of social situations. The "freedom from" of solitude also makes it a place for replenishing depleted resources of attention, focus, and memory.

To explain how this might work, we can also draw upon theories related to the benefits of being in nature. *Attention restoration theory* was first proposed by the University of Michigan environmental psychologists Rachel Kaplan and the late Stephen Kaplan. To illustrate this perspective, picture someone walking down the sidewalk of a busy urban street. A lot of things demand their attention. They are constantly scanning for possible obstacles in their path, including other pedestrians, dogs, and, increasingly these days, e-scooters.* As they cross a busy intersection, their eyes dart back and forth, constantly vigilant for trams, cars, and bicycles. And all the while, there are countless other assaults on their senses, all demanding and competing for their immediate attention: the honking of horns, the shrieking of sirens, the pounding of a jackhammer, and the constant drone of

* I think we can all agree that e-scooters represent a clear and present danger for society at large.

conversations. I don't know about you, but my head starts to hurt just thinking about this.

Now imagine the same person walking down a moss-covered path bound by trees. They can hear the faint whispers of a babbling brook in the distance, the wind gently weaving through the leaves, and the slightest hint of birdsong. Up above, glints of sunlight streak through the thick foliage, interrupted only by the slow-moving presence of puffy white clouds. I don't know about you, but I feel better already.

Both of these descriptions are a little over-the-top. But they are meant to illustrate the stark contrast between urban and natural environments in terms of sensory input. When we are in nature, everything slows down, and our body reacts accordingly. According to attention restoration theory, one of the major contributors to this slowing-down process is the difference between what is called hard and soft fascination. *Hard fascination* forcefully grabs and holds our full attention, like a car honking as we step into a crosswalk in a crowded city intersection. Hard fascination is intrusive and jarring. It does not allow the mental space for us to process our thoughts. Instead, it forces us only to react, again and again.

Soft fascination does not demand anything. It asks nicely. It gently and effortlessly nudges our attention, like the cresting of waves on a beach as the tide comes in. Soft fascination leaves space for us to think and reflect and, most important, for our minds to wander. It is this extra mental bandwidth that helps to restore our cognitive battery, and this can have powerful rejuvenating effects.

In an effort to quantify this dynamic, a group of researchers led by the University of Chicago psychologist Marc Berman compared the effects of exposure to urban versus natural environments on people's attention and memory. In one of their studies, college students began by completing thirty minutes of taxing memory tests that were designed to drain their cognitive reserves. Then half the participants took an hour-long walk by themselves downtown, whereas the other half spent the same amount of time walking in a nearby arboretum. After students completed their walks, they received another series of tests designed to measure their current levels of concentration and memory, such as hearing a sequence of numbers and then having to repeat it backward.

The results were clear. Participants who walked in nature performed substantially better on these cognitive tests than those who walked in an urban center. Subsequently, Berman repeated the experiment, but instead of walking downtown or in the arboretum, students spent ten minutes simply looking at either pictures of nature or pictures of urban settings. Amazingly, the results were the same. Just spending a few minutes glancing at pictures of nature was enough to provide measurable cognitive restoration.

Soft fascination also helps to explain why natural environments may be among the best places to spend time alone. Recall that most people find sitting alone with just their thoughts painfully boring, even aversive—to the point that self-administering an electric shock while alone was preferred over doing nothing. But being alone in nature offers us things on which to focus our attention. Furthermore, unlike an urban setting, where sensory input is more likely to be jarring and draining, the sensory input in nature is peaceful and renewing. In this way, a solitary walk through the woods or a park allows us to reap the emotional and cognitive benefits of both solitude and nature together in one calming and scenic package.

Here, it is worth asking again if the benefits of being alone in nature have more to do with nature or with solitude. This remains a complex question that is difficult to answer. In one of the only studies to date that specifically addresses this issue, my PhD student Alicia McVarnock and I compared how undergraduate students felt when asked to vividly imagine themselves in different hypothetical scenarios, including being alone indoors, with others indoors, alone in nature, and with others in nature. The results were complicated and differed depending upon the types of feelings that were assessed. But there appeared to be something unique about the combination of being alone and being in nature. For example, participants reported that they would feel more peaceful (a low-arousal positive emotion) alone than with others in nature, but this was not the case when they imagined themselves indoors. In contrast, participants indicated that they would feel less happy (a high-arousal positive emotion) alone than with others inside, but this was not the case when they imagined themselves in nature.

It is also worth acknowledging that, depending on the circumstances, spending time alone in nature can feel unsafe. If you're concerned about being mauled by a bear or getting lost, you are not going to feel very chill or be able to soak up those positive nature vibes. Being with others in nature might reduce safety concerns, but it may also increase social input and diminish the effects of feeling "freedom from."

So, it's complicated. Personally, I suspect personal preferences and motivations have a significant effect. That is, what we get out of solitude, be it sitting in a small room with the door closed or hiking up a rocky crag, depends very much on our motivations for choosing to spend time alone in the first place. Let's tackle that idea next.

Freedom To: Self-Determination Theory; or, It's the Autonomy, Stupid!

In 1972, the actress and author Marlo Thomas released *Free to Be . . . You and Me*, a record featuring a series of songs and stories performed by notable actors, singers, and other celebrities of the time, including Alan Alda, Michael Jackson, Shirley Jones, Roberta Flack, and Diana Ross. The record had a simple aim: to teach children about life. I think it is fair to say that it achieved this goal with a lot of children. To this day, *Free to Be . . . You and Me* remains a bestselling album. Although the content of this album focused broadly on helping children thrive in a rapidly changing world, its title perfectly encapsulates why solitude can help all of us thrive. In solitude, we are free to be . . . anything we want.

The psychological importance of "freedom to be" has its roots in humanistic psychology, which emerged in the 1950s as an alternative approach to understanding the human psyche. Prior to this, prevailing psychological approaches included Freudian psychoanalytic theory, which focused on unconscious desires, and behaviorism, which focused on how people's behaviors were learned from the environment through processes such as "conditioning."* Humanistic psychology focuses on fostering well-being by promoting self-awareness, individuality, and intentionality. From this perspective, humans are considered to be more than the sum of our parts, and true happiness comes from seeking meaning, value, and creativity.

Emerging from this perspective was the notion that humans have essential needs that extend beyond the basics of survival. Ideas like this were popularized by the American psychologist Abraham Maslow during the 1940s. He described a *hierarchy of needs*, comprising a rank-ordered progression of universal needs that we must satisfy in order to ultimately achieve our full potential. This hierarchy is often visually depicted as a pyramid. At the bottom are the basic necessities of life, including food, shelter, and sleep. Further up the pyramid are needs related to love and social connection, including friendship, intimacy, and trust, as well as needs related to aspects of the self, including feelings of accomplishment, self-confidence, and independence. According to Maslow, fulfilling each stage of this hierarchy of needs would allow us to reach the top of the pyramid. Here we would achieve

* A classic example of this process is when the Russian psychologist Ivan Pavlov "conditioned" his dogs to associate the sound of a bell ringing with food. He did this by ringing a bell every time he fed the dogs. After a while, he just needed to ring the bell, and the dogs would begin to salivate.

the crowning achievement of *self-actualization*, a process (somewhat fuzzily defined, in my opinion) that Maslow believed would allow for people to essentially be all that they can be.

Some of the specifics of Maslow's hierarchy of needs have since been disputed. For example, strong evidence never really emerged to support his assertion that all the stages represent essential human needs that must be satisfied in this specific order. Nevertheless, although not everyone agrees with Maslow's specific list, it is now widely accepted that there are fundamental and essential contributors to our health, well-being, and happiness beyond the basic needs of food, water, and shelter.

The American psychologists Edward Deci and Richard Ryan identify and highlight the importance of several of these needs in their influential *self-determination theory.* We have already talked about the need to belong, which relates to our inborn drive for social connection. Deci and Ryan described a similar concept, calling it the need for *relatedness*, but also outlined other core necessities. For example, the need for *competence* is about the importance of mastering different tasks. Simply put, the need for competence is more likely to be satisfied when we feel capable and adept in our lives.

Deci and Ryan also highlighted the need for *autonomy*, which is perhaps most relevant for solitude. When we have autonomy, we feel in control of things. We are steering the ship. In short, autonomy is when we are the star of our own stories. This type of personal self-government paves the pathway to growth, fulfillment, and flourishing.

Making the choice to choose solitude. Think back to my piano lessons story at the outset of this chapter. At first, my piano-playing behavior was driven by extrinsic motivations, which included being forced to practice by my parents, feeling guilty and not wanting to let my parents down, and the desire to avoid being punished. Under these circumstances, my choice to play piano was nonautonomous and not self-determined; unsurprisingly, it led to me hating practicing and quitting my lessons. In contrast, when I was older, my choice to play piano reflected an intrinsic motivation. Playing piano became personally important to me. I wanted to improve, and I genuinely enjoyed it. My motivation for playing piano became autonomous and self-determined, and to this day it remains a great source of joy for me.

So, how does this apply to solitude? Solitude offers the potential of freedom. It can provide the freedom to think your own thoughts, feel your own feelings, and be your true self. In short, solitude can offer the freedom to choose. But—and this part is critical—to access this potential, to reap and revel in these freedoms, you must *choose* solitude as a place you willingly want to be.* If your approach to solitude is governed by intrinsic motivations, if you autonomously elect to spend time alone, you will "flip the switch": solitude will turn from an empty and lonely void to a full and fulfilling favorite place.

Results from several recent research studies demonstrate the power of choice in determining experiences and implications of solitude. The American psychology researchers Virginia Thomas and Margarita Azmitia asked adolescents and young adults about their reasons for spending time in solitude by having them complete the sentence "When I spend time alone, I do so because . . ." Some respondents highlighted extrinsic motivations, such as seeking solitude because they felt uncomfortable or disliked being around others. These participants, whose choices to spend time alone were not self-determined, were more likely to report loneliness and depressive symptoms, as well as poorer-quality relationships with others. In contrast, other respondents described intrinsic motivations for spending time alone, including enjoyment, valuing privacy, and the freedom to pursue their own interests and activities. These self-determined choices for

* But not, as we have discussed, as a place where you end up because you are avoiding social situations perceived as stressful, anxiety-provoking, or unpleasant.

solitude were not related to depression, loneliness, or other negative outcomes but instead predicted greater well-being.

A team of UK-based psychology researchers led by Netta Weinstein reported a similar pattern of results in a study of adults aged thirty-five and older. They tracked episodes of daily time alone and daily time with others over a three-week period. Overall, results again highlighted the duality of solitude, with increased time alone predicting loneliness and lower life satisfaction but also reduced stress. However, the negative effects of solitude were nullified on days when solitude was *chosen*. Meanwhile, the stress-relieving function remained.

Similarly, the University of Vienna psychology researcher Jana Nikitin explored how episodes of solitude were experienced by adults aged eighteen to eighty-eight years. Overall, participants who spent time alone primarily "due to my wish/decision" reported more positive emotions, greater well-being, and even greater feelings of social connection than those whose experiences of solitude were nonautonomous. Taken together, studies like these provide a pretty clear demonstration of the power of choice when it comes to the implications of solitude.

So, to recap, there is growing evidence explaining how and why solitude can be good for us. Time alone provides us with freedom from the constraints and stresses of being around others and gives our nervous system a break from the barrage of social input that almost always demands our attention. This respite allows us to relax and recharge. Solitude also affords us the freedom to be ourselves—to choose our own adventures. When we make the choice to choose solitude, it makes us feel better about ourselves and others.

This is great news. You could even describe it as a "fairy-tale ending" for the study of solitude's benefits. With that in mind, we now turn our attention to a critical question about the benefits of solitude: How much time alone is best for our well-being? As it turns out, one particular fairy tale is quite instrumental in helping us understand the answer.

Chapter 6

When Solitude Is "Just Right"

Aloneliness and the Goldilocks Principle

What would the story of "Goldilocks and the Three Bears" look like if it was told as a breaking news story happening today? The headline would probably be something like "Bear Family Shaken After Violent Home Invasion!"

> The suspect, described as a young woman with golden hair, broke into the house while the family was out and proceeded to wreak havoc. She consumed food, including a bowl of porridge, and damaged property, including a small chair. When the Bear family returned home, they were shocked to find the suspect asleep in one of their beds. She escaped through an open window and is still at large. Police dogs are now being employed to scour the forest in search of her scent. A DNA sample extracted from the used porridge spoon is also currently being tested for matches with known offenders. Mama Bear described the experience as harrowing and feared for the safety of her young child. Papa Bear was seething with anger at the brutal violation of their homestead. Anyone with information pertaining to this incident should immediately contact Crime Stoppers or their local police station.

This classic fairy tale first appeared in print in the 1800s. It makes extensive use of a literary device sometimes called the *rule of three*. Goldilocks examines three sets of items in the house: bowls of porridge, chairs, and beds. In each case, the first two are unsatisfactory in opposite ways, such as the porridge being too hot and then too cold, followed by the third one being just right. Now let's consider what the story of Goldilocks would look like if the main focus was on solitude.

Once upon a time, a young girl named Goldilocks went to visit the Bear family. She planned to stay with them for three weeks. During the first week of her visit, the entire family left very early in the morning, before Goldilocks even woke up. Papa and Mama Bear went to work, dropping off Baby Bear at the local day care. It was a tremendously busy time for the family, and they did not return each day until well into the evening. Goldilocks was left pretty much all by herself for the entire week. She tried to make the best of this unplanned alone time, but with each passing day, she felt more and more sad and lonely.

During the second week of Goldilocks's visit, the Bear family had a week off work and decided to enjoy a staycation. Suddenly, the small home felt crowded and noisy. Papa and Mama Bear were very sociable. They loved talking and constantly engaged Goldilocks in heated debates about politics, religion, the merits of pineapple on pizza, and other hotly contested topics. Then they taught her how to play Settlers of Catan, and they all became deeply immersed in an intense series of highly competitive games. (It turned out that Papa Bear was a bit of a sore loser.) Young Baby Bear was full of beans himself and peppered Goldilocks with repeated requests to play. At first, Goldilocks enjoyed the whirlwind of conversations and activities. But as the week progressed, she began to feel edgy, grumpy, and even a bit sad. She was not really sure why.

During the third week of Goldilocks's visit, Papa and Mama Bear went back to work, Baby Bear went back to his day care, and everyone was on a more regular schedule. Goldilocks had breakfast with the Bears each morning. Then she would spend part of the morning reading an engrossing mystery novel while sipping on a cup of warm cocoa. At midday, she took to exploring the surrounding forest in each direction, and by late afternoon, she busied herself with a bit of light housework and prepped dinner for the Bear family's return. She hung out with the Bear family in the evening and went to bed each night feeling calm and content. By the time her visit came to an end, Goldilocks was already looking forward to returning for another visit in a few months.

The moral of this story would probably be something like: Sometimes solitude can be too much, sometimes it can be too little, and we should all strive to spend time alone in a way that is "just right" for us. Written like that, it seems like such a simple and intuitive idea. Why didn't this light bulb go off in my head years ago?

The history of science is filled with tales of eureka moments. Some of these accounts have reached the realm of mythos, like the apple falling out of a tree and hitting Sir Isaac Newton on the head, providing the catalyst for his theory of gravity. Or Albert Einstein surmising the underlying premise of the theory of relativity while riding a streetcar away from a clock tower in Bern, Switzerland. Over the course of my entire thirty-plus-year career of studying solitude, I have had precisely one experience like this. Don't get me wrong, I have developed some unique ideas, answered some interesting questions, and I like to believe I have been a valued contributor to the steady growth of knowledge in my field. But only once have I felt that aha feeling.

I had already spent years exploring the causes and consequences of solitude across the lifespan and in different cultures. Like many academic researchers, my work is heavily dependent upon the success of grant applications to fund my research and support my graduate students. Over a period of several weeks, I had grown increasingly frustrated as I tried to work through the details of my next such proposal. After a few particularly busy days filled with teaching classes, a seemingly endless succession of meetings, driving kids to and from their various activities, and other social commitments, I was stressed and grumpy. Then, miraculously, like the proverbial parting of the Red Sea, a break suddenly emerged in the steady stream of my commitments, and I got a chance to go for a walk.

As soon as I was out of sight of other people, I started to calm down. I began to think more clearly. I wondered where this wave of negative emotions had come from and why I had just experienced this abrupt release. The answer, in that moment, became suddenly clear: I had been feeling so on edge because I was craving alone time. What I really needed was just a chance to catch my breath, rest, and focus on delving into my work.

It also occurred to me then that although many people must feel this way at times, I could not remember ever specifically hearing or reading about this phenomenon in the psychological literature. Sure, people wanting some "me time" was not really a new idea.* However, I couldn't think of a word that could be used to define the negative feelings that arise from not getting enough time alone. So I made one up. Since "loneliness" describes what you feel when you are getting too much time alone, and I viewed this feeling as loneliness's mirror image, I called it *aloneliness*: the bad feelings that result from not getting enough time alone.

I first introduced the concept of aloneliness during a symposium presentation I delivered at a developmental psychology conference

* According to the *Oxford English Dictionary*, the first usage of the term "me time" can be traced back to the early 1980s.

in March 2019. Little did I know that almost exactly one year later the entire world would be unimaginably upended by the COVID-19 pandemic. Suddenly, everyone was talking a lot more about solitude, and experiences of both loneliness and aloneliness were thrust into the spotlight as never before.

The Importance of Getting Things "Just Right"

As I mentioned earlier, the Goldilocks story exemplifies a literary device known as the rule of three: the first chair that Goldilocks encounters is too big, the second one is too small, and the third chair is just right. And so on, with the porridge and the beds. In doing so, the story highlights a broader general concept, which, in honor of the fairy tale, has been at times labeled the Goldilocks principle, the Goldilocks rule, the Goldilocks effect, or the Goldilocks zone. Its primary premise is that moderate values are often preferable to their more extreme counterparts. In other words, there is an optimal range for things that is "just right."

This relatively simple idea has evolved to widespread appeal, and it has been applied across diverse disciplines and domains, from the exotic and grandiose to the modest and mundane. For example, there is evidence of the Goldilocks principle at work in the fields of macroeconomics, chemistry, climate science and ecology, statistical analyses, medicine, and astrobiology. In his 2010 book *The Grand Design*, the physicist Stephen Hawking wrote, "Like Goldilocks, the development of intelligent life requires that planetary temperatures be 'just right.'" It has also been applied to create effective pricing strategies, to explain the appeal of social media influencers, and to improve the process of fitting people with hearing aids.

Within the realm of psychology, the Goldilocks principle has been drawn upon to better account for what sounds might draw a baby's attention when they are learning how to talk, to unravel the mechanisms that underlie how people are affected by stress, and to reveal the cognitive processes involved in decision-making. In more applied contexts, the Goldilocks principle has been a helpful tool for everything from optimizing motivations for training among elite athletes to facilitating teachers' efforts to communicate new ideas to students.

The psychology researchers Andrew Przybylski and Netta Weinstein tested if the Goldilocks principle could be applied to technology use in a sample of more than 120,000 teenagers in the UK. They measured adolescents' digital screen time during the week and on weekends, including watching videos, gaming, surfing the internet, and scrolling social media. During this period, the teenagers also reported on aspects of their well-being, such as happiness, life satisfaction, and social functioning. Overall, the researchers found that both too much and too little technology use predicted poorer well-being among the teenagers. As an aside, this is but one example of a carefully designed research study debunking a popular myth about technology use, namely that all screen time is bad for children and adolescents. We will sink our teeth into this meaty debate later.

Finding SolAS. I simply applied the Goldilocks principle to solitude. As we have seen, the history of the psychological study of solitude is, understandably, fraught with concern over the implications of spending too *much* time alone. As a result, everyone is familiar with loneliness, the word used to describe negative feelings that arise when we perceive a deficit between our desired and actual social connections. Loneliness is a dissatisfaction with our social lives, and it occurs when our need to belong is not met. Humans have understood this for a very long time.

But what about the other side of this coin? What happens when we don't get enough solitude? I coined the term "aloneliness" to describe negative feelings that result from a deficit between our desired and actual experiences of solitude. Armed with this initial idea, my colleagues, graduate students, and I set out to see if this was really "a thing." We started by brainstorming ways to ask about this and talking to groups of people about how they would describe this phenomenon. This helped us generate a series of items that we used to develop a questionnaire. We asked people how much they agreed with a series of statements, including:

> "I need to make it more of a priority to do things alone each week."
>
> "I never seem to have enough time by myself."
>
> "Other demands too often take away chances for me to just be alone."

With the help of some statistical machinations, we selected the twelve statements that appeared to best represent the notion of not getting enough solitude and created the final questionnaire. We labeled it the Solitude and Aloneliness Scale, which was abbreviated as SolAS. The initial development of this measure showed us that people understood the questions and tended to reply to them in a consistent way. Because the concept of aloneliness had never been formally studied before, the next step was to try to determine if what we actually measured meant what we thought it did.* To do that, we had to demonstrate that our measure of aloneliness was related to stuff that aloneliness *should* be related to, based on our theory of the phenomenon. So, we conducted a series of studies to try to do exactly that.

One of the first things we found across several studies was that people who reported higher aloneliness also tended to have more positive attitudes toward solitude. To me, this made good sense: generally

* This is called establishing *construct validity* and is considered a critical part of the process of creating a new measure.

speaking, people who really like something would be expected to more often feel like they are not getting enough of that something. For example, I am a big fan of hot banana peppers, so I often feel like a pizza place has skimped on them on my pizza and find myself wanting more. But I have never, and I mean never ever, craved more (or even any) pineapple on my pizza. Taking this a step further, if I lived in a house with someone who had an anaphylactic reaction to hot banana peppers, I would likely feel routinely deprived. However, if my housemate was allergic to pineapple, it would probably not even register with me when we ordered pizza.

We also found that aloneliness predicted lower overall satisfaction with life. In terms of demonstrating what aloneliness was supposed to be, this was important. Aloneliness was theorized to represent a dissatisfaction with a particular domain in our life: our experiences of solitude. If we are dissatisfied with one aspect of our life, we should see this reflected, at least in part, in our more general life satisfaction.

Across all our studies, we also found that aloneliness is *not* typically directly related to a fixed overall amount of time people report spending alone over the last week. For me, this was perhaps the most critical evidence that aloneliness was tapping into something unique and potentially important. Instead, we found that aloneliness arises based on people's individual *perceptions* of whether the amount of time they are spending alone is too much or too little. Critically, the "just right" amount of time for each of us is different.

For example, let's say that three different people, we'll call them Moe, Larry, and Curly, each tend to spend about three hours a day in solitude. If they were participants in one of my research studies, they would each report having spent about twenty-one hours alone over the last week. We would then interview them and ask them about how they view their respective experiences of twenty-one hours of solitude over the last week. Let's say that during the first interview, Moe laments that three hours of solitude a day feels like way too much, and when we asked him to complete the SolAS, he scores really low in terms of aloneliness. In short, he doesn't at all feel like he is not getting enough time alone (with apologies for the double negative). Relatedly, it would not surprise us to learn that Moe is actually feeling lonely. When we talk with Larry, he confides to us that three hours of solitude a day is just about right for him, a fact reflected in his moderate aloneliness scores. Then comes Curly. He arrives for the interview agitated and in a foul mood. After taking a moment to collect himself, he confesses that three hours of solitude a day is just not enough for him. He is deeply craving more "me time." Consistent with this, his aloneliness score is off the charts.

As this example illustrates, just knowing the overall amount of time someone spends alone each day does not really tell us anything about their aloneliness. The crucial information is how they are *feeling* about that time alone: Too much? Too little? When we considered these initial findings collectively, we felt increasingly reassured that our new measure of aloneliness meant what we thought it did. Armed with this confidence, we then set out to see what else aloneliness could help us explain and understand in terms of people's experiences of solitude and the resulting implications.

It occurred to me that we might be able to use the concept of aloneliness to provide more evidence about the positive aspects of solitude. My rationale here was that if solitude can have benefits, then the feeling one is being deprived of enough of it should manifest negatively in various ways. We already know that getting too much solitude can make us feel lonely, which leads to all kinds of bad outcomes. I figured we might expect similar sorts of things for aloneliness. And that is exactly what we found. Across several studies, aloneliness predicted feelings of increased stress, negative mood, and even symptoms of depression. Feeling like you are not getting enough time alone can make you feel stressed out, grumpy, and sad.

We published our findings, and it was not long before it became evident that the concept of aloneliness resonates with lots of people. I began to receive a steady stream of emails from people telling me about their personal experiences related to aloneliness. Here are some excerpts:

> I just read an online article about your research about the flip-side of loneliness, that you call aloneliness. It resonated with me on a huge level and I thank you very much for putting into words, and giving a name, to validate something I have struggled with for many years.

> When I am alone, in solitude, doing an activity I enjoy with nobody around and no interruptions, I can mentally and physically FEEL my body recharging, refreshing, rebooting. When I nurture that alonely feeling and get the solitude time I desire and need, I experience more clarity in my thinking about everyday stresses and situations that are difficult. When I'm constantly around others, my mind gets muddled with too much incoming information with no time to process it or clarify it. This causes me to be stressed, overwhelmed, and to have emotional meltdowns.

> Sometimes the guilt of taking "me time" away from my family still creeps in. And sometimes I wonder about how much solitude time is considered too much . . . I love my family a lot, but sometimes I just want to escape from it all (chores, expectations, decision making, so much time together, etc.) and desire a vacation away, just me, for a long time, to do the things I want and enjoy to do. Many mothers often feel like this.

As these snippets emphasize, aloneliness appears to have been a pretty common experience long before I put a name to it. And then COVID-19 happened—and shone a bright spotlight on our understudied, misunderstood, and hugely complex relationship with solitude. Many people were forced to endure the pain of loneliness and social isolation during these times. But, importantly, many others also suffered the ill effects of aloneliness, never able to find a moment to themselves.

At the height of the pandemic lockdowns and social distancing measures, my daughter was among the millions of children who attended school online. Her high school homeroom teacher had two young children of her own who, of course, were stuck at home with her. Day after relentless day, this poor overwhelmed and exhausted teacher would try to engage a class of sullen, tuned-out teenagers, while simultaneously trying to manage the trials and tribulations of her housebound toddler and preschooler. I don't know for sure, but I would bet good money that she was suffering from intense feelings of aloneliness.

A colleague of mine who is a clinical psychologist spoke often to me about encountering such challenges during this same period. Like many other mental health professionals, he was somewhat overwhelmed by the combination of a significant increase in demand for his services and having to migrate his in-person practice to telephone and video sessions. Many of his patients sought his counsel in the face of social isolation and loneliness. But perhaps just as often, a client would need to hold their telephone session with him from a parked car outside their home or apartment, having escaped to the only place where they could find the needed privacy to speak openly.

Now, a few years later, it has become increasingly clear that aloneliness is a phenomenon that still deserves our attention. Along with some international collaborators, we have conducted studies of aloneliness in several other countries, including Italy, China, and Indonesia. The results have been very similar: aloneliness is consistently associated with negative mood, feelings of stress, symptoms of depression, and other indicators of ill-being.

Other researchers have also expanded the study of aloneliness into new domains that I had not even considered. For example, the Texas Christian University psychology researchers Julie Swets and Cathy Cox explored how aloneliness impacts romantic relationships. In their first study, they found that aloneliness predicts feelings of anger and hostility more strongly among members of a couple than people who were single. Swets and Cox surmised that people in romantic relationships faced the added dilemma of balancing their different individual needs for alone time against their (and their partner's) needs for time together, a potential stressor that could promote frustration.

They tested this hypothesis more directly in a second study. All the participants in this experiment were married or in a committed relationship. A random half of the participants were primed to think about aloneliness. This was done by having them read a passage explaining the concept and then write for a few minutes describing their previous experiences with it. The other half was deemed the comparison group; they read a blurb about daily routines and were asked to write about theirs.

Following this, all participants completed a measure assessing how angry they felt right in that moment. They also participated in a procedure called the *voodoo doll task*, which was developed to provide an indirect measure of feelings of aggression toward someone. Participants were shown a virtual image of a doll and told that it represented their romantic partner. They were then informed that this part of the study was meant to "release any negative energy you experienced in the study." To do so, they were given the choice to click a button to stick the doll with one or more virtual pins. Participants could choose not to stick any virtual pins in the doll, or they could continue and stop at any point up to a maximum of about fifty pins.

Participants who had been primed to think and write about aloneliness reported feeling more anger afterward than those in the comparison group. Just thinking about aloneliness made people mad in that moment. But notably, participants primed to think about aloneliness also specifically directed more virtual aggression toward the voodoo doll representing their romantic partner than the comparison group. In fact, on average, they stuck the voodoo doll with more than twice as many pins! As the authors wrote in their conclusion, this was "further evidence that a perceived lack of solitude is a marker of poorer well-being with serious consequences."

Balancing the Social-Solitary Seesaw

One interesting tidbit that emerged from several of my studies was that some participants reported high scores of both aloneliness and loneliness. At first glance, this seems somewhat counterintuitive. How can someone simultaneously feel like they are getting both not enough and too much time alone? It turns out that how we feel about solitude and social connection depends not just on how much time we spend alone and with others but also on the *quality* of that time.

As we have already discussed, people can experience loneliness even while in the presence of others. This has happened to me many times. I go to a party where I don't know the other attendees very well. Maybe I am not in the best mood to begin with, maybe I am just not a good fit with that particular crowd, or maybe the other guests are just not that friendly and welcoming. Whatever the reason, I spend the evening engaging in occasional spurts of small talk but not really connecting with anyone. Meanwhile, everyone else seems to be having a really good time. From my corner of the room, standing awkwardly trying to look like I am enjoying myself, I see people sharing an inside joke and laughing unabashedly together. Others are completely immersed in deep conversations, gesturing grandly to emphasize a particularly salient point. After spending several hours in this social company,

I often leave feeling lonelier than when I arrived. For me and many others, such "poor-quality" social experiences do not really contribute much to satisfying our need to belong.

I wondered if the same principle might apply to solitude. Is all alone time really the same? We decided to try to find out by testing this idea in a study with a large group of high schoolers. We looked at how much time teenagers spend alone over a week and their most common solitary activities, as well as measures of their mood, enjoyment of time spent alone and time with others, and their feelings of aloneliness. The findings were complicated and reinforced the important notion that there is no one-size-fits-all recipe for how each of us should best spend our time.

For example, some teenagers in the study spent relatively little time alone and were pretty happy about it. For discussion purposes, let's label this group as the "socialites." These teens preferred spending time with others, and despite their low frequency of solitary activities, they did not report wanting more alone time. For them, this was enough to satisfy their personal need for solitude. Although we did not ask them to sit alone in a room for fifteen minutes, I suspect that many in this group would be among those who reached to press that button for an electric shock.

But there were other teenagers who spent relatively little time alone and were not at all happy about it. This group reported higher levels of aloneliness as well as high negative mood. We will call them the "alonely-ists" because they demonstrate the prototypical characteristics of what the concept of aloneliness is thought to represent. Importantly, these teens spent about the same amount of time alone each week as their socialite counterparts, but for them, it was not enough. They craved more solitude and were grumpy as a result of not getting it.

There were also groups of teens who spent comparatively more time alone over the course of the week. Like the two groups I just described, they also differed in terms of how they felt about it. Some teens who reported more frequent solitude seemed quite happy about it. For now, we will label them the "happy aloners."* They enjoyed their time alone and did not report high aloneliness. Their more frequent "me time" was just right for them.

But there were other teens who also reported more frequent solitude and were not very happy about it. However, somewhat counterintuitively, despite spending about the same amount of time alone as the happy aloners, members of this group *still* reported high levels of aloneliness and negative mood. So, let's call them the "dissatisfied aloners."

So, what was going on here? Why wasn't spending time alone more frequently meeting the need for solitude among the dissatisfied aloners? After taking a closer look, we found that although dissatisfied aloners spent about the same time alone as happy aloners, they differed in terms of what they tended to do when they were alone. The happy aloners were more likely to spend alone time engaged in leisure activities: hobbies, reading for pleasure, listening to music, or being outside. We figured that these types of solitary activities most likely reflected *intrinsic* motivations (reminder: intrinsic motivations are driven by enjoyment, meaning, and purpose). In turn, such "high-quality" time alone would be more likely to satisfy the need for solitude and thus be more effective in reducing aloneliness.

In a follow-up study led by my graduate student Alicia McVarnock, we found similar results with a sample of university students. Participants who more frequently spent time alone engaging in leisure activities reported feeling less alonely. In contrast, those who spent their alone time in less productive ways, such as "doing nothing," ruminating, or worrying, reported feeling *more* alonely, despite spending about the

* In the next chapter, we will have an extensive discussion about the challenges in finding an appropriate label for people with these characteristics.

same time alone. These two studies provided some of the first evidence to suggest that all solitary activities may not be created equal when it comes to quenching our thirst for solitude.

So, what should we take away from all of this? To be satisfied with both our social and solitary lives, we not only need to spend *sufficient* time alone and with others, but we must spend *quality* time alone and with others. This is why it is possible to feel both lonely and alonely at the same time. This also underscores an important lesson: finding the right balance between good quality time alone and time with others is really good for us!

Some recent studies provide some direct support for the benefits of getting this balance "just right." For example, a group of Swiss researchers led by Theresa Pauly and Minxia Luo tracked daily episodes of solitude and social interactions over a three-week period in a large sample of older adults aged sixty-five to ninety-four. Participants who displayed patterns of routinely alternating episodes of solitude and social interactions reported the highest life satisfaction.

Cycling back and forth between episodes of alone time and social interaction seems like a good recipe for well-being. However, a couple of crucial caveats must be considered. First, as we just discussed, quality matters. Going back and forth between solitary and social activities that are boring, cumbersome, or aversive is not going to bolster well-being. And hearkening back to the last chapter, choice also matters . . . a lot. As we have seen, the differences between chosen and unwanted solitude are significant. The same appears to be true for socializing, perhaps even more so.

The Israeli researchers Liad Uziel and Tomer Schmidt-Barad tracked how university students spent their time. For ten consecutive days, participants received text messages every day in the morning, at noon, and in the evening, prompting them to answer a series of questions about their current circumstances. These included whether they were alone or with others, how they were feeling, how meaningful their current situation felt, and how satisfied with life they were feeling at present. They also indicated whether their current social circumstances, alone versus in the company of others, were a result of "their choice" or because of "external demands."

Overall, participants reported better mood and higher life satisfaction in moments when they were with others than they did in moments when they were alone. This is consistent with the general notion that social situations typically make us feel happier. Additionally, consistent with the last chapter's discussion about autonomy and self-determination, when participants had chosen what they were doing, whether solitary or among others, they generally felt happier and more fulfilled. Interestingly, the impact of choice was more pronounced in social settings than solitude. Being forced to spend time with people seemed to be a more negative experience than being forced to spend time alone.

The flip side of this finding could also be interpreted to suggest that unchosen episodes of solitude are preferable to being forced to be around others. For many people, being with others because of "external demands" can be stressful and activate feelings of discomfort, wariness, and self-consciousness. An unwanted social scene also has more constraints than unwanted solitude: not only did you not choose to be among these people, but you also have to modulate and restrain your words and actions because of their presence. In contrast, although unwanted solitude comes with its own well-known substantial downsides, at least some elements of autonomy remain: you have some choice as to what you do while you are alone.

Finally, and perhaps most important when it comes to understanding the balance between solitude and socializing, there is no one-size-fits-all pattern that is optimal for everyone. Allow me to step up on my soapbox one more time and shout out to the masses: we all experience solitude and socializing differently, and we all need to find our own "just right" amount of each—within reason. For the vast, vast majority of people, it is not healthy to spend all or almost all of one's time either alone or with others. No matter how much you personally prefer spending time alone or with others, both contexts make important and unique contributions to your health and well-being.

Of course, I am hardly the first person to make this suggestion. As inevitably happens in many scientific disciplines, I am routinely humbled by coming across a historical reference of someone advocating an idea that I thought was new and exciting decades or more before I was born. *The Voice of Experience*, published in 1933 by an anonymous author,* was billed as a book of advice on different aspects of life. In one chapter, the unnamed author tackles the topics of solitude and socializing. Here is some of their advice: "Social life is an essential ingredient of human happiness, but social life without some solitude is like a meal without salt." They also write: "Too much of a good thing is just as bad as not enough of it . . . the true way to happiness lies in the judicious alternation of social activity and solitude." I wonder if this anonymous author read Epictetus in the original ancient Koine Greek.

* The identity of the author of this book remains unconfirmed to this day. However, it is of note that there was a popular 1930s radio advice show called *The Voice of Experience*, hosted and narrated by Marion Sayle Taylor.

Chapter 7

Loners & Homebodies & Introverts, Oh My!

The Memes Versus Realities of Preferring Solitude

During the first few months of COVID-19 pandemic lockdowns and social distancing in 2020, we were treated to the following headlines in big, bolded font:

"The Introvert's Guide to Social Distancing"
(CNN, March 23, 2020)

"For Introverts, Quarantine Can Be a Liberation"
(Bloomberg, March 28, 2020)

"Hey Introverts, Stop Loving This Crisis so Much"
(*The Daily Telegraph*, March 30, 2020)

"No Parties, No Problem: Introverts Don't Mind Sheltering at Home"
(Reuters, April 5, 2020)

"For Introverts, Lockdown Is a Chance to Play to Our Strengths"
(*The Guardian*, May 2, 2020)

"Check on an Extrovert Today"
(*The New York Times*, May 19, 2020)

Social media was also flooded with memes (half) joking that introverts were now finally getting to live their best lives, could be happy that they no longer had to think up excuses for not going out on Friday night, and were just now finding out that their normal daily lifestyle was called "quarantine." But did introverts really thrive during the pandemic? Did they really end up doing so much better than their more extraverted counterparts? There have now been several research studies that sought to answer these exact questions. And the results may surprise you . . .

I often reflect upon the first class I ever taught as a university professor. It was an unmitigated disaster. When I interviewed for the position in the psychology department at my institution, I was asked if I would feel comfortable teaching an introductory class on psychology research methods and statistics. Of course I enthusiastically said yes. To be honest, I would have happily agreed to teach a class on underwater basket weaving if I thought it would have helped me land the job.

Sure enough, soon after I was hired, I received my teaching schedule for my first term, and I had been assigned to teach that very course. These days, most graduate students take seminars on pedagogy, course design, and other critical elements of university teaching as part of their education. But back then, most of us received no formal training on how to teach before starting our careers as professors.* All this to say: I had no idea what I was doing. At all. And I certainly didn't realize that courses on research methods and statistics were particularly difficult to teach because many psychology students feel stressed taking any class that they perceive as having anything to do with math.

Fortunately, I had some time to prep before the semester started. So, I set myself to work organizing the curriculum and putting together lecture notes and slides. I diligently plugged away, highly motivated to

* . . . and we had to walk to class uphill in the snow . . . both ways!

make a good first impression on my students and the people who had hired me. My course was scheduled as one three-hour class each week. By the time the first lecture was upon me, I figured I had prepped about ten to twelve hours of content—more than enough material for the first three or even four classes. I was ready. Or so I thought.

I walked into the auditorium and got myself organized. Stepping up to the lectern, I gazed out at the sea of faces looking back at me. I was nervous but not overly so. I took a deep breath and cleared my throat. *I got this*, I told myself. Then I introduced myself as a new professor in the psychology department, welcomed the students to the class, and launched into my first lecture.

My memory gets a bit fuzzy after that. I think I must have entered into a bit of a fugue state. I do remember talking . . . a lot . . . at a relentless pace. The words just seemed to pour out of my mouth. At one point I think I wondered why none of the students were asking any questions. But I just kept on talking, plowing forward, head buried in my notes, furiously flipping through slide after cellophane slide, illuminated by the glare of the single light bulb in the old-fashioned overhead projector.

I stopped only when I reached the end of my notes and my last slide. My throat felt parched, so I took a quick sip of the glass of water that had been sitting by the lectern, having ignored it up to this point. Coming back to myself, I glanced up at the clock at the back of the lecture hall and noted with some surprise that less than an hour had elapsed since I started talking. *Oh well, not too bad,* I thought. Although I did not get the timing exactly right for my first lecture, I figured I could recalibrate a bit before the next class and adjust the rest of the content accordingly.

It was then that I realized the depth of my "miscalibration." I had not just presented the material for my first lecture in under an hour's time. I had blasted through the entire corpus of lecture content and slides for *all* of what I had prepared for the course so far. Everything. The entirety of the material I had assumed would make up my first three or four weeks of classes.

It was absolutely silent in the classroom. I looked out again at the faces of the students sitting in tiered rows laid out in front of me. They were stunned. An entire class of deer in the headlights, with wind-blown hair from the typhoon stream of hot air that had blasted from my mouth over the past hour. It turned out I absolutely had not "got this." At least not yet. I had a lot more work to do, and clearly, I needed some help.

I asked around for advice about who could show me the ropes and help me improve my teaching. Everyone I spoke to mentioned the same person, a colleague in the psychology department named Brian, as the exemplar of an amazing lecturer. Here was someone we could all aspire to be like when it came to teaching. Brian had won several prestigious awards for his teaching, and whatever "it" was, he definitely had it. And if I wanted it, I needed to emulate his approach.

Brian regularly taught a very popular course on the psychology of personality. There was always a long waiting list of students desperately hoping to enroll. I sheepishly asked him if I could sit in on some of his lectures, with a goal of observing and learning from his teaching style. He graciously agreed. The first time I attended one of his classes, I quietly made my way to the back of the room, trying not to draw any attention to myself, took a seat, and pulled out my notepad. Brian stepped up to the lectern and engaged the class. What I witnessed that day was a virtuoso performance of high energy, humor, and intellectual stimulation. His passion was palpable and contagious. Brian seamlessly weaved back and forth between core lecture material, amusing anecdotes, and answering a continual flurry of student questions. He just spoke, confidently, but in an easygoing, conversational style, and entirely without notes. The lecture hall was packed with several hundred students, and they were hanging on Brian's every word. It was a joy to watch. I was in awe. It all just seemed to come so naturally for him.

About halfway through the three-hour class, Brian paused and announced that the class would be taking a short break. I stood up and made my way through the throng of students to the front of the classroom, with the hope of complimenting Brian on being an absolute teaching rock star. But he was nowhere to be found. About fifteen minutes later, I watched him reenter the classroom, walk back up to the lectern, and resume his lecture. This same pattern of Brian disappearing during the class "intermission" repeated itself each time I attended one of his classes. I didn't think too much of it at the time. I learned a lot from watching Brian and did my best to adapt aspects of his powerhouse teaching style into my own approach.

It was only years later that Brian let me in on what was going on for him during those breaks: he was a card-carrying, full-blown, off-the-scale introvert. Brian truly loved teaching and was really good at it. But having to be so "on," continuously having to perform for and interact with all those students during his lectures, was absolutely exhausting for him. He confessed to me that during the scheduled pause at the halfway point of each lecture, he would immediately flee to the bathroom, go into a stall, close the door, and stand on the toilet so no one would know he was there. He would spend the fifteen minutes there in silence, recharging his battery in the serenity of blissful solitude (despite the less-than-idyllic setting). This brief respite allowed him to muster enough energy reserves to complete the second half of his lecture. For Brian, this time alone was absolutely essential for him to be able to do his job up to the level that he was capable of.

With that in mind, it is time to address the quiet elephant in the room. Let's talk about introverts. The topic of introversion has increasingly made its way into the spotlight in recent years—ironically, a place where I am sure many introverts would rather not be. Introversion is now the subject of an ever-expanding array of articles, social media accounts, podcasts, and popular press books. For these reasons, there are now many famous introverts who are the subjects of societal acclaim: Albert Einstein, Bill Gates, Lady Gaga, Emma Watson, Meryl Streep, and countless others.

Introversion is inexorably linked to solitude. Yet, although introverts may tend to enjoy and seek out regular time alone, introversion is also a lot more than that. And, of course, extraverts can also appreciate some "me time," just as introverts can also value and nurture their social connections. Also, perhaps not surprisingly, many popular conceptions about introversion do not align with what we have learned from psychological research on this topic. So, let's put on our reading socks, curl up under a blanket by the fire, and spend a Friday night alone learning about introverts.

When One Is Company and Two Is a Crowd

> I find it wholesome to be alone the greater part of the time. To be in company, even with the best, is soon wearisome and dissipating. I love to be alone. I never found the companion that was so companionable as solitude.
>
> —Henry David Thoreau

Think of someone who values and finds pleasure in spending time with others. Social engagement is important to them, and they find interacting with others rewarding, energizing, and enjoyable. What words would you use to describe this person? There are several that immediately come to my mind, such as "sociable," "outgoing," "gregarious," "affable," "friendly," and, of course, "extraverted." For me, all these terms seem to have fairly positive connotations, which likely reflects a generally positive view of sociability in Western cultures. In short, this hypothetical "social butterfly" we just imagined possesses characteristics that are typically highly valued, and the language we use to describe this person reflects these beliefs.

Now imagine someone who values and enjoys spending time alone. They are not nervous or anxious around others. But solitude is important to them, and they find time alone engaging, rewarding, and restorative. For me, the quote by Thoreau at the outset of this section perfectly encapsulates this type of person. What word or words would you use to describe them? The words that come to mind are probably along the lines of "shy," "reclusive," "antisocial," "aloof," "loner," or "hermit." It seems to me that many, if not most of the words that could apply here have more negative connotations. The most "positive" one I could think of would be something like "homebody." In the English language, we have the phrase "social butterfly," but no one talks about a "solitary caterpillar."

In the psychology literature, various terminologies have been proposed over the years to describe the characteristic of "enjoying solitude." As is the case more often than we care to admit, psychologists do not agree on the most appropriate nomenclature for this trait. Common psychological jargon terms used in this regard have included "unsociability," "affinity for aloneness," "solitropic orientation," and "social disinterest."* Frankly, I think these are all pretty awful and certainly in no danger of coming into common usage outside the realm of psychology.

Along with my graduate student Tiffany Cheng, I sought to understand more about the language used to describe these individuals who enjoy and value spending time alone and what that might tell us about societal attitudes toward solitude. To do this, we asked thousands of adolescents and adults what words they would use to describe a person with these characteristics. The most common term generated by

* I came up with this last one earlier in my career. Looking at it now, all I can say is: *What was I thinking?*

participants was "introvert." This didn't surprise me at all, given contemporary pop culture's portrayal of introverts as solitude loving. But I would argue that this is just one of many ways that the personality trait of introversion is misrepresented to the general public. We will circle back to this idea in a moment.

What did surprise me about the results, and pleasantly so, was the composition of the other words that people used to describe the hypothetical individual who enjoyed and valued spending time alone. Although some participants offered the more negative-sounding words I'd anticipated, such as "loner," "loser," and "antisocial," these responses were in the minority. Most respondents characterized the hypothetical solitary-loving person with either more neutral words, such as "homebody," "normal," and "independent," or more positive-sounding words, such as "confident," "mature," and "peaceful." Indeed, many of the participants seemed to identify with this hypothetical person, replying with words such as "me" or my personal favorite, "my spirit animal."

Despite these findings, I would still argue that language remains an issue here; the more positive-sounding generated words do not really evoke solitude in the same direct way that the more negative-sounding words do. For example, if I described someone as confident, mature, or independent, their relationship with solitude does not immediately leap out as a central feature, nor is it even highlighted to the same degree that it would be if I described them as a loner, hermit, or recluse.

That is why I think we need a new "positive" word to describe someone who enjoys and values spending time alone. Feel free to submit your candidates to me directly. In our research, we failed to elicit a generally agreed upon term from respondents. As a result, we ended up having to provide a label that we made up, just so that we could more easily ask them questions about this hypothetical character. The word we came up with was "soloist."* Since "someone who prefers, enjoys, and values solitude" is an awkward and clunky phrase to keep having to repeat, and there is not a better word available, I will use the term "soloist" moving forward to simplify things.

I was encouraged by the frequent use of these more positive-sounding words in my study, which perhaps was at least some indication that attitudes about solitude are changing for the better. It turns out that the COVID-19 pandemic may have had something to do with this. The Tilburg University psychology researchers Dongning Ren and Olga Stavrova explored whether the experience of COVID-19 lockdowns and social distancing protocols impacted people's general beliefs about solitude in a series of studies conducted during the first wave of the pandemic. Participants were asked about their lives before versus during the pandemic and to indicate how negatively others would view them if they engaged in solitary activities. Across all studies, participants felt that spending time alone would be judged less negatively during the pandemic. Thus, experiences during the pandemic appear to have reduced the social stigma associated with choosing to spend time alone. However, it still remains to be seen if these attitudinal shifts will persist as these experiences continue to fade into memory.

But there may also be a bit of a double-edged sword here. In another series of studies with participants from the United States, the UK, and the Netherlands, Ren and her colleagues looked at whether having a preference for solitude was beneficial during times of pandemic lockdowns and social distancing. They presented participants with descriptions of hypothetical individuals who differed in terms of how much they preferred/enjoyed solitude. In terms of people's beliefs, they

* We later found out that someone else had actually used this term before. The New York University psychology researchers Jill Katz and Ester Buchholz used the term "soloist" to describe preschool children who enjoyed playing alone at school. More on their research in a later chapter . . .

found that regardless of how much they valued and enjoyed solitude themselves, participants expected soloists to suffer less from loneliness during times of social distancing compared with their more sociable counterparts.

Yet, it turns out that the participants' beliefs did not accurately reflect reality. Ren and her colleagues looked at the actual links between preference for solitude and well-being at various points during the pandemic. Overall, they found that people greatly overestimated the "protective" role of being a soloist during the pandemic. In reality, soloists fared only slightly better, if at all, in terms of their reported loneliness and life satisfaction. Ren speculated that this could ultimately be problematic for those who prefer solitude; if others think they are okay and are less willing to allocate social resources to them, soloists may end up being overlooked—and suffer more as a result.

Introducing Introverts

After all this discussion about why we borrowed the term "soloist" as a label for people who value and enjoy solitude, it would be entirely reasonable for you to be wondering why we didn't instead just use the much more familiar and common term "introvert." The short answer to that question is although there may be some overlap, not all soloists are introverted and not all introverts are soloists. The longer answer is more complicated. And because the term "introverted" is used so pervasively in popular culture, we need to get into the weeds here a bit to try to untangle some of the myths from the realities.

The first use of the term "introverted" is attributed to the Swiss psychiatrist and psychoanalyst Carl Jung in the early 1900s. In his 1921 book *Psychological Types*, Jung outlined a conceptualization of introverts and extraverts that, for better or worse, remains widespread today: extraverts are energized by the outside world; introverts are energized by the internal world. A classic metaphor used to exemplify this dichotomy refers to how people's "batteries" get charged or drained. If an extravert is feeling low, they will seek out high-energy social situations. Going to a party would be just the ticket, as being where the action is helps to recharge their batteries. When the party is over and an extravert is left sitting alone in a quiet room, this will feel draining for them, and they will typically not tolerate it for very long.

In contrast, if an introvert is feeling low, they will seek out that same quiet room (or other favorite solitary place) to recharge their batteries. For them, as was the case with Professor Brian mentioned at the outset of the chapter, being among the hustle and bustle of others takes a toll, and they need some "me time" to help replenish their energy stores. Importantly, however, being around others does not necessarily make introverts feel anxious or self-conscious. It mostly just makes them feel run-down.

In the 1940s, the German psychologist Hans Eysenck spearheaded the defining characteristics, measurement, and study of introversion-extraversion as a core personality trait. Eysenck's conceptualization of this trait was broader, extending beyond Jung's core notion of energy. Eysenck believed that extraverts were also more sociable, active, assertive, and impulsive than their more introverted counterparts. This approach is still largely prevalent today in the psychological study of introversion/extraversion.

Apart from being a well-studied personality trait in psychology, introversion has also morphed into a mainstay topic in popular culture. In 2011, the first World Introvert Day was celebrated on January 2. According to its website, the push to establish a World Introvert Day was spearheaded by the psychologist and author Felicitas Heyne, who put out the call for "a day for us quiet ones."

In 2012, the author Susan Cain published *Quiet: The Power of Introverts in a World That Can't Stop Talking*, catapulting introversion into the realm of cultural phenomenon. In her book, Cain presents a compelling depiction of the historical negative biases against introversion that have permeated Western culture. She argues that, particularly in the United States, societal views are dominated by the "Extrovert Ideal," which promotes and values assertion, dominance, and action. In contrast, introverts are either dismissed, undervalued, or even viewed as pathological.

Personally, I think it is laudable that Cain and many others have raised awareness and promoted the many positive aspects of introversion. Yet, for all the attention paid to it, I would argue that this personality trait remains largely misunderstood by the public at large and significant misconceptions persist. This is likely due, at least in part, to the substantial disconnect between "popular culture" introversion and the introversion conceptualized, measured, and studied by personality psychology researchers and theorists. I mean, if the memes are to be believed, introversion can be boiled down to loving solitude, reading a lot of books, and some stuff with cats. This is not quite accurate.*

Are you really my type? Let's start with the purported "prevalence" of introversion. I have seen scientific and nonscientific estimates that anywhere between 15 and 50 percent of the population are introverts. I put the word "prevalence" in scare quotes because, in my view, the notion that we can easily classify people as either an introvert or an extravert is questionable at best. For a lot of reasons, this is not a straightforward procedure at all.

To begin with, based on the content of social media feeds, most people are either extremely extraverted or intensely introverted. This is simply not the case. Individual personality traits form a continuum. Thus, introversion and extraversion represent opposite ends of a broad spectrum. Because of the wide range of possible values on the scale,

---

* . . . although it sometimes can be.

when you ask if someone is an introvert or an extravert, you're really not asking a yes-or-no question. Imagine we give one hundred people a well-established psychological assessment of personality traits that includes an introversion-extraversion scale.* The introversion-extraversion scale includes twenty-five items describing characteristics related to this trait, such as "I hate spending time alone," "I do not enjoy reading books," or "None of my best friends are cats."† For each item, people indicate how much this statement describes them on a 5-point scale, with responses ranging from 0 = "not at all" to 4 = "very much." We then calculate people's totals such that higher scores are more reflective of extraversion and lower scores more indicative of introversion. This way, scores on the introversion-extraversion scale could range from 0 to 100. Got it? Sorry, I know that nobody told you there would be math in this book.

My point is that everyone is introverted-extraverted to a certain degree. Sure, some people may score really high or really low on this scale. But importantly, there is no standard cutoff for placing someone in the category of introvert or extravert. And problems remain even if we could all agree on an approach to classification. For instance, using our hypothetical measure, we could decide that only scores above 75, or 90, or even 95 would be required in order to meet the criterion of extravert. Likewise, scores below 25, 10, or even 5 could be the standard for a designation of introvert. But any decisions about these cutoff values would be entirely arbitrary. And even if everyone agreed on the criteria, which they certainly do not, you are still faced with some serious issues. Whatever the cutoff, is someone who scores one or two points away from that value really that different from someone

* These include the International Personality Item Pool (IPIP), Myers-Briggs Type Indicator (MBTI), Eysenck Personality Inventory (EPI), NEO Personality Inventory (NEO PI), and many others.

† Because of copyright issues, my sample items are drawn from memes.

who just barely meets the criteria for the designation of introvert? Do we think that differing by two points on a score that ranges from 0 to 100 really represents a meaningful difference in personality in the real world? The difference in scores could be accounted for by the extraverted respondent checking the boxes for two items in the scale that indicated "a little," whereas the introvert checked the ones denoting "not at all" for the same two items. Would it really be possible to distinguish these two individuals based on their day-to-day behaviors in this regard?

Related to this, we could graph the individual scores of our introversion-extraversion scale to help us visualize how they are distributed along their continuum. Typically, they would form the shape of an inverted U, with more scores falling in the middle range and fewer at the tails. This pattern is called a *normal distribution*, and it is common to almost all personality traits (and many other phenomena in nature). In the case of our hypothetical introversion-extraversion scale, with possible scores from 0 to 100, about two-thirds of people would tend to score in the 40 to 60 range. This means that they likely rated some items reflecting both introversion and extraversion as "somewhat like them." In other words, this middle group would possess attributes of both introverts and extraverts. As such, they would be neither intensely introverted nor extremely extraverted. Such individuals are often called *ambiverts*, and they represent the majority in the population.

We could continue to debate the merits of procedures for classifying people into different categories of personality "types." Indeed, this is a long-standing—and very much ongoing—historical dispute among personality psychologists. However, misinformed assumptions about the prevalence of extreme introverts among humans is only one issue with the popular concept of this trait. The root problem is how introverts are portrayed. In this regard, I think it is fair to say that as far as popular culture depictions are concerned, liking or needing solitude represents the core dominant feature of being an introvert. To be fair, there is some truth to this. Generally speaking, introverts do tend to report preferring solitude and spending more time alone than extraverts.* But these differences are not huge. It is not as if studies show that introverts spend many more hours a day alone compared with extraverts. Furthermore, to reinforce the point I made earlier, although there may be some overlap, it is certainly not the case that all introverts are soloists—that is, people who enjoy and value solitude. Nor should we assume that all soloists are introverts.

This underscores what I think is the most important thing we tend to get wrong about introversion: it is not a unidimensional trait. Introverts are not one-trick ponies wholly defined by their need for solitude. Overall, although introverts may indeed find social interactions more taxing and seek solitude as a means of recharging their batteries, the introversion-extraversion dimension is about much more than just solitude and sociability. As Eysenck argued more than eighty years ago, introverts and extraverts tend to differ on a broader array of characteristics that also include assertiveness, impulsivity, activity level, and sensation seeking, which represent components that are not really related to solitude per se. In short, there are many different ways to be introverted.

On top of that, introversion-extraversion represents only one dimension of personality. Current psychological theories of personality include multiple traits. A popular approach is the Big Five model, which has been a dominant conceptualization of personality traits since the 1980s. Along with an introversion-extraversion dimension,

* Despite my rant against the arbitrary assignment of individuals who vary on a continuum to discrete categories, I am still going to talk about introverts and extraverts. This is just much easier than always having to say "individuals who scored particularly low (or high) on a scale assessing the personality dimension of introversion-extraversion."

this model also includes four other traits, each of which also ranges along a wide spectrum.

Openness to Experience: practical, preference for routine ← → curious, unconventional

Neuroticism: emotionally stable, calm ← → self-conscious, irritable

Agreeableness: stubborn, demanding ← → trusting, empathetic

Conscientiousness: disorganized, impulsive ← → organized, dutiful

There remains some debate as to how strongly these different traits might be related to one another. Nevertheless, individual personality "types" reflect the combination of all five of these characteristics. This means people who are all highly introverted might be *very* different from one another in other facets of their personalities. For example, some introverts might be stubborn and irritable, others calm and trusting, and yet others impulsive and curious. With this in mind, I think we should be wary about making sweeping statements about "introverts" in general.

These other personality traits also appear to impact experiences of solitude. Another study led by Dongning Ren found that different Big Five traits predict different priorities when it comes to the positive functions of solitude. For example, although introverts were indeed more likely to value time alone because it helps them relax and recover, people higher in neuroticism sought solitude because it was a place where they could deal with negative emotions. Those high in conscientiousness, on the other hand, particularly appreciated the productivity that solitude afforded them. These findings highlight not only the wide range of benefits solitude can offer but also how people with different personality traits tend to differentially prioritize and value these different positive functions.

So happy together? Other common (mis)portrayals of introverts include that they don't want or need to spend time around other people, that they find being in the company of other people stressful or even aversive, and that they are only happy when they are alone. Again, the science simply does not bear out these claims.

For example, a group of European researchers led by Susanne Buecker conducted a meta-analysis reviewing and synthesizing the findings from more than a hundred studies over the last forty years that explored the links between Big Five personality traits and loneliness. A clear pattern emerged. Buecker found a robust positive link between introversion and loneliness. In short, despite their proclivity for solitude, introverts generally reported being *lonelier* than extraverts. And importantly, this effect held even after accounting for other personality traits that could also predict loneliness, such as neuroticism. Although we have already (I hope!) firmly established that loneliness is not the same as solitude, I think this finding calls into question the notion that introverts are happiest when they are alone.

And what about the stereotype of introverts "hating people" and generally not relishing being around others? As we have already discussed, introverts really do not appear to "hate" socializing, although it may make them feel tired after a while. And there is also considerable research demonstrating that even if we "force" introverts to be more sociable (to act like an extravert), they end up enjoying it. The Canadian researcher John Zelenski and his colleagues have extensively explored the impact of asking introverts and extraverts to act *dispositionally* (that is, in keeping with their actual personalities) versus counter-dispositionally (that is, not like their true selves). In a series of controlled studies in lab settings, adult participants engaged in various social activities for a period of twenty minutes with instructions to act like either an introvert (e.g., "reserved," "quiet," "passive") or an extravert (e.g., "bold," "talkative," "assertive"). They found that participants who acted like an extravert experienced a post-interaction boost in their positive mood, regardless of whether they were actually introverts or extraverts. Interestingly, they did not find any evidence, at least from these relatively short social episodes, of introverts being "drained," either emotionally or cognitively, from their socializing. Instead, the opposite occurred. Following a social episode where they were "forced" to act quietly and passively, dispositional extraverts displayed the poorest performance on a test of attention and concentration. It seems as though acting like an introvert, even for a brief period of time, comes at a cognitive cost for extraverts.

The University of California, Riverside, psychology researchers Seth Margolis and Sonja Lyubomirsky extended these findings to the real world. Instead of acting like an introvert or extravert for a twenty-minute social episode, participants did so for an entire week at a time. Half the participants were instructed to act like an introvert for the first week and an extravert for the second week, whereas for the other half, this order was reversed. Again, the findings were consistent. Overall, acting like an extravert increased reports of positive mood for all participants, regardless of their initial reported levels of introversion-extraversion.

So, it seems that acting like an extravert makes us happier, regardless of our disposition toward introversion or extraversion. This is certainly consistent with our earlier discussion of how humans evolved to live in groups—and again reinforces the important role of social interactions in promoting well-being. However, there is at least some recent research to suggest that acting like an extravert may indeed come at a cost for introverts, particularly over a more sustained period of time.

The Australian researcher Rowan Jacques-Hamilton and his colleagues conducted another study where half the adult participants were randomly assigned to the "act extraverted"* condition and the other half were instructed to "act introverted"† for a one-week period. As with the previously described studies, overall, people who acted extraverted reported a greater boost in positive mood than those who acted introverted. However, in this case, there was some evidence that acting against their true nature came with a cost for introverts: after an entire week of acting like extraverts, introverts reported feeling more tired and less authentic than extraverts who behaved in the same way.

This research does provide scientific support for the social media–fueled stereotype about introverts finding social interactions "draining." Of note, this does not appear to be the case in smaller doses. So, introverts can still reap the mood-boosting benefits of company, but they likely need to balance these episodes with time alone to recharge.‡ This sounds like very good advice to me! I will go even further in the next chapter and recommend that extraverts can also benefit from spending time alone, even if it is for shorter periods.

Pandemic paradise? Let's finish by returning to the issue of how introverts were misleadingly portrayed in the Western media at the start of the COVID-19 pandemic. As we saw at the outset of the chapter, the prevailing message was pretty much that introverts were not just going to survive but that they would actually thrive in a world of lockdowns and social distancing. Unfortunately, and particularly so for introverts, the early headlines and memes got it wrong. In reality, there is emerging and consistent evidence to suggest that introverts actually fared much *worse* than extraverts during the pandemic.

---

* The exact instructions were: "In your interactions with other people across the next week, act in a bold, talkative, outgoing, active, and assertive way, as much as possible."

† The exact instructions were: "In your interactions with other people across the next week, act in an unassuming, sensitive, calm, modest, and quiet way, as much as possible."

‡ However, hearkening back to the commuter train experiment we discussed earlier in the book, introverts likely still need to push themselves a bit to socialize, since they might be underestimating how much they will enjoy talking to someone.

The Australian psychology researchers Jeromy Anglim and Sharon Horwood compared data on personality and aspects of well-being among young adults collected before and during the pandemic. Overall, young adults reported poorer well-being during the pandemic, including worse mood and lower life satisfaction. However, both before and during the pandemic, extraversion was positively related to well-being. That is, despite the significant change in social lifestyle brought about by pandemic lockdowns and social distancing, people who were more extraverted tended to cope better than those who were more introverted. This again reinforces the notion that introversion is about a lot more than liking solitude.

A team of American and European researchers led by the German psychologist Lara Kroencke conducted a series of studies during the pandemic testing links between personality and well-being. Their participants included thousands of adults from fifty-nine countries around the world. They employed different methods, including time-consuming experiential sampling, which involved having participants report who they were with, what they were doing, and how they were feeling at random intervals during the day. They also collected data before, during, and after lockdowns were in effect. In short, this was one of the most comprehensive and extensive studies of this topic that had been attempted to date. Their results clearly indicated that, overall, extraverts reported greater happiness and life satisfaction than introverts.

Taking all of this together, what can we conclude? Well, there is no question that people can differ widely in terms of the trait of introversion-extraversion and that these differences have real-world implications for many aspects of our lives, including our experiences of solitude. However, as I think is so often the case when we compare memes or headlines to reality, the details are considerably more complicated than social media implies. It turns out that it is not so easy or even useful to broadly classify large swaths of the population as either introverts or extraverts. Introversion is also about much more than just "loving solitude," and people who score similarly high on the trait of introversion can be quite different from one another in terms of other core personality traits. Furthermore, our popular conceptions of introverts are quite misinformed, at best oversimplified or exaggerated ("introverts are only happy when they are alone!") and at worst blatantly false ("introverts thrived during the pandemic!").

But I think we can learn at least two important lessons from introverts when it comes to solitude. First, having a positive attitude toward solitude helps to optimize many of the potential benefits of spending time alone. Second, people are not very good at predicting how they will feel in situations where they believe they will have to act in a way that is not consistent with their personality. In the case of introverts, they tend to think that even short episodes of social interaction will be unpleasant and tiring for them. In reality, short social exchanges make them feel happier, without any real "costs."

It turns out that the same thing applies in the case of people who think they do not like solitude. A group of international researchers led by the Japanese psychologist Aya Hatano found that not only do people tend to significantly underestimate their capability to enjoy solitude, but this also makes them proactively avoid opportunities to just be alone. In other words, thinking we don't like solitude often leads us to not even give it a chance. But, as it turns out, there is some very practical advice on how we can all improve our relationship with solitude.

Chapter 8

Learning to Play Solo

How to Do Solitude Better

I hate tomatoes. I mean, really hate them. This is not a casual distaste or a passing whim. This is active loathing. In fact, my animosity toward tomatoes was actually a deep-seated part of my personal identity when I was growing up. And I was not at all shy about it. I wanted people to know this about me. Without provocation, I would launch into a soapbox sermon about the horrors of tomatoes and joke that we should not eat them for religious reasons: "If God had meant for us to eat tomatoes, he would have made them taste good." I would describe, in tortuous detail, the outlandish plot of the outrageously bad 1978 movie *Attack of the Killer Tomatoes!* In this classic spoof of B movies, mutated tomatoes go on a murderous rampage. Politicians and scientists must band together to prevent these killer berries from the *Solanum lycopersicum* plant from taking over the world.*

When asked why I hated tomatoes so vehemently, I would passionately disclose the true story of the "traumatic" tomato experience I had when I was a young child. It all started when my mother planted her

* The original movie spawned no less than three sequels (*Return of the Killer Tomatoes!*, *Killer Tomatoes Strike Back!*, and *Killer Tomatoes Eat France!*), as well as a cartoon TV series for kids and several video games.

first herb and vegetable garden in the backyard of our suburban home. Among the growing clusters of oregano, cucumbers, and green peppers, there were several vines of cherry tomatoes, interwoven around bamboo poles for support. When the first batch was ripe enough to pick, my mother excitedly called for us all to come out and see. As fate would have it, I was the only one home, so I came running to see the literal fruits of her labor—and faced my date with tomato destiny.

My mother held several bright red cherry tomatoes in her hands and eagerly offered me the coveted first taste. I, of course, reminded her that I did not like tomatoes, although at this point, it was really nothing more than a mild aversion. My mother was undeterred. She enthusiastically exclaimed that these were not ordinary tomatoes: "They taste so sweet . . . just like candy!" Immediately upon hearing the word "candy," my six-year-old self instantly grabbed a fistful of cherry tomatoes and greedily shoved them right into my mouth. To my horror, these purported "candies" did not taste like any candy I had eaten before. These "candies" tasted exactly like . . . tomatoes. I was dumbfounded and devastated by this hurtful ruse and profound betrayal. And after that, I made it my mission in life to spread the word and raise awareness about the perils of eating raw tomatoes.

When I was older, I made a point of nibbling a raw tomato every once in a while, just to see if my taste had changed. It never did: I am still a loud and proud tomato hater. But the thing is, as much as I continue to boast about how much I abhor tomatoes, it turns out that, like most things in life, it is not quite that simple. You see, I like ketchup on my fries. I like spicy salsa with my tortilla chips. I like tomato sauce on my pasta. I even like a steaming bowl of tomato soup on a cold day and get weird cravings for tomato juice when I am on an airplane.* I still

* According to a study conducted by the Cornell University researchers Robin Dando and Kimberly Yan, chronic loud noises like we experience on a plane mess with our sense of taste, dulling sweet-tasting foods but also enhancing the flavor of savory foods like tomato juice.

hate biting into raw tomatoes. But if I am being honest with myself, it would certainly seem that I do like tomatoes, at least in some sense. So where does this leave me in terms of me actually hating tomatoes?

I share this story because I probably thought I hated tomatoes about as much as some people think they hate solitude. But like me, they may hate it only in particular forms. Remember those students who preferred receiving an electric shock to just sitting alone with their thoughts? For them, sitting alone with their thoughts might just be their equivalent of me biting into a raw tomato. If they tried solitude in other ways, like going for a walk, knitting, or doing a crossword puzzle, they might actually find that one or more of those things turns out to be their version of drinking tomato juice on a plane.

Have Solitude Your Way

One moral of my tomato story is that solitude is not just one thing. We're all individuals* with our personal tastes when it comes to solitude. As we saw in the previous chapter, people with different personality traits value different positive functions of spending time alone. This is yet another reason experiences of solitude are so personal—and why solitude works best for people who *personalize* it. This translates into some very simple advice: when it comes to solitude, you do you.

In my studies with samples of adolescents and young adults, we have tried to track what people most often do in solitude. The main results can be summarized in just one sentence: people do a lot of different stuff when they are alone. Some folks seem to be more focused on getting things done when they are alone, be it homework, chores around the house, running errands, or other parts of their daily routine. Others are

* Whenever I hear that particular phrase, I immediately think of the balcony scene in the classic Monty Python movie *Life of Brian*. Brian shouts out, "You're all individuals!" and the crowd below immediately (and in unison) responds with . . . "Yes, we're all individuals!"

more apt to make use of solitude for leisure activities, such as watching videos, making or listening to music, pursuing hobbies, and exploring creative outlets. Yet others seek wellness in solitude, taking walks outside, exercising, meditating, and engaging in other forms of self-care.*

Importantly, these different solitary activities all tend to reflect *intrinsic* motivations, which, as we have seen, suggests that this alone time is self-directed, meaningful, and enjoyable. It is under these circumstances that people are most likely to appropriately satisfy their need for solitude. But again, this wide range of possible solitary activities also highlights the many different functions of solitude and, in turn, reflects the multiple and unique pathways that can individually optimize opportunities for reaping the benefits of alone time.

Of note, some of the adolescents and young adults in our studies told us that they tended to do mostly nothing while they were alone. Their list of solitary "activities" included things like lying in bed, being bored, worrying, and thinking bad thoughts. As we have seen, most people really do not enjoy sitting alone with their thoughts. In line with this notion, across all our studies, we consistently find that people who tend to do *something* (really almost anything) in solitude report more positive mood, less loneliness, lower levels of distress, and higher overall well-being than people who tend to do nothing when alone.

I would say that in some ways, this represents a good-news-versus-bad-news scenario. In terms of the good news, there is a lot of flexibility here; people can find their own best way to spend their alone time. The perhaps not-so-good news is that people need to find their own best way to spend their alone time. How do we do this, exactly? Although everyone's optimal solitary experience may differ, we have already discussed several different principles that can be applied to help us hone

* And, of course, for many people, whatever they choose to do while alone is done with their phones. Much more on this in chapter 10.

our experiences of solitude. First, we must take ownership over our solitary lives. For many of us, this is probably not even something we have ever concretely considered to any degree. Taking responsibility for our solitude means prioritizing some time and energy to customizing how we do alone time. This is not hard to do, and it offers the potential for a substantial return on a relatively small investment.

How to keep a "solitude diary." One easy way to get started is to document your alone time. This is the first official entry in our user's manual for solitude. On your phone or in an old-fashioned paper journal, try keeping track of how you spend your solitary time during a typical week. The entries don't need to be long or complex. Before going to bed each night or first thing in the morning, try spending just a few minutes detailing your episodes of solitude over the last twenty-four hours. For each solitary event, indicate how long you spent alone, what you were doing during this time, and your general mood after each solitude episode as either negative, neutral, or positive. You can use emojis here as well if you prefer: ☹, 😐, or ☺. Finally, for each twenty-four-hour period, indicate whether your time alone felt like it was "too little," "just about right," or "too much."

Your goal here is to produce a log of your typical daily patterns of behavior when it comes to solitude. Don't worry, it doesn't have to be perfectly accurate. In some ways, the creation of this solitude journal is more important than its actual content. That is because this exercise will make you more concretely aware of how often you are spending time alone each day, how you are making use of this solitude, and how it is impacting your mood. Just putting some eyeballs on these experiences can be very helpful in itself.

With that in mind, spend some time looking over what you have recorded. The results may surprise you. What sticks out? Did you spend more or less time alone than you would have predicted? Were you aware of how much of your alone time you spent doing each of the activities you listed? Can you spot any patterns in terms of how your solitude spent in different ways connects to your mood? Were you satisfied with your solitary life on most days, only some days, or ever at all?

Most people have an idealized perception of how they spend their time. And as we have already seen, we are also all pretty bad at forecasting how different solitary or social experiences are going to make us feel. Documenting these things helps to disavow us of these notions. Just raising our awareness about how we are actually spending our alone time is an excellent first step toward taking ownership of our solitary lives.

Once we have collected and analyzed this snapshot of our solitary patterns, the next step is to consider making some tweaks to optimize and personalize it. Again, and importantly, there is no one-size-fits-all solution here. It is now up to each individual to figure out what works best for them. If the answer is not immediately apparent, just try some stuff out! For example, one thing to look for is where and under what circumstances you are spending time that you consider to be "alone." Is most of your solitude in the physical presence of others, like riding to and from work on a crowded commuter train or sipping coffee while on your laptop in a busy coffee shop? If so, make the choice to also try to fit in some episodes of "physical" separation from others and see how that impacts your mood and energy levels. Again, this does not have to be a seismic life change. You could make the decision to take a fifteen-minute walk before or after work on most days, or spend fifteen minutes of your lunch hour sitting in a quiet place alone, reading a book, doing a sudoku puzzle, or listening to music. Whatever you decide, just make a plan and stick to it.

The primary goal here is to make our solitary time more deliberate. As much as it is feasible for you, try to put yourself on a schedule, continue to track what you do and how it makes you feel, and then continually make adjustments based on what you find. A critical component of this endeavor is to make a conscious and conscientious effort to devote some of your (inevitably limited and divided) resources toward working to improve the quality of your time alone. When seeking out your personal best-for-you solitary activities, your aim should be to find things to do in solitude that are some combination of enjoyable, meaningful, and satisfying.

The ultimate goals and results of these specific chosen activities are likely to be entirely unique for different individuals. And that is okay. Some people may choose to focus on relaxation, others on self-care, others on leisure, and yet others on getting stuff done. Your goals or chosen activities for solitude may fluctuate over time, depending upon your life circumstances or even your mood on any given day. And that is okay. Come up with a strategy and give it a whirl. Then try some different things and document the results. Keep doing this until you hit upon what seems to be the best combination that works for you. It may take some time, and that is also okay.

Solitude: Mind over Matter

Over the years, I have spent a lot of time playing piano in bars, restaurants, and coffee shops. In many cases, I have found it to be an interesting form of solitude, or at least of being alone in a crowd. People are not really there to see me—I am more like part of the decor. And that often suits me just fine. I find it very relaxing and even meditative to play. Often, I almost forget that there are people there who are listening.

When I do interact with people, it is most often someone coming up to the piano to request a specific song. But what to do if you have never even heard of the requested song? Most piano players are very motivated to play the requested song, as this often leads to receiving a generous tip. What I do in these situations is basically . . . fake it. I go for the full-on bluff, project confidence, and hope for the best. After getting the person requesting the song to hum a few bars and then playing that short snippet back to them, I proceed to basically play anything, literally anything, just to keep the music going. For the next few minutes, anytime I register that person turning their attention to me, I switch back to the small section of the song that they previously hummed or sang. It doesn't always work, but most of the time, and for most people, this is more than enough to convince someone that you know their song at least a little bit and thus secure the coveted tip.

I was quite surprised when I learned that a version of this technique could be similarly applied to solitude. You don't actually have to know that much or even anything about solitude to start taking advantage of its many benefits. Indeed, if you have made it to this point in the book, you, lucky reader, now actually know a lot more about solitude than most (and you will know even more if you read until the end). In fact, as it turns out, you don't even have to like it. You just have to *pretend* to like it. This translates into our next piece of simple advice for reaping the benefits of time alone: if you don't enjoy solitude, fake it till you make it.

It really does seem to be a case of mind over matter. As our favorite ancient Greek philosopher Epictetus wrote more than two thousand years ago, "Men are disturbed not by things but by the principles and notions which they form concerning things." Put simply, and as Epictetus told us even way back then, the power of positive thinking is a real thing. There is a tantalizing tidbit related to this in one of the studies I previously described by the UK-based researchers Nguyen and Weinstein. They found that participants who were instructed to just "think happy thoughts" reported a more positive mood after sitting alone for fifteen minutes than those who did not receive the instruction. Could it really be that easy? Is just deciding to believe that solitude is good for you enough to really make it so?

The scientific name for a process relevant to this is *cognitive reappraisal*, which basically means "thinking about things differently." This is an amazingly powerful tool. For example, the Harvard psychology researcher Jeremy Jamieson and his colleagues applied this principle to the issue of college students' test anxiety. In one of their studies, they had half the student participants read a short passage describing how it is normal to feel anxious before a test, how there are often advantages to feeling this way, and that they should remind themselves during exams that feeling nervous could even sometimes improve their performance. The other half of the students did not receive any specific information ahead of time. Then all the students took the same exam. Both before and after the exam, participants also provided saliva samples, which the researchers tested for levels of alpha-amylase, an enzyme that has been shown to be a marker for stress.

The results were striking. Students who simply read a short passage instructing them to think differently about their test anxiety were not only less stressed after the exam (as measured by the levels of their stress enzyme) but also significantly outperformed their counterparts who did not read this passage. To me, these results are a remarkable example of the power of positive thinking.

Can this same approach be applied to solitude? The psychology researcher Micaela Rodriguez provided the first preliminary support for this very idea. She designed a study that combined aspects of the student test anxiety experiment with the previously much discussed "sit alone with your thoughts and shock yourself if you want" experiment. In the Rodriguez study, one group of college student participants read a short excerpt about the benefits of solitude, another group read a short excerpt about the prevalence of loneliness, and a third group read about an unrelated topic. Then all three groups sat alone for ten minutes. The results showed that participants who read the brief snippet about positive aspects of solitude were more resistant to the mood-dampening effects of sitting alone compared with the other two groups. In other words, just reading about the possible benefits of solitude made the experience of sitting alone more pleasant for them.

In a more extensive follow-up study using a larger community sample of adults, Rodriguez and her colleagues provided additional support for this phenomenon. This time, they only included people who scored in the medium-to-high range on an initial screening measure of loneliness. As we have previously discussed, people who are prone to being lonely tend to have more negative experiences of solitude in general. So, this approach made the study an even more stringent test of this effect.

The design was the same as the previous experiment. Participants read short blurbs about either the benefits of solitude, the prevalence of loneliness, or an unrelated topic and then sat alone for ten minutes. As with the previous study, the results were striking. Overall, participants who read the positive solitude snippet reported greater low-arousal positive emotions than those who read about an unrelated topic. That is, they felt calmer, more content, and more peaceful after sitting alone. Thus, even people who were already prone to loneliness experienced greater mood-boosting benefits from time alone after simply reading a short passage about why solitude can be good.

I find these results extremely intriguing. These effects were triggered by a relatively tiny action: reading a two-hundred-word blurb describing the benefits of solitude. And it even worked for people who tended to be lonelier at the outset, and thus more prone to negative experiences of solitude. If reading a short excerpt helped these participants appreciate their solitude time more, just think about how much you might benefit from reading this entire book!

So, we have more to add to our user's manual for solitude. Everyone needs to figure out their best way to do alone time. And whatever you end up doing alone, educating yourself about the positive aspects of solitude and just generally thinking positive thoughts while you are alone will help you tap into the many benefits of a healthy dose of solitude.

Practicing Solitude Makes Perfect

If you already enjoy solitude, you are more likely to prioritize spending at least some time alone as part of your daily routine. But if solitude is not really your cup of tea, it is more than understandable that you might feel as though you just do not have enough time to add anything new to your schedule (even if that anything might be good for you). Many people live very busy lives, and it is just not feasible for them to take a two-hour solitary walk in the woods every day. Or even one hour. Many wouldn't even want to if they had the time.

I have two responses to this. First, I offer this quote attributed to the sixteenth-century Catholic saint Francis de Sales: "Half an hour's meditation each day is essential, except when you are busy. Then a full hour is needed." Saint de Sales was referring to the practice of daily prayer here, but I think we can apply this principle more generally to solitude. It is when you feel like you have the least amount of extra time at your disposal for solitude that you may most need to take that time. And taking some of that "me time" will likely help you make better use of all the rest of your time. Remember, solitude can be restorative, making us feel calmer, refreshed, and revitalized. Solitude can recharge our emotional and cognitive batteries. This makes us more attentive, improves our memory, and ultimately makes us more productive. In this sense, if you take some time for solitude—even when it feels like you don't have any time to spare—you will almost certainly get a solid return on your investment.

Also, like any other skill, doing solitude right, and just right for you, takes some practice. It may come easier to some people than it does to others, but practice makes perfect. Just give it a bit of time. And while we are talking about time, remember that you don't need much solitary time to generate results. Research shows that as little as fifteen minutes of alone time a day can have demonstrable and lasting effects. That is my next piece of advice for our user's guide: engage in micro-moments of solitude. It is okay to start small. A little bit of "me time" can go a long way. So, grab a few minutes here and there throughout the day. Take a short walk in the morning before you start your busy day. Find a quiet place to drink an afternoon cup of tea. Sit in your car for a few minutes at the end of your day before going inside to your busy and bustling home. But as an important reminder, these moments will work best if they are planned, intentional, and prioritized.

For some people, this relatively little bit of time each day will be the "just right" solution for them. Everyone's daily solitude quotient is different. So don't stress about how much time works best for you. Having said that, if you want to increase your dosage of alone time, just approach it like you would if you were trying to increase your stamina for jogging. When people start to jog, they do not begin with marathons. Instead, a common approach is to start with a short distance and combine running with intermittent walking. Gradually, slowly but surely over time, they increase the proportion of their time spent running versus walking by small increments and progressively lengthen the total distance that they cover. It is a process that leads to slow but steady improvements. After a while, and a string of those additional small steps,* noticeable change becomes evident.

We can do the same thing with solitude. Start small and don't be too hard on yourself. It will take some time to build up your stamina for solitude. For some, it will be like developing muscles you have never used before. There will be ups and downs, advances and setbacks, and that is all okay. As they say, practice makes perfect. (Personally, I

* In the case of jogging, this process is taken literally one step at a time.

prefer the phrase "practice makes *better*.") Track your progress, stick with it, and over time, you will see noticeable improvements not only in your capacity for solitude but also in the quality of your solitary experiences—and the rewards that come with this.

Approaching Solitude Versus Avoiding Socializing

The last part of this chapter is not about how much time you can comfortably spend in solitude; it's more about the importance of prioritizing quality over quantity. As we have already seen, the quality of our alone time depends upon several factors, including what we are doing and how we are thinking about it. However, as we already discussed at some length, it also has a lot to do with *why* we are spending time alone. So, let's give some attention to individuals who already tend to spend a lot of time alone, not because they are actively seeking out solitude but more because they are ending up alone as a result of avoiding social situations.

The COVID-19 pandemic forced millions of people around the world to come face-to-face with solitude in a way they never had to before. Personally, however, my first experience with pandemic-induced social isolation came over a decade earlier. In 2009, I accepted an invitation to serve as a visiting professor at the University of Melbourne in Australia. My family came along. We rented a great little house and enrolled our two young children in the local elementary school. It did not take us very long to settle in, although adjusting to the whole driving-on-the-other-side-of-the-road part was a personal challenge for me and there were many times I was a clear and present danger to myself and others. Oh yeah, there was also all the local fauna that had the real potential to kill us.*

During the latter part of our stay, we faced an entirely different kind of danger: the initial emergence of the H1N1 flu pandemic. At the time,

* Australia is home to some of the world's most deadly venomous spiders and snakes.

almost nothing was known about this new flu strain. Rumors were flying around about how serious it was, and people were understandably very scared. Given the uncertainty of the risk, we decided that it would be best for the rest of my family to return home early, while I remained alone in Melbourne for an additional month to fulfill my remaining work commitments. For those next several weeks, in an effort to avoid the virus, I almost never left the house. I spent this time alone looping through an ever-growing and spiraling list of worries and staring into what I perceived as the endless void of my solitary space.

Fortunately, I stayed healthy, and soon enough, I returned home to rejoin my family. In the intervening years, I have reflected on why that particular experience of solitude was so unpleasant for me, especially since I have enjoyed and greatly valued my time alone on many other occasions. Ultimately, it was about my motivations—that is, the reasons I sought solitude to begin with. I spent almost all that time in Melbourne alone because I was seeking to avoid social situations that I perceived to be a threat to my health and well-being. It wasn't fun, but the experience helped me understand what can happen when people seek solitude primarily to avoid being around others.

I don't like being the center of attention. Feeling somewhat anxious when meeting new people or when having to speak in front of a group is a common experience, even for relatively outgoing people. However, for particularly shy individuals, the mere fact of being around others can trigger feelings of unease and self-consciousness. Like most personality traits, shyness is neither inherently "good" nor "bad." Rather, it can have both benefits and disadvantages, as we discussed a few chapters ago in the parable of shy and bold cavemen. As a reminder, on the good side, people who tend to be shy also tend to be more sensitive to others' feelings, good listeners, and thoughtful decision-makers. Shyness also comes with an advanced "early-warning system" that can more easily detect potential threats and problems. On the not-so-good side, being shy can also make people prone to worry, particularly about what others might be thinking about them.

When such negative feelings become too much, a natural response is to simply avoid the perceived causes of this distress. In the case of shyness, this means keeping away from others, which means spending more time alone. But this type of solitude is not intentional. It's a side effect of social avoidance. As a result, the table is not set for a positive solitary experience. Instead, when people are avoiding others, they tend to spend that alone time thinking about exactly why they are avoiding others, what happened the last time they were with others, and what will happen the next time they are with others. Then they think about that again and again, and then again some more. This self-perpetuating whirlwind of bad thoughts is called *rumination*.

Rumination is repetitive and persistent negative thinking about yourself and others. In the context of social avoidance, these negative thoughts focus on upsetting social experiences and concerns about being poorly perceived by others. Although I have tried to emphasize the wide range of solitary activities that can promote well-being in solitude, ruminating is one of the things people do alone that is definitely not on this list. When people sit alone with their thoughts and those thoughts are ruminative, it can have significant negative consequences.

The UK-based psychologists Edward Watkins and Henrietta Roberts reviewed previous research on the impact of chronic rumination on people's well-being. This is a well-studied topic, and the findings are very consistent. Rumination is insidious because it disrupts several different aspects of people's positive functioning. For example, rumination amplifies negative emotions such as worry, sadness, and anger, and it aggravates sleep problems. This all serves to further intensify symptoms of anxiety and depression. This maladaptive pattern of thinking also impairs people's ability to cope with stress and solve problems effectively. As a result, chronic rumination makes people vulnerable to more serious mental health problems, including major depressive episodes, anxiety disorders, and substance abuse.

The University of Cincinnati researcher Joseph Fredrick and his colleagues provided some direct illustrations of these effects during the COVID-19 pandemic. A large sample of early adolescents (ages twelve to fourteen years) participated in the study at three points in time. The results showed that adolescents' self-reported stress about COVID-19 at Time 1 (May–June 2020) predicted rumination at Time 2 (October–November 2020), which in turn predicted symptoms of anxiety and depression at Time 3 (March–April 2021). In short, rumination is the process that seems to turn stress into episodes of anxiety and depression.

This leads to another item for our user's guide for solitude: when alone, don't worry, be happy. Of course, this is often easier said than done. However, there are many effective strategies for reducing rumination, including distraction, writing out your thoughts, and making concrete plans for addressing your worries. Importantly, there are also very well-established therapeutic techniques, such as cognitive behavioral therapy (CBT), which focus specifically on challenging and altering patterns of negative thoughts. Psychological "talk therapies" are really good at this and have been proven to be extremely effective in combating rumination. In short, thinking "bad" thoughts does not have to ruin people's experiences of solitude. However, they need to take active steps to combat it.

I hate people. Finally, some people avoid social situations not because these episodes make them nervous or self-conscious but because they just don't enjoy them very much. To paraphrase the writer Charles Bukowski, "I don't hate people, I just feel better when they aren't around." Or as Jean-Paul Sartre wrote in his play *No Exit*, "Hell is other people."

It has become somewhat fashionable of late to boast about how much you hate people. A quick Google search of "I hate people" will reveal endless memes devoted to this cause and even a song—"I Hate People"—sung by Willow Pill on *RuPaul's Drag Race*. The lyrics for this song are a laundry list of things that Willow loves, followed at the end of each verse with a restating of the central theme of hating people.

Of course, most folks who say "I hate people" are exaggerating; they wouldn't really prefer total isolation. But "I hate people" is a real thing. In psychology, it is called *social anhedonia*, a phenomenon wherein an individual fully or partially lacks the ability to derive pleasure from social interactions.* As we have discussed, people generally tend to feel happier when they are around others. Social anhedonia interferes with that process by blunting the happiness boost that typically comes with positive social engagement.

The psychology researcher Thomas Kwapil and his colleagues explored the impact of social anhedonia on college students' social and solitary lives. They tracked participants' experiences of solitude and socializing over the period of one week. Not surprisingly, students with higher initial scores on a measure designed to assess social anhedonia tended to spend more time alone. Individuals with social anhedonia also reported being alone by choice more often and in a better mood when they were alone compared with when they were around other people.

From this description, social anhedonia does not sound so bad, particularly in the context of a book espousing the benefits of solitude. However, as I have tried to also emphasize, too much time alone for any reason can be problematic. We all need both solitude and socializing. Perhaps more troubling, in its more extreme forms, social anhedonia appears to impart a vulnerability for the development of some significant mental health problems, including avoidant personality disorder and schizophrenia. Thus, although "I hate people" may currently be a fashionable and somewhat tongue-in-cheek topic for memes and social

* More generalized anhedonia, where a person fails to derive pleasure from things that typically made them happy, is also a core feature of depression.

media, we should be careful not to water down the phenomenon of social anhedonia too much.

I gave out a lot of advice about solitude in this chapter. To help keep everything straight, here is a summary of the main entries in our user's guide for solitude:

User's Guide for Solitude

KNOWLEDGE ABOUT SOLITUDE IS POWER.

→ Keep a solitude diary where you track your time alone, solitary activities, and mood every day for a week. Afterward, examine it for patterns, make some tweaks, and see if you can improve your moods.

WHEN IT COMES TO SOLITUDE, YOU DO YOU.

→ Everyone needs to find their personal "just right" amount of solitude and to personalize their alone time with their preferred solitary activities.

IF YOU DON'T ENJOY SOLITUDE, FAKE IT TILL YOU MAKE IT.

→ Just thinking positive thoughts while alone can improve experiences of solitude, and being reminded of the benefits of solitude can improve the strength of those effects.

ENGAGE IN MICRODOSES OF SOLITUDE.

→ Spending as little as fifteen minutes alone a day can have measurable and lasting positive effects. And remember, "practice makes better" applies to alone time as well. Make a plan for how you can integrate a little bit of solitude into your routine on most days—and stick to it!

WHEN ALONE, DON'T WORRY, BE HAPPY.

→ If you find yourself ruminating while alone, try to distract yourself with another activity, write out your thoughts to get them out of your head and onto paper, or make some concrete plans to address your worries. If you still struggle with these negative thoughts, consider seeing a therapist. There is really good help available, and it can make a huge difference.

Chapter 9

Making It Alone

How Solitude Can Enhance Your Creative Side

I'm a walker. Not as in a zombie from the long-running postapocalyptic TV show *The Walking Dead*, but as in someone who needs to get outside for a walk pretty much every day. Before step count was a thing, and long before there were apps that could track your distance traveled, pulse, and other vital stats, walking was my main form of "me time." If there are choices available, I typically prefer routes that bring me by some water or through some trees, but ultimately, I will walk anywhere and in any weather.

I know that walking is good for my physical health. A daily stroll provides regular cardiovascular exercise and gets me outside and often into nature. I also know that walking is good for my mental health, giving me a chance to catch my breath, recharge my emotional batteries, and satisfy my personal need for solitude. But what I learned only by doing was that walking would become my most invaluable "space" for thinking and problem-solving. There is just something about the rhythm of stepping heel to toe that clears my mind and opens it up to new perspectives. I call it putting my thoughts into my feet.

I simply would not have been able to write this book without my daily treks. As almost all writers will tell you, sometimes you just get stuck. It's certainly happened to me. Many times. In what I think is a particularly apt example, taking walks helped me figure out how to write this very chapter on solitude and creativity. I spent several days stewing over how to best organize the content. I just could not figure out how to cohesively present all the different ideas I had in mind to include here or what examples or anecdotes I could include to bring them all to life. I also struggled with how to make some of the more complex psychological processes involved in the links between solitude and creativity more accessible and engaging.

Each time I hit one of these proverbial walls, I took myself out for a walk. When I was out ambling around my neighborhood, my eyes roaming over the passing landscape, I tuned in to the steady pulse of my footsteps, and I tried to free up my mind to go wherever it drifted. Inevitably, something would shake free. Each moment of insight, each moment of realization, each little "aha!" and I would pull out my phone and dictate a voice note with my new idea. It was amazing how *not* thinking about the problem for a while allowed me to approach it from a new perspective. And the irony is not lost on me that I needed to let my mind wander so I could figure out the best way to write about mind wandering in this chapter.

In ancient Greek mythology, the Muses were goddesses who served as inspirations for writers, artists, and scientists. The exact number of Muses is still the subject of some debate. However, according to an account by the Greek poet and mythmaker Hesiod, who lived around 700 BCE, the Muses were the nine daughters of Zeus and Mnemosyne. Each Muse was thought to offer inspiration in different domains, including Urania, the Muse of Astronomy; Erato, the Muse of Poetry; and Terpsichore, the Muse of Dancing. For the purposes of this chapter, I propose an honorary tenth Muse, Monaxiá,* as the Muse of Solitary Creativity.

---

* The Greek word for solitude.

Suffering for One's Art, Alone?

Back in chapter 5, I described Christopher Long and James Averill's classic psychological treatise on the benefits of solitude. In it, they also discussed the long-standing connection between solitude and creativity, stating that "the link between creativity and solitude is so ubiquitous that it has become almost a cliché: the scientist alone in a laboratory, the writer in a cabin in the woods, or the painter in a bare studio." History is indeed filled with many well-documented examples of philosophers and artists retreating to solitude in pursuit of new ideas and perspectives.

Authors as diverse as Virginia Woolf and Stephen King have discussed the essential value they place upon having a quiet and solitary space for their writing. Some of the world's most influential thinkers and innovators jealously guarded their solitude as a place for ideation and contemplation, including Sir Isaac Newton, Nikola Tesla, and Albert Einstein. Bill Gates has spoken often about his "think weeks," during which he isolates himself in a remote cabin in the Pacific Northwest for seven days of brainstorming. There is also a long list of artists who produced some of their greatest works in solitude, including Frida Kahlo, Georgia O'Keeffe, and Edward Hopper. As Pablo Picasso famously said, "Without great solitude, no serious work is possible."

Sometimes, the lines between solitude, creativity, and art can get pretty blurred. For example, the Taiwanese artist Tehching Hsieh made isolation a primary ingredient of his art. For *Cage Piece*, the first of his famous set of five *One Year Performance*s, Hsieh had a cell installed inside his New York studio. On September 30, 1978, he locked himself in the 11'6" x 9' x 8' cage and did not emerge until September 29, 1979. In a statement issued at the start of this performance art piece, Hsieh outlined the restrictive conditions of his solitary confinement, which included no talking, no reading, no writing, no listening to the radio, and no watching television. One photo was taken each day to document his experience, and the public was invited to view the "exhibition" on several days each month. Hsieh states on his website that the goal of this performance art was to make art and life simultaneous using long durations. As Hsieh himself has said, "Isolation, being solitary, is very important to me."

In many ways, Hsieh fits the well-trodden trope of tortured artists who must suffer for their art. This archetypal persona is well represented in history (and continues to trend online). As supposedly noted by Aristotle more than two thousand years ago, "No great mind has ever existed without some touch of madness." Modern-day Greek psychologists Evangelia Galanaki and Konstantinos Malafantis identified and described a common pattern of solitude, loneliness, and loss in the childhoods of the gifted writers Hans Christian Andersen, Edgar Allan Poe, Robert Louis Stevenson, and Beatrix Potter. Childhood traumas experienced by these authors included loss of parents by death or abandonment, extreme poverty, severe mental health problems, and substance abuse among family members.

These experiences led to extended episodes of social isolation and loneliness and, according to Galanaki and Malafantis, caused these writers to feel that there were aspects of themselves that could not be understood by others. In turn, these feelings of separateness led them to retreat into inner worlds of their own creation, which could only be explored in solitude. Galanaki and Malafantis conclude by citing another example of a paradox of solitude: gifted writers are prone to intense experiences of both painful and beneficial solitude, which serve as both a cause and result of the writing gift. As the author Ernest Hemingway said in his Nobel Prize acceptance speech, a writer "does his work alone and if he is a good enough writer he must face eternity, or the lack of it, each day."

So, is there any truth to the "mad genius" hypothesis? According to the University of California, Davis, psychology researcher Dean Keith Simonton, the answer is far from simple. The differences in results across the many studies in this area are likely due to differences in who we are studying (for example, scientists versus artists),* what symptoms and types of mental disorders are studied, and how creativity is defined and measured. There are also chicken-or-egg-type issues to contend with: Does being creative make you more vulnerable to mental health problems, or is there something about the experience of mental health symptoms that somehow unlocks or amplifies creative channels?

When we add solitude to the mix, it gets even more complicated. For example, in a study of young adults conducted by my frequent collaborator Julie Bowker, a connection was found between preferring solitude and creativity. The same causality issue arises here, though. Do people who prefer solitude tend to become more creative, or does creativity nudge us into seeking solitude as a place to engage in artistic or innovative pursuits? We have already talked about the complex links between solitude and mental health, but now we have the triumvirate of creativity, solitude, and mental health, which appear to be deeply entangled in a way that may be almost impossible to tease apart.

It is easy to get bogged down in the potentially fine line between genius and madness—and the role that solitude might play in delineating that line. In the end, it may be that great artists tend to seek solitude to pursue their work, and they may suffer, at least partially, as a result. But for our purposes, we are more concerned with questions about how and why spending time alone might stimulate creativity and how we can use solitude to help us boost our creative pursuits.

---

* The Swedish researcher Simon Kyaga and his colleagues conducted a large-scale study of the link between creativity, mental illness, and suicide in a sample of more than 170,000 people. Overall, they did not find much evidence of a link between creativity and mental illness, except among authors!

Autopilot, Daydreaming, and Getting Ideas in the Shower

My parents live about two hours away from me. They are both in their eighties now and living in a retirement community. I make the drive in to see them as often as I can. The route is mostly on a multilane highway, and I often take the trip myself. When I am alone in the car, I usually start off trying to sort out the best way to deal with my busy upcoming schedule or contemplating the most pressing personal or professional issue of the day. But inevitably, my thoughts start to drift, and at some point, and it is never clear to me for how long, I will realize that I have been driving on autopilot. My body seemed to know what to do, but I was not actively focused on it. It is a bit of an unnerving feeling. Some part of me was making small adjustments to my speed, steering around curves, and possibly even changing lanes. Yet, I would have no real recollection of these events, having been almost completely lost in my thoughts.

It turns out that this is a very common experience, particularly when people are driving on familiar routes. How common? In one study, the psychologist Carryl Baldwin and her colleagues found that participants engaged in "mind wandering" about 70 percent of the time during a twenty-minute driving scenario. There remains some debate as to how much daydreaming while driving is directly responsible for car accidents, but obviously we all need to keep focused on the task at hand as much as possible.

The other place where my mind wanders all the time is the shower. I will drift off into random thoughts, and, some undetermined amount of time later, I will have to check to see if the bar of soap is wet to confirm whether I have actually washed myself. When I get a really good idea in the shower, it poses more of a logistical challenge than when I am walking: I have to continually repeat it to myself until I can exit the shower and write it down. Brainstorming in the shower is not uncommon. In fact, there's a name for it: the *shower effect*. The Australian psychology researcher Linda Ovington and her colleagues explored "aha" moments in a sample of more than one thousand adults. They found that the most common places where people have creative insights include in the shower, during transport, while exercising, and in nature.

What is it about these settings that seems to kick-start creativity? One thing they have in common is that they are all pretty typical contexts for solitude. As we have seen, one reason time alone is "good" for us is that it offers both "freedom from" and "freedom to." It turns out both these conceptual processes play a big part in understanding how and why solitude might specifically get our creative juices flowing and spark innovation.

Solitude gives us a respite from our direct connections to the social input that we are exposed to in the presence of others. This input is funneled through all our senses, with our ears catching snippets of conversation, our eyes glimpsing different facial expressions, and our noses detecting wisps of bodywash or aftershave. We process this constant information stream both consciously and unconsciously. When we get a break from all this input, it has an impact on how our brain functions and therefore on how we think. In short, solitude is an ideal place for our mind to wander.

A group of international researchers led by the Canadian neuroscientist R. Nathan Spreng found evidence to suggest that solitude leads to greater activation in a collection of brain areas known as the *default mode network*, which is believed to be involved in creative thought. This suggests that when we are alone, our brain is primed to activate a range of different cognitive processes that allow for the consideration of multiple perspectives. Thus, to (perhaps over-)simplify, solitude offers our brain some additional flexibility to think about things in different ways. This can directly stimulate outside-the-box approaches, which are a foundation of creative thinking.

To connect all this back to driving, showering, and taking a walk, the default mode network is also associated with mind wandering. However, being lost in aimless thought is not always a good thing. For example, there is some evidence to suggest that mind wandering can promote negative moods. This may be because for many people, meandering thoughts can end up looking a lot like rumination, the pattern of negative repetitive thoughts that can bolster feelings of anxiety and depression. It turns out that what we are daydreaming about plays a role in determining how beneficial mind wandering can be. The psychologist Florence Ruby and her colleagues found that mind wandering focused on the past and on others was more likely to put people in a bad mood. In contrast, daydreaming about the future and with a focus on oneself was found to increase positive mood.

This leads to our first piece of advice for this chapter: when you are alone, look forward to letting your mind wander. In other words, it can be good, even productive, to daydream. But be mindful of your mind wandering. For some people, daydreams can morph into daymares. Although this is not always easy to prevent, it's possible. We already talked about one simple, evidence-backed method for boosting your mood in solitude: just try to think happier thoughts. Another strategy involves taking a moment to acknowledge and appreciate positive feelings. This process is often referred to as *time-savoring*. The Swiss researcher Miriam Wallimann and her colleagues found that older adults (age sixty-five to ninety-two years) who specifically engaged in time-savoring felt less lonely and depressed when spending time alone compared with their counterparts who did not tend to time-savor.

So, thinking happier thoughts and focusing on positive feelings can help to ward off some of the negative consequences of solitude. Notwithstanding, it turns out that to truly unlock the creative potential of a good solitary mind wander, both timing and what you are doing while daydreaming also matter.

Incubate and Switch

In his 1926 book *The Art of Thought*, the British psychologist Graham Wallas proposed one of the first comprehensive models of creativity, which remains a popular theory today. According to Wallas, there are several stages that are common to the creative process. He called the first stage "preparation," which basically involves working on the problem for a while. The second stage, which is most relevant for our discussion, he labeled "incubation." During the incubation phase, people stop consciously working through the issue and just let their ideas gestate. This is thought to lead to the third phase, which Wallas named "illumination": the aha moment where something shifts and a new solution to the problem at hand emerges.

There is considerable research to support the notion that taking a break from something you are working on can really help. The psychology researcher Shelly Gable and her colleagues at the University of California, Santa Barbara, conducted a series of studies with participants from two highly innovative yet distinct occupations: professional writers and theoretical physicists. Their studies focused on how these two types of "creatives" came up with their most creative idea each day. Overall, they found that about 20 percent of creative ideas came to both writers and physicists during instances when they were engaged in an activity other than working. Or if they were working, it was on something unrelated to the new idea that they came up with. This supports the notion that our minds continue to churn away on a problem even when we are engaged in other activities.

Ken Gilhooly and a group of UK-based psychologists tested this notion directly. In their experiment, they used two different tests of creativity. Measures of creativity, also sometimes called *divergent thinking*, essentially challenge people to think outside the box. For this study, half the participants completed a verbal measure of creativity, which involved having to list as many different unusual uses for everyday objects they could come up with. For example, participants were shown a picture of a brick and asked what else they could use it for besides construction. The other half of the participants were tested using a spatial measure of creativity: they were shown pictures of five different shapes (circle, square, rectangle, triangle, and the letter C) and asked to combine them to form as many different recognizable objects as they could.

Both groups worked on their respective creative tasks for five minutes. Following this, some participants spent five minutes working on unscrambling the letters in anagrams to form words before returning to their original creative test for five more minutes. This was the "verbal incubation" period group. Other participants spent five minutes mentally rotating objects before returning to their original creative test. This was the "spatial incubation" period group. And the rest continued working on their original creative test. These last participants were in the "no incubation" period group.

Their results showed that taking a break helped people be more creative afterward, but the degree of the benefit depended on specific combinations of the type of creative test and what people did during their breaks. On the verbal test of creativity, participants who completed a spatial task during incubation performed best, but on the spatial test of creativity, participants who completed a verbal task during incubation performed best. In other words, people came up with the largest number of new ideas when they took a break and did something different from the problem they were trying to solve.

This underscores our next piece of advice for our user's guide for solitude: to help get unstuck, incubate and switch. Simply put, if you need to figure something out and you are feeling blocked, stop directly working on the problem. Take a solitude break and do something else for a while. Although you will be consciously focused on your new activity, your mind will still be working away in the background. For those of you who are more averse to solitude or continue to struggle to squeeze in "me time," this is yet another reason to justify prioritizing time alone: think of it as a productivity tool!

However, to again further complicate things, it also seems to be the case that what you are doing when you switch it up matters. The psychology researchers Benjamin Baird, Jonathan Smallwood, and their colleagues had participants complete the same verbal creativity test I just described. This is the test where the goal is to list as many unusual uses as possible for a series of common objects, like bricks or paper clips. After working on this task for several minutes, participants were randomly placed in one of four different groups.

The first group spent twelve minutes engaged in an activity that demanded a considerable amount of their attention. The task involved having to remember if certain previously presented numbers on a computer screen were even or odd. The second group spent the twelve-minute break completing a far easier assignment; they simply had to indicate if occasionally appearing numbers on a screen were odd or even. The third group was told to rest and sat alone with their thoughts for the same period of twelve minutes. All three of these groups then returned to the creativity test. The fourth group, however, was not given any time at all in between their two attempts at the creativity test.

The results were striking. Participants in the undemanding task incubation group produced more new ideas than all other groups. Interestingly, there were no differences in new ideas among participants in those other three groups. It did not matter if participants engaged in a demanding incubation task, did nothing during the incubation period, or had no incubation period at all: they all generated a similar number of new ideas. So, what does this all mean? First, incubation periods can boost creativity, but not all incubation periods are the same. A specific type of activity appears to be most helpful in terms of allowing the brain to solve problems: one that is mildly engaging, unrelated to the challenge at hand, and not overly difficult. Why? Because it is these types of activities that appear to naturally promote mind wandering, which, as we've seen, is a process that helps us solve problems we are already working on consciously.

This really hits home for me. It helps explain why, when I have something on my mind that I am trying to sort out, it feels like I do my best thinking when I am in the shower, driving on the highway to visit my parents, or out on a long walk by the water. During these not-too-demanding tasks, my mind is free to wander, and it goes places that basically help me connect the dots in my head.

As another caveat, although less demanding tasks are better than demanding tasks, there appears to be a sweet spot in terms of exactly how demanding. This hearkens back to our previous discussion of the Goldilocks principle. A group of US-based psychologists and philosophers led by Zachary Irving found that people were more creative following an incubation period where they participated in a moderately engaging task, in this case watching a clip from the movie *When Harry Met Sally . . .* , compared with an incubation period spent in a boring task, in this case watching a video of men folding laundry.

I realize how many caveats and buts I've already asked you to consider, but there is one final complication to note: the important and unique roles of both solitude and collaboration in the creative process. The University of Texas researchers Runa Korde and Paul Paulus compared the number of new ideas generated while brainstorming alone, brainstorming with a group, and in a hybrid context where participants alternated between solitary and group sessions. Across three studies, they consistently found that participants in the hybrid sessions were most creative, producing the greatest number of new ideas. Thus, in some phases of the creative process, periods of solitude will be helpful to fully develop ideas, engage in intense research, or allow for mind wandering to encourage outside-the-box thinking. However, it is also important to be exposed to others' perspectives, bounce one's ideas off others, and seek their feedback.

So where does this leave us in terms of the benefits of mind wandering and incubation periods for creativity—and, more generally, for well-being? The short answer definitely appears to be: it's complicated! To help get unstuck with a problem, take a solitude break and do something else. During this break, activities that let your mind wander will be the most helpful. Optimally, you will choose an activity that is unrelated to the type of problem you are working on. This is a good way to help shake loose new ways of solving an old problem. However, we all need to figure out what activities best facilitate this process for each of us. Ideally, we are likely looking for something that, for us, is right between not too boring and not too engaging. For me and many others, this activity is walking. But it could be something else like knitting, coloring, folding laundry, or whatever—and it will likely take some time and experimentation to figure this out.

In the same vein, we can further optimize the flow of our creative juices by alternating between solitary and social settings. However, as with the choice of activity, how this plays out best is not the same for everyone. As Paulus and his coauthors Jared Kenworthy and Laura Marusich conclude in their essay on solitude and creativity, "It is not feasible at this point to provide a precise recipe for the balance of solitude and social interaction for creativity. This will depend on the personal characteristics of the individuals involved, the type of task, and the phase of the creative process." So, although more sociable people will probably seek out more collaborative settings, soloists will prefer to retreat to solitude to pursue creative endeavors. The reality is that both contexts will likely provide unique benefits for this process.

Let It Flow, Let It Flow, Let It Flow

The only creative outlet of mine that I can't pursue when I am walking is writing music. I like to write songs, but composing music does not come easily for me at all. It is always a struggle. What seems to work best is to sit myself down at the piano bench, close my eyes, put my fingers on the keys, take a deep breath, and just . . . play. Anything. After a while, I am able to allow my fingers and my mind to wander, and I see where they both take me. Solitude provides me with a safe haven where I can try out musical ideas, no matter how unfinished or weird, and not worry about what it sounds like for anyone except me. Like the proverbial million monkeys sitting at a million typewriters, I sometimes stumble upon something interesting.

Occasionally, when I have done this, something truly wonderful has happened. It is hard to describe. I am playing, exploring different chord combinations and experimenting with melodies that might sit on top of them, and something just seems to click. Right at that moment, I am absolutely dialed in. Thinking but not thinking. My hands moving without me consciously knowing what notes I will play next. When this happens, I lose almost all sense of time and place. I am completely at one with the music. And it feels amazing. It's a huge rush but, at the same time, completely peaceful.

Experiences like this are known as entering the state of *flow*. The concept of flow was developed by the Hungarian American psychologist Mihaly Csikszentmihalyi, a hugely influential researcher in the domain of positive psychology. Csikszentmihalyi conceptualized flow as an "optimal experience," which is a state where people feel deeply involved and absorbed in a specific activity. Activities that inspire flow are typically challenging, but not so daunting that you don't feel confident that you have the skills to meet that challenge. Flow is being "in the zone"—losing track of yourself and your surroundings, completely focused in the moment, and feeling confident and unselfconscious. According to Csikszentmihalyi, flow experiences are *autotelic*, meaning that the activity contains its own primary purpose. When we are in a state of flow, our drive and meaning come from within.

The concept of flow is commonly described and studied in the realm of sports, particularly among elite athletes. However, researchers have also documented states of flow among writers, artists, outdoor adventurers, students in learning contexts, and computer programmers. In one study, Spanish researchers led by Xiaowei Cai identified and measured flow as a common experience among frequent video game players.

Flow experiences make us happy—and provide a context for creativity, learning, and achievement. Although it has been argued that solitude is a required context for achieving states of flow, there remains considerable debate as to the exact role of social context. In this regard, there is some evidence to suggest that flow is more enjoyable when experienced in groups. Again, as has turned out to be the theme with this chapter (and the continual impetus for me to take more walks as I have tried to write it), it is complicated.

For example, in one of the last studies published before his death in 2021, Csikszentmihalyi and the University of Houston researcher Tingshu Liu explored the role of introversion and extraversion in people's experiences of flow, when they are alone versus with others. Overall, they found that people were just as likely to report occurrences of flow when they were in solitude compared with when they were in social settings. However, the context where people reported flow events—and the intensity of those flow experiences—was very much dependent on personality. Participants who were more extraverted reported more frequent flow during social activities, whereas introverts were more likely to experience flow while in solitude. Interestingly, the *intensity* of flow experiences did not differ for extraverts across solitary versus social contexts. But for introverts, the presence of others reduced the intensity of their flow states.

Near the end of this research paper, Csikszentmihalyi and Liu commented on this particular finding and noted the many other benefits of solitude for creativity that we have already discussed. With this in mind, they offered the following advice: "Interacting with others can be a good source of an enjoyable life, but one has to learn to enjoy solitude as well to complete some life tasks that demand absolute concentration." That seems like a very good way to end this chapter.

User's Guide for Solitude

WHEN YOU ARE ALONE, LOOK FORWARD TO LETTING YOUR MIND WANDER.

→ Use time alone as an opportunity to let your mind wander. But be mindful that your daydreams do not deteriorate into daymares. Although this can be challenging, thinking happy thoughts and focusing on positive feelings can help.

TO HELP GET UNSTUCK, INCUBATE AND SWITCH.

→ To boost creative solutions to stubborn problems, take a solitude break and switch to a different activity. Ideally, this activity should not be too engaging, not too boring, but "just right." Take some time and experiment with different approaches to find your own optimal activity for this.

FIND YOUR BALANCE BETWEEN SOLITUDE AND SOCIALIZING.

→ To help with the creative process, and to generally boost your mood and well-being, alternate between episodes of being alone and time with others. Again, this balance will require some time to figure out, and it will look different for different people.

SOLITUDE IS AN OPPORTUNITY TO GO WITH THE FLOW.

→ Time alone can also be an opportunity to achieve a state of flow. Find an activity that you enjoy, find challenging, and feel motivated to pursue. Dive in, immerse yourself in the experience, and let it lead you wherever it goes.

Chapter 10

Me, Myself, and AI

How to Be Alone with Your Phone

The year was 1980, and I was twelve years old. On a Friday afternoon in late May, one of my friends at school passed me a floppy disk with the word "Adventure" scribbled on the label in smudged pencil. "You have got to try this game!" was all he said. After supper that night, I went downstairs and turned on the new computer, with its fancy monochrome monitor, that my parents had recently purchased and placed in a small room off the basement in our suburban home. As I waited, not very patiently, for the machine to boot up, I had no concept of how my life was about to change.

I inserted the disk in the drive and typed the command to start the game. After a few moments, the first lines of text appeared on the screen, in all caps: "YOU ARE STANDING AT THE END OF A ROAD BEFORE A SMALL BRICK BUILDING. AROUND YOU IS A FOREST. A SMALL STREAM FLOWS OUT OF THE BUILDING AND DOWN A GULLY." Below the text was a blinking cursor, apparently awaiting my directive. My twelve-year-old self had never seen anything remotely like this before. With a broad smile on my face, I carefully typed "enter building" with my two index fingers and pressed the return key.

Adventure (also known as *Colossal Cave Adventure*) was among the first interactive fiction computer games designed to emulate the experience of the popular fantasy tabletop game Dungeons & Dragons. Dennis Jerz, an English professor at Seton Hill University, wrote extensively about the impact and legacy of this program. *Adventure* was originally created by Will Crowther in the mid-1970s and expanded upon a few years later by Don Woods. The basic premise of the game is to explore a series of deep, dark caves in search of treasures, and unsurprisingly, given the title of the game: adventures.

From the very moment when those first lines of all-caps text appeared on my screen, I was absolutely hooked. And by hooked, I mean all-in, absolutely manic, can't-think-about-anything-else hooked. As I explored every corner of those caves, I collected objects to help me in my quest for treasure. I was also routinely confronted by, and eventually managed to overcome, a series of increasingly deadly threats, including snakes, bears, pirates, trolls, and giants.

I am not really sure why, but I pursued this new obsession entirely alone. It simply became something I wanted to do by myself, just for me, in private and in solitude. I did not talk to my family or friends about it. And of course, in those days, there was no internet, so I could not access hints, cheat codes, or Reddit threads.* I played the game compulsively, retreating to that little room in the basement as often as I could. I even started sneaking down to the basement in the middle of the night to get in some extra gameplay time.

The hours stretched into days. After a couple of weeks, I finally found myself at the climax of the game. In its shouting, all-caps font, *Adventure* informed me of my greatest challenge yet: "YOU ARE IN A SECRET CANYON WHICH EXITS TO THE NORTH AND EAST. A HUGE GREEN FIERCE DRAGON BARS THE WAY!" I took a deep breath. It had taken a lot to get here, but I was ready. With steady resolve, I

* . . . and we had to walk to school uphill in the snow every day . . . both ways!

confidently typed in the instruction to "kill dragon" and immediately received the response "WITH WHAT? YOUR BARE HANDS?"

Okay, no problem, I can do this, I remember thinking. I followed up with a series of commands to kill the dragon with a knife, then a sword, then an axe, then a rock, until I had exhausted each and every one of the objects that I had accumulated during my extended time playing this game. Nothing worked. I stayed up most of that night trying anything and everything I could think of, and then again most of the next night . . . and then the one after that.

Finally, exhausted and exasperated beyond description, and faced with the heartless and soul-crushing repetitive taunting of "WITH WHAT? YOUR BARE HANDS?" I simply replied "yes." There was a slight pause, and then on the screen in front of me appeared the words: "CONGRATULATIONS! YOU HAVE JUST VANQUISHED A DRAGON WITH YOUR BARE HANDS! (UNBELIEVABLE, ISN'T IT?)"

I was gobsmacked. I just sat in stunned silence for several minutes, before suddenly breaking out in maniacal laughter. My outburst was so loud that it woke my parents, who were none too pleased to find their twelve-year-old son awake at 2:30 a.m. on a school night playing computer games and making an unholy racket to boot.

With the wisdom of experience and hindsight, I can see now that this intense period in my life very much exemplified how technology can serve to both detract from and enhance experiences of solitude. On the downside, as I progressed deeper into both the literal and metaphorical cave of the game, I gradually devolved into the classic stereotype of the brooding teenager who shirks school and familial responsibilities, as well as personal hygiene, to play computer games alone in his parents' basement. It was pretty bad. I was perpetually exhausted, distracted, and irritable. I suffered and, as a consequence, made those around me suffer as well.

But at the same time, my admittedly obsessive experience down this solitary cave-based rabbit hole also marked a formative period for my twelve-year-old self. It unlocked parts of my identity that had previously lay dormant: a love of puzzles, a passion for literary fantasy and science fiction, and a deeper understanding of my capacity for focus and dogged determination in solving complex problems.

Looking back, I can see how my behavior bordered on the unhealthy, and this focused period of obsession could easily have deteriorated into a prolonged addiction. Today, video gameplay is ubiquitous, starting in early adolescence, if not sooner. But do teenagers really get *addicted* to video games? The Brigham Young University psychology researcher Sarah Coyne and her colleagues conducted one of the most extensive research studies of potentially problematic video gaming in adolescence. They recruited a sample of almost four hundred teenagers around the age of fifteen years and followed them for six years, tracking video gameplay and aspects of mental health over time. Coyne found that about 10 percent of teens displayed a behavioral pattern of high and increasingly worsening symptoms of gaming addiction across the six years of the study. Compared with the other teens in the sample, this smaller group of "pathological gamers" demonstrated the most negative mental health outcomes at the conclusion of the study, including higher levels of depression, anxiety, and aggression.

As a result of studies like this, as of 2019, the World Health Organization now includes a formal diagnosis of "gaming disorder" in its most recent version of *International Classification of Diseases* (*ICD*). The criteria for this disorder include: (1) impaired control over gaming, (2) prioritization of gaming over almost all other activities in life, and (3) continuation of gaming despite negative consequences. For a diagnosis of gaming disorder, these behaviors need to result in a significant impairment of functioning in the individual's personal, family, social, and educational (or work) life over a period of at least twelve months.

So, for about 10 percent of teenagers, video game addiction really is a thing and definitely something we should be aware of and pay attention to. But when we consider the flip side of this statistic, it is also true that 90 percent of teenagers who play video games are not doing so in a way that is considered to be pathological.

As for my initial foray into solitude and gaming, I have reached my own conclusions as to its longer-term impact on my personal development and well-being. All these years later, I vividly remember the sense of accomplishment, growth, and burgeoning self-identity that emerged as a direct result of my quixotic quest in the colossal caves. But I do not have the faintest recollection of what punishment my parents bestowed upon me for sneaking down to the basement in the middle of the night, waking them up, and failing to hand in a series of assignments during those fateful days in May.

Flash-forward a few decades, and the most advanced video games of my youth look quaint, akin to typing in your responses to a Choose Your Own Adventure book. I cannot even imagine how my twelve-year-old self would have responded to today's offerings. There continues to be enormous (and much warranted) debate about the impact of technology on our social lives. But as we will see, and of particular relevance for our experiences of solitude, the ubiquitous use of smartphones has transformed the very meaning of what it is to be "alone." And it is not an understatement to say that contemporary technologies threaten the very existence of solitude.

Don't Leave Me Alone in Displace

Let's start with a brief discussion of how technology has forever altered the social world. In 1998, the Carnegie Mellon University researcher Robert Kraut and his colleagues sounded the alarm about the potentially devastating detrimental impact of the internet on our health and well-being. In an article published in *American Psychologist*, these researchers reported the results of a study they conducted tracking links between internet usage, social interactions, loneliness, and depression over time.

Kraut and his colleagues began their article by noting that almost 40 percent of US households owned a personal computer, with one-third of these computers connected to the internet. For their study, they recruited families in the Pittsburgh area who, at the time, did not own a computer and were not connected to the internet. They provided the families with a new computer and internet access. Family members also received "a morning's training on the use of the computer, electronic mail, and the World Wide Web." The computers included software that monitored how often people were connected to the internet, how many email messages they sent and received, and the number of unique sites they visited on the web.

At the outset of the study, before families were given access to the internet, family members completed some initial measures of their friendships and social networks, as well as their loneliness, depression, and other indicators of well-being. About two years after being given access to the internet, family members again completed these same measures. In this way, the researchers could test how internet access changed the lives of these families. The results were quite clear. The greater the increase in family internet use over the two-year period, the greater the reduction in family communication and the size of participants' social networks, and the greater the increase in loneliness and depression. The authors noted the paradoxical nature of these findings: a technology that was supposed to build and maintain social contacts and make us happier was instead making us feel lonelier and more depressed. Reading this article today, it is truly astounding how much—and how quickly—technology has reshaped the world in the last quarter century.*

* Kraut and his colleagues made note of this phenomenon even back then. Near the end of their article, they cited a possible limitation of this study was that the internet itself changed during the course of their research: "group-oriented software, like America Online's Instant Messenger or Mirabilis' ICQ, which allow people to monitor the availability of selected individuals and to immediately swap messages with them when they go online, was not available during the early days of this trial."

Much has been written about how continued rapid advances in technology have impacted almost every facet of our lives, from the mundane to the metaphysical. A sizable portion of the discussion has been focused on how screen time reduces, disrupts, and impoverishes our social lives. One of the most prominent and enduring explanations that arose from early studies like the one I just described is the *displacement hypothesis*. This theory warns that online interactions will replace in-person social engagement. Essentially, this argument boils down to the idea that because there are only so many hours in the day, the more of them you spend online, the less you will spend in the face-to-face company of others.*

This notion echoes some of the earliest warnings about the potential "dangers" of solitude that we discussed closer to the outset of this book. Namely, time in solitude is potentially problematic because it takes away time from social interactions. The American psychology researcher Kaitlyn Burnell and her colleagues argued in a recent essay that although this notion remains popular, there is only mixed research support for such effects, with some studies even demonstrating that digital interactions can also strengthen real-world relationships.

During the COVID-19 pandemic, there were numerous studies demonstrating this phenomenon. For example, the Austrian researcher Anja Stevic and her colleagues found that the use of smartphones to communicate with friends strengthened these relationships over time. In turn, this helped to reduce anxiety during the first COVID-19 lockdown in Austria. In collaboration with the psychologist Mona Bekkhus and other researchers at the University of Oslo, my team and I found similar results in a study of Norwegian adolescents at the outset of the pandemic. Teens who texted more with others were less lonely and experienced

* According to *Digital 2024 Global Overview Report*, published by DataReportal, the average human spends more than 6.5 hours per day online (and that number is more than 7 hours in the United States).

fewer symptoms of mental health problems. In contrast, teens who spent more of their alone time scrolling through social media were more likely to feel lonelier and experience heightened mental health problems during lockdown. These findings highlight a critical issue that we will discuss much more: not all screen time is the same when you are alone.

Of course, there remains considerable debate in academia and elsewhere as to the impact of technology on our social lives. However, somewhat ironically, and certainly most relevant for this book, there is now also growing discourse on the role of such technology in our *solitary* lives.

Tech-nically Alone

A technological "recalibration" of our definition of solitude is currently underway. For example, the researchers Scott Campbell and Morgan Ross recently proposed that we should do away with the now seemingly archaic criterion of "physical separation from others" when attempting to define solitude. Instead, they argue that solitude should be reconceptualized as *noncommunication*, which would include all forms of both face-to-face and virtual interactions.

In some of my own research, I am finding that it may be even more complicated than that. In a series of studies I mentioned earlier, we asked large samples of teenagers and young adults to tell us what they did most often when they were alone. In perhaps the least surprising research result ever, the activity they most commonly reported doing in solitude was being on their smartphone. However, what did surprise me was that many teenagers and young adults included types of virtual social engagement as part of their "solitary" pursuits, including texting, talking to their friends, and even using FaceTime. This really made me think. Do young people consider themselves to be alone when they are alone in their room with the door closed but engaged in a group video chat with five of their closest friends?

To explore this idea, my graduate students and I conducted a follow-up study where we asked teenagers exactly that. We presented adolescents with a series of hypothetical scenarios involving the use of technology while alone. In the first case, they were asked to imagine themselves alone in their room with the door closed, but not using any technology—no phone, no tablet, etc. Next, they were instructed to imagine themselves alone in their room using their phone, but not directly engaging with others socially. This type of "passive" technology use included watching videos, visiting websites, and scrolling on social media. Next, we asked them to imagine being alone in their room and using technology more "actively," such as communicating with others via texting or DM. In the final scenario, participating teens were asked to imagine themselves in their room using audiovisual communication with others, such as FaceTime or Zoom.* In each hypothetical situation, we asked the participants to tell us if they would consider themselves "alone." They replied by indicating how much they agreed with that statement on a 5-point scale ranging from "strongly disagree" to "strongly agree."

Our results showed that, across each of these different scenarios, the teens considered themselves to be in different *degrees* of solitude in each scenario, with the degree of perceived solitude gradually diminishing with increasing amounts of digital communication. This really made me stop and think about how deeply technology is impacting our fundamental conceptualization of solitude. Until very recently, "Are you alone?" was a simple yes-or-no question: Are you or are you not in the presence of others? But at least among teenagers today, this no longer appears to be the case. For them, solitude appears to be more of a gradient, with increased levels of virtual interaction serving to

* Video games are trickier to classify. Playing a "solo" game of *Candy Crush* on your phone seems like passive technology use. In contrast, playing *Call of Duty* in multiplayer mode with a headset looks a lot more like audiovisual communication.

gradually reduce their perceptions of being alone. As Campbell and Ross suggest in their essay, it seems we should now be thinking about different *shades* of solitude.

In terms of implications for our advice about solitude and technology, this means that we need to consider the impact of being alone but using our phone in different ways. And as it turns out, these issues are further complicated (aren't they always?) by our personal characteristics and how we generally feel about solitude.

Technical Assistance or Interference?

Conducting and publishing psychological research takes time. Once you come up with your original idea, you typically then have to secure funding for your particular study. After that, you need to design the study itself and go through the often tedious (albeit entirely justified) process of obtaining approval from the university board of ethics and all relevant participating organizations. Then you collect the data, which often takes years. After that, you still have to code the data, conduct statistical analyses, and write up the findings. Then you have to go through the (often protracted) editorial and peer-review process. After all that, if you are lucky, your research article will eventually be published. So, in many cases, the gap between the onset of your idea and your article appearing in a scientific journal can actually stretch to several years.

This makes conducting research about the impact of technology particularly challenging, as the tech landscape changes much more quickly than the speed of scientific inquiry and publication. For example, in the late 2000s, psychologists began publishing a series of articles about teenagers' use of Facebook. This was all well and good, but by the time most of this work made it through the aforementioned process and got published in academic journals, teenagers had fled Facebook for other social media apps. This was understandable. If you are a teenager, once your parents and grandparents start showing up in your social media feed, you are out of there.

So, I understand the risk I am taking here by writing about what the "latest" studies are telling us about technology and solitude. As I sit here typing these words, it is entirely possible that by the time you are reading this book, things will have already changed. Nevertheless, with that caveat established, studies are now starting to tease apart some of the complex connections between technology and experiences of solitude.

For example, in the study I just described, we also asked teens to rate how strongly they would feel different emotions in each scenario. Their responses depended not only on the different technologies we asked them to imagine using while alone but also on aspects of their personalities. Teenage soloists, who generally enjoyed and valued time alone, anticipated being more content, less bored, and less lonely in the solitude scenarios with either no technology or only limited passive tech use. In contrast, in the solitude scenarios that included texting and audiovisual communications, this particular group of teenagers expected to feel more negative emotions. This suggests that for soloists, introverts, and others who generally enjoy spending time alone, once technology use crosses into the realm of social communication, it starts to interfere with the emotional benefits that solitude affords them.

In contrast, teenagers who tended to be more shy reported that they were happiest in solitude scenarios where they engaged in some, but not too much, virtual interaction with others. Thus, shy students did not like being alone without their phone, presumably because this would likely lead to rumination and other negative thoughts. They also did not like audiovisual communications, presumably because even virtual face-to-face exchanges can make shy teens feel self-conscious and uncomfortable. For them, the "sweet spot" was communicating by text, presumably because they do not have to fret about being seen and can take some time to formulate their thoughts before replying.

A group of US-based researchers led by the psychologist Virginia Thomas found similar results in their study of technology use and solitude among college students. After collecting initial information about students' personalities and preferences for solitude, they tracked time spent alone and with others, use of technology alone and with others, as well as loneliness and other indicators of well-being over a one-week period. Several interesting findings emerged. First, the loneliest students were also the ones who reported using social media most often, either while alone or when with others. This is consistent with the considerable amount of previous research that consistently indicates that scrolling through highly curated images of shiny, happy people tends to make us feel worse about ourselves.

Thomas and her colleagues also found that college students who generally enjoyed time alone were just as happy in solitude with or without their devices. In contrast, students who indicated that they generally prefer not to spend time alone were much happier in solitude with their phone than without it. Similarly, in a large survey of adults, the German psychologists Sarah Diefenbach and Kim Borrmann found that compared with people who generally dislike spending time alone, people who enjoy solitude are less likely to use their smartphones during alone time, including while in transit, in a waiting room, and when they are alone in bed.

So, what can we take away from these three studies? First, we have some convergence in the pattern of results across three different types of studies with three different types of samples. In the first, teenagers were asked to imagine themselves in different situations; in the second, college students reported their feelings in real time across similar situations; and in the third, a broader sample of adults described their general behaviors using questionnaires. For all three of these different studies, the findings suggest that people's responses to the intersection of solitude and technology depend both on how they generally feel about solitude as well as what types of technology they are using.

For example, if you are a soloist or introvert, then solitude without any technology is likely going to be best for you, not only in terms of optimizing your enjoyment of time alone but also in terms of maximizing the benefits that these episodes of solitude can impart. Using your phone in noncommunicative ways also seems to be okay. But once you move past the threshold into more active forms of technology use, the possibility of "interference" starts to increase. For people who tend to be shy, technology appears to provide a bit of a social crutch when they are alone, allowing them to help compensate for their perception of solitude as an empty space where they worry and ruminate.

For soloists, this makes the resulting advice relatively straightforward: if you enjoy spending time alone, consider turning off your phone for a while so that it does not interfere with your experiences of solitude. For others, I think the takeaway is a bit more layered: if you find solitude anxiety-provoking, boring, or aversive, your phone can be helpful in terms of making your time alone more pleasant. However, be mindful of *how* you are using your phone from a social interaction perspective. If you find that most of your "solitary" time is spent video chatting with friends, you are likely missing out on a lot of the "freedom from" and "freedom to" that solitude has to offer. Consider at least turning off your notifications and refraining from the more "social" uses of your phone. One piece of advice that I think essentially applies to everyone: spending too much time scrolling through social media can ruin your alone time—and will likely make you feel bad about yourself under almost any circumstances.

Putting in a Plug for Unplugging: Digital Detox, FOMO & JOMO

In the Jewish religion, one day each week, known as the Sabbath, is reserved for rest. During this time, it is customary to turn off all electronics. In 2003, drawing upon this ritual, the annual National Day of Unplugging was launched, created as a twenty-four-hour break from technology from sundown to sundown. In 2009, this practice evolved into the Global Day of Unplugging, now celebrated annually on the first Friday of March.

As stated on the Global Day of Unplugging website, "Whether it is 1 hour or 24 hours, people all over the world, will step away from their screens and intentionally shift into an offline activity, an in-person interaction, a real-life gathering or simply a meaningful conversation about their relationship with technology." Understandably, and importantly, the primary goal of this event is to encourage in-person social interaction. Nevertheless, I appreciate that at least one of the options suggested for how to spend your unplugged time is "an offline activity," which the website does not explicitly stipulate as necessarily being social in nature.

The idea of unplugging is gaining popularity. The *Oxford Learner's Dictionaries* now defines the term "digital detox" as "a period of time when a person does not use digital devices such as smartphones or computers, especially in order to reduce stress and relax." Somewhat ironically, there are a growing number of apps that are meant to assist with this process.

As we have seen, there are some very compelling reasons to consider turning off your phone when you want to spend time alone. However, as with most of the topics we have discussed related to solitude, there is not a one-size-fits-all solution for this either. A group of European researchers led by the German psychologist Theda Radtke supported this notion after reviewing the available research exploring the effectiveness of digital detoxes in improving outcomes such as health, well-being, and social relationships. They uncovered decidedly mixed results. For example, some studies reported that unplugging led to less anxiety, depression, and stress as well as better sleep, whereas other studies tested for but did not find these same effects. Some studies also found that digital detox predicted higher life satisfaction, better mood, greater social connectedness, and lower loneliness. However, again, other studies tested for but did not find any effects for these outcomes. And even more confusing, others found the exact opposite results, with unplugging leading to lower life satisfaction, more negative mood, decreased social connectedness, and higher loneliness!

Radtke and her colleagues offered several possible explanations for these widely divergent results. I think some of their ideas are particularly relevant for how to best incorporate technology in cultivating a healthy and positive solitude practice. First and foremost, there is no one way to do a digital detox. People may choose to schedule their regular period of unplugging to last for one hour, one day, or one week. For some people, digital detoxing might mean completely shutting off their phone and other devices for this predetermined period, but for others it might be taking a break from using social media or other specific apps. Results also varied based on how often people use their phones to begin with and how anxious, depressed, or stressed they are in general, as well as their personality and other characteristics.

These differences are particularly evident in the different ways that people tend to react to not having access to their phones. And in a lot of ways, I think they mirror the profound differences that we have already seen in terms of how people experience solitude. At one end of the spectrum, some people feel discomfort, stress, and worry about being separated from the social connections that these devices provide. This is often referred to as *fear of missing out*, abbreviated as FOMO, which is defined as a preoccupation with missing out on or being excluded from activities within one's social network. The concept of FOMO has been studied by psychologists since the early 2010s, with a commonly used measure of this phenomenon developed by a group of researchers led by Andrew Przybylski in 2013. Since that time, FOMO has been consistently found to worsen feelings of loneliness, anxiety, and depression and to negatively impact our well-being.

More recently, a more generalized and acute distress about being cut off from technology in general has been dubbed *nomophobia.* An abbreviated form of "no-mobile-phone phobia," nomophobia is a state of anguish and fear of being cut off from immediate access to information, communication with others, and other common smartphone functions. As noted in a review of this phenomenon by the Spanish researcher Antonio-Manuel Rodríguez-García and his colleagues, nomophobia is becoming increasingly common and is now being considered as a damaging mental health problem.

On the other side of this spectrum are feelings of freedom and relief when one is disconnected from the constant stream of alerts and information emanating from their smartphone. For some people, turning off their phone leads to the *joy of missing out* (JOMO). This term is believed to have first been coined by the tech entrepreneur and writer Anil Dash in 2012 and has remained a hot topic on social media and in the popular press. However, JOMO has only recently begun to be studied by psychologists.

The Washington State University psychology researcher Christopher Barry and his colleagues developed a new measure of JOMO and explored its implications among adults. In one of their studies, they identified groups of participants based on JOMO and other factors. The group with the highest JOMO, representing about 10 percent of the sample, also displayed a somewhat mixed set of characteristics. For example, compared with other groups of participants, the JOMO group reported high life satisfaction and mindfulness but also higher scores on social media use, stress, anxiety, and depression. This made me think a bit about aloneliness. Perhaps the high-JOMO participants were reporting more stress and depression because they enjoyed disconnecting from social media but, for a variety of reasons, were not doing so enough. However, I think we still have a lot to learn about this phenomenon.

I do think that JOMO is something we can all *aspire* to. When spending time alone or taking a break from your phone, try to reframe this "time-out" as a joyful respite. Instead of worrying about unseen notifications or whatever else that is going on that you might not be a part of during this time, embrace being disconnected and the freedom it offers. Even if it is for a few minutes at a time, we should all try to cherish the chance to revel in missing out!

So, What the Tech Should I Be Doing Here?

What can we take away from all of this? I believe there is some good advice about technology and solitude that we can extract from this somewhat "messy" set of research findings. In terms of an overarching message, I think we can make a small tweak to some of the general advice I imparted earlier in this book: when it comes to solitude and technology, keep in mind what you want to do is not necessarily what is going to be best for you. I *want* to eat fudge ripple ice cream with caramel sauce, mini-marshmallows, and sprinkles pretty much every night. But I don't, at least most nights, because I know that this is a better eating choice for my health and well-being. So yes, the best ways to incorporate and/or limit the use of smartphones and other devices while alone are different for everyone. But given the addictive siren call of our smartphones, most of us will have to exercise some restraint.

For those people who crave the most freedom in solitude, shutting off your phone for periods of time is likely going to be required. For those who hate the thought of being alone but are trying to cultivate a healthier solitude practice, turning off notifications or limiting use of specific apps while in solitude will likely be the way to go. But be wary of global and generalized advice about technology and solitude that does not take into account your own specific personal characteristics.

Simply stated, when you are alone, try to use technology in ways that are most likely to benefit you. We know that too much of certain digital behaviors can be harmful to our well-being, such as obsessively monitoring your social media timelines or doomscrolling through anxiety-provoking news headlines. We should all self-monitor in terms of such activities and be mindful of their impact on our mood. Being mindful in this context means having a plan in place to take a break, detox, or disconnect from such activities in a way that works best for you. It also means being aware of how specific apps and tech activities might be interfering with our experiences of solitude.

Yet, it is overly simplistic to make the blanket statement that "technology interferes with solitude." Technology can also be used for "good" when we are alone. Many people use their phones or other devices for reading, listening to music, engaging in hobbies, or playing low-key games that facilitate mind wandering. There are also a growing number of specialized apps specifically designed to promote mindfulness, meditation, breathing, exercise, and other positive aspects of solitude.

In the end, we all need to figure out how to sprinkle technology into our personalized recipe for what works best for us when we are alone. For some people, a clean break from technology while alone is the way to go. For others, using technology in specific ways offers quick and easy stress relief while alone. As a caveat for this, though, if you are spending all your "alone" time using technology to engage with others, you are probably missing out on a lot of the "good" that solitude has to offer.

User's Guide for Solitude

IF YOU ENJOY SPENDING TIME ALONE, CONSIDER TURNING OFF YOUR PHONE FOR A WHILE.

→ For soloists and introverts, optimal alone time likely entails no or minimal use of technology. Too much tech can interfere and distract from positive experiences of solitude.

IF YOU FIND SOLITUDE ANXIETY-PROVOKING, BORING, OR AVERSIVE, YOUR PHONE CAN BE HELPFUL IN TERMS OF MAKING YOUR TIME ALONE MORE PLEASANT.

→ Be mindful of using your alone time exclusively to interact virtually with others. You are likely missing out on a lot of "freedoms" that solitude has to offer. Consider at least turning off your notifications and refraining from the more "social" uses of your phone.

WE SHOULD ALL ASPIRE TO FEEL SOME JOMO.

→ Try to reframe each solitary "time-out" from technology as a joyful respite from your phone's constant demands for your attention. Relish and revel in all the stuff you are (temporarily) missing out on.

WHEN ALONE, TRY TO USE TECHNOLOGY FOR "GOOD" INSTEAD OF FOR "EVIL."

→ Aim to reduce obsessive monitoring of social media timelines or doomscrolling through anxiety-provoking news headlines and be mindful of how such activities impact your mood. Instead, focus on activities that reduce your stress, such as reading, listening to music, engaging in hobbies, or playing mindless games that facilitate mind wandering.

SPENDING TOO MUCH TIME SCROLLING THROUGH SOCIAL MEDIA CAN RUIN YOUR TIME ALONE—AND LIKELY MAKE YOU FEEL BAD ABOUT YOURSELF UNDER ALMOST ANY CIRCUMSTANCES.

→ This advice is presented without caveat!

Chapter 11

Growing Up Alone

How to Promote Healthy Solitude in Children

I was very fortunate to be able to spend time with all my grandparents when I was growing up. My grandmothers both passed away while I was in my mid-twenties. Both of my grandfathers lived several years after that as widowers. Although they shared this experience, in almost every other way, my grandfathers could not have been more different from each other.

On my mother's side, there was my grandpa Sid. He was the very definition of a people person. He worked in insurance, regularly starred in Gilbert and Sullivan musicals produced by local theater companies, and was generally the life of the party, a performer in every regard. Time spent with him always involved being regaled by his jokes and stories about his life. One of my favorite tales from his youth was the one about when he crashed his sled through the living room window of his house—and somehow talked his friends into paying for the damage. My grandpa Sid had the gift of gab, and he passed this gift on to his daughter, my mom. From this side of the family, I inherited my musicality, social skills, and inherent comfort with being the center of attention when I need to be.

On my father's side, there was my grandpa Lou. Lou was the epitome of a man of few words. He worked as an accountant and spent his leisure time reading books and doing crossword puzzles. He was extremely intelligent and had a sharp wit, which would often be displayed under his breath when he was forced to socialize. I used to love sitting next to him on such occasions, so I could pick up these biting but soft-spoken comments. In the latter part of his life, Grandpa Lou lived in a retirement community not far from my family home. I visited him there regularly. Without fail, whenever I came to see him, I would find him in his room alone, sitting on his small couch, diligently working his way through a *New York Times* crossword puzzle. He would also always sit on the same side of the couch, and over time, that particular armrest became darkened by pencil lead. He passed on his formidable intellect, quiet demeanor, love of crosswords, and affinity for solitude to his son, my dad. From this side of the family, I inherited my work ethic, voracious appetite for books, puzzles, and crosswords, and need for alone time.

I thought of my grandfathers as I sat down to write this chapter on how parents can foster the development of a healthy relationship with solitude in their children. Their lineage remains strong in my son and daughter, who are now young adults themselves. Both are performers who enjoy being "onstage," be it playing music, acting, or hosting a podcast. I would also say they each have their own versions of the gift of gab. Yet, they both have also caught the crossword bug, as well as a need for daily solitary walks. I find it fascinating to trace the seeds of these traits back through the generations.

Mother Knows Best . . . About Solitude

A common experience among parents is having their young children pepper them with questions about . . . pretty much anything. "Why is the sky blue?" "Where do babies come from?" "What is the airspeed velocity of an unladen swallow?" A few days after my grandpa Sid passed away at the age of ninety-four, my extended family and I were sitting around the dinner table reminiscing about him. During a lull in the conversion, my then-five-year-old son called across the table to me, for everyone to hear, “Daddy, what happens when we die?” Suddenly, you could hear a pin drop. All eyes turned to me as I struggled to formulate my reply, knowing full well that this could very well be a critical moment in the life of my young son. As I opened my mouth to respond, he suddenly blurted out, “Wait, wait, wait . . . I have a more important question! Who is faster, Superman or Flash?” I was exceedingly happy to answer this question, and that was the end of all talk about death—for that day at least.

Setting aside the interesting hierarchy of priorities inside the mind of a typical five-year-old, children ask parents so many questions because parents are smart and they know stuff. Developmental psychologists also like to ask parents lots of questions for these very same reasons. Accordingly, I designed a study to ask parents what they thought about the role of solitude in their children's development. I was particularly interested in parental beliefs about the potential costs and benefits of solitude for children of different ages.

I should note that when we recruit “parents” to participate in our studies, we cast a wide net. We are always quite happy to include mothers, fathers, stepparents, foster parents, grandparents, or anyone else who is serving as the primary guardian for a child. However, although this continues to gradually change with each passing year, it is mothers who most often respond to our questionnaires.

For our study, we were able to recruit more than five hundred mothers whose children ranged in age from four to eighteen years. We presented the participating moms with two fairly straightforward statements, which they were instructed to consider while thinking about the current age of their child.* The first was “At this age, it can

* If they had more than one child, mothers were instructed to answer the questions thinking about the child whose birthday came next. This was our way of having them pick one of their children essentially at random.

be a problem for children to spend time alone because . . . ," followed by "At this age, it can be beneficial for children to spend time alone because . . ." Moms were instructed to complete each statement with up to three open-ended responses. A small army of student research assistants then coded all these responses for broad themes and specific content.

Overall, moms most commonly reported potential perceived "costs" of solitude related to mental health concerns. These included worries that time alone could worsen loneliness, depression, and anxiety. Other notable concerns included the fear that spending time alone would interfere with the development of children's social skills, which would lead to problems making and keeping friends. There was also apprehension about the lack of supervision when children are alone, which may lead to misbehaviors or bad decisions. Moms also foresaw the potential for solitude to be a direct conduit for excessive screen time.

On the flip side, the potential perceived "benefit" of solitude most often reported by moms was that time alone helps children to develop autonomy by promoting independence and fostering the ability to entertain oneself. Other positives included the belief that solitude could be a place for restoration by providing children with a means of stress reduction and time to think. Solitude was also seen as an opportunity for children to engage in leisure activities, pursue hobbies, and complete homework and other tasks. Moms also viewed solitude as a place where children could develop and hone a wide range of skills, most notably related to creativity and problem-solving, and learn about themselves and explore their own blossoming and fluctuating sense of identity.

I know moms are usually right about most stuff. But it was particularly striking to me just how much these maternal beliefs lined up with what is now decades' worth of psychological research about the potential costs and benefits of solitude for children and adolescents. Clearly, we could have saved a lot of time by just asking moms in the first place!

Solitude During Early Childhood: Learning to Play Alone

When my son was little, his thing was Thomas the Tank Engine. I read him Thomas books, we watched Thomas videos, and then slowly but surely, he began accumulating some *Thomas & Friends* trains and railroad tracks. My son was completely enamored with his trains. He spent countless hours building tracks, pushing his trains around, re-creating scenes from books and videos, and setting off on his own train adventures. Although I sometimes joined him in his rich imaginary world of trains, he most often wanted to play with his trains alone. At bedtime, after we had read a Thomas storybook for the umpteenth time—he knew every one by heart—my son would spend a few minutes by himself studying the *Thomas & Friends* toy catalog. This would entail learning and listing the names of each character and prioritizing which ones he wanted next for his birthday. For many months, this was the only thing that would grab and keep my son's attention while he was alone. To this day, I remain very grateful to Thomas and his train friends for affording me an occasional break. Parents sometimes need some alone time too.

In our study of maternal beliefs about solitude, mothers of younger children were most likely to report concerns about safety issues due to lack of supervision when their child was alone. As any parent will tell you, it does not take long for a toddler to make mischief when they are left unmonitored. Generally, children of this age need to be kept in earshot, if not within a direct line of sight. For this reason, true experiences of solitude are relatively rare among young children. For example, in collaboration with my PhD student at the time, Kristen Archbell, we had parents keep a daily log of how their child (aged six to eight years) spent their time outside of school over a two-month period. We found that, on average, children in this age range spent only about 10 percent of their waking hours alone.

As an interesting contrast to this, although time alone outside of school tends to increase as children age and become adolescents, the opposite pattern is true regarding time alone at school. For young children, playing alone is very common and normative even when there are other children around. If you watch preschool children during free play, as I spent all those hours doing during the early part of my career, you will certainly see some pairs or small groups playing together. These early social interactions are important because they provide opportunities for children to hone their developing social, emotional, and language skills. However, because these skills are still largely underdeveloped, such interactions tend to be relatively brief. It is common to see young children play alone. They also more frequently spend time playing next to, but not with, other children. This is called *parallel play*.

In one of my earlier studies of kindergarten children's play behaviors, we observed that, on average, children played alone* about one-third of the time during free play periods. Most commonly, solitary play at this age involves either making something, such as building a tower with Lego blocks or drawing a picture, or pretending, such as animating a doll or pretending to be a superhero. These types of solitary experiences serve important functions in young children's development, providing them with unique opportunities to practice burgeoning skills and abilities. Of course, you may not be surprised to hear that moms of younger children in our study already seemed to have learned about this, specifically citing benefits of solitude related to opportunities for leisure time and skill development during this age period.

Of note, while conducting observations in kindergartens, we also found that some children spent a considerable amount of time engaged in what we called *reticent behaviors*. This was a term we used to denote

* In this case, "solitary" play was coded when the child was more than three feet away from other children and focused on their own activities.

wandering around aimlessly, staring off into space, and watching other children play but not attempting to join in. On average, this type of behavior was observed to occur only about 10 percent of the time. However, although most children hardly displayed any reticent behavior at all, a smaller group was found to do mostly this during opportunities for free play.

This is something for parents and educators to keep an eye on, because just as we have seen among adults, doing *something* while alone is often better than doing nothing. Reticent behavior during play is often a sign of nervousness and anxiety. Children who spend too much time watching others are often caught in what is called an *approach-avoidance conflict*. They are interested in what the other children are doing and genuinely want to play with them. That's the approach part. At the same time, however, they are nervous and anxious about the prospect of having to ask the other kids to play or interact with them. This makes them want to avoid the situation altogether. These two opposing forces can make the child get stuck in between, hovering on the edge of where other children are playing but never pushing past the threshold to engage with them.

Finally, in our study of maternal beliefs, we found that compared with mothers of older children and teens, mothers of younger children were also more likely to worry that their child was not mature enough to spend time alone. This was especially the case with regard to the perception of young children's inability to tolerate solitude. This is certainly understandable and likely a response to many young children's persistent complaints about being bored or having nothing to do when alone. However, I will argue that it is not always in the child's best interest if parents give in to these complaints and demands for attention too easily.

Although it has not received as much attention as arguments in favor of the importance of social interactions, I am hardly the first developmental psychologist to promote the value of solitude for young children. One of the earliest was Donald Winnicott, a British pediatrician who gained prominence in the 1950s as an expert on child development. He is best known for describing the notion of the *transitional object*, an item used to provide comfort in stressful situations. Examples of this phenomenon would be a young child snuggling with a favorite teddy bear to help them fall asleep or the security blanket carried by the classic *Peanuts* cartoon character Linus.

But Winnicott also argued that the *capacity for solitude* is one of the most important developmental achievements in life. He believed that experiences of solitude in children fostered creativity and allowed them to understand their "true selves." With this in mind, Winnicott preached that parents had a critically important responsibility to help foster children's ability to spend time alone.

In 1999, the New York University psychology researchers Jill Katz and Ester Buchholz published an impactful essay espousing the necessity of "solo play" for young children.* They highlighted a number of benefits that solitude can afford at this age, including promoting independence and autonomy, providing relief from stress, and offering an environment where young children can safely express needs, exert control, and work through the "big feelings" that can overwhelm them at this age.

In terms of specific advice for parents of young children, I think we can incorporate suggestions from the very smart moms in our study of beliefs about solitude with some of the insights that can be drawn from the work of developmental psychologists. First off, learning to play solo is an important task for young children, and parents can help foster their child's development of this capacity. Try to build in

* And as I mentioned earlier, before we independently coined the same term, they labeled children who enjoyed playing alone as "soloists."

some alone time as a regular part of your child's routine. But like all skills, learning to spend time alone can take time: children will need to build up and flex their solitude "muscles." And as with adults, this will come easier for some children than others. Don't give in too easily to complaints about having nothing to do. Remember that boredom can be a gateway to imagination and creativity.

What constitutes solitude will of course look a bit different depending upon the age and stage of any given child. As we mentioned, for toddlers it may be better to have them in your sights or at least within earshot. But preschool-aged children are often old enough to spend time alone in their room with the door either open or closed. In terms of what your child does while they are alone, they should have as much agency over this as is safe and reasonable for their age. Remember, the benefits of solitude involve having the freedom to choose how we spend this time. For young children in particular, solitude offers an opportunity to try stuff out, practice newly developing skills, and have some means of control over their environment. However, young children do not always know what is best or safe for them to do, so some monitoring will always be required.*

A quick note about screen time for very young children. The American Academy of Pediatrics updated its published guidelines related to this in 2016.† Although specific limits for screen time among older children are in flux these days, the message for young children remains fairly clear: screen time should not be a solitary activity at this age. Specifically for children younger than eighteen months, screen time should be discouraged. The occasional video chat, with grandparents who live out of town, for instance, is considered an exception to this guideline.

For parents of children aged eighteen to twenty-four months who

---

* This is sometimes true of adults as well.

† At the time of this writing, this was the most recent update. As we have already discussed, things change quickly when it comes to tech.

want to introduce digital media, choose high-quality and educational apps. It is also optimal to engage in these activities together with your child, because this is how toddlers learn best. Here the academy also specifically recommends avoiding letting toddlers use media by themselves. For children aged two to five years, try to limit noneducational screen time to about an hour per day, and again, ideally, these should be shared experiences between the child and parents.

Advice around how and how often young children spend time on screens remains a topic of great debate (and the same is certainly also true for older children and adolescents). However, when it comes to the intersection between solitude and technology for young children, the message is very clear. Parents should strive to foster the development of a capacity for solitude by providing opportunities and encouraging their young children to engage in a wide range of solitary activities. However, ideally, young children should not be using technology while alone.

Finally, with all this in mind, parents and teachers should not worry too much about children who like to spend time by themselves at school. However, as with most things, solo play is best in moderation, as too much time playing alone may mean children are missing out on all the good stuff they get from playing with others at this age. Parents and teachers should also be mindful of the reasons children are spending time alone at school. If it seems to be because they are choosing and enjoying these experiences, that's great. On the other hand, if children are being ostracized or victimized, this warrants immediate attention. Signs that solitary children are avoiding others out of social unease and anxiety are also cause for concern. Some shy children may need a gentle push and appropriate support to get them over the hump of their approach-avoidance conflict. In the end, as is the case with adults, each young child will benefit most from finding their own "just right" balance between alone time and time with others—and parents can play a critical role in helping them figure this out.

Solitude During Middle and Later Childhood: Making Some Space to Be Alone

I was a child of the 1970s. Life was different then. From an early age, I would wake up at the crack of dawn on Saturday mornings and help myself to a bowl of cereal. Some combination of my three siblings would sometimes be around. But they liked to sleep in on weekends, so this was often a period of quiet solitude for me. On such occasions, I would walk down the stairs to the family room and sit with my face right up close to the small TV to watch the Saturday morning cartoons. My first exposure to classical music came via Bugs Bunny. This was the only time you could watch these cartoons. They were only broadcast Saturday mornings, and you got whatever happened to be showing that day on the channels that your TV could receive. On a clear day, if I adjusted the antenna just right, we could get up to four channels. It was a different world.

By the time I was ten years old, my mom would shoo me out of the house after lunch on those weekend days and send me off to play. Her simple instructions were to come back in time for dinner. In 1970s suburbia this was common practice. I was a free-range kid. Often, I would spend these days playing tag, hide-and-seek, street hockey, and other games with the kids on my block and around my neighborhood. But sometimes, even back then, I'd happily just wander around by myself.

On one such occasion, I ended up at a small park down the street from my house. The park bordered train tracks, with only a dilapidated fence acting as a barrier. Without thinking twice, I slid through a gaping hole in the fence and peered down the track to hear, and then eventually see, a large train approaching. I am sure that I was way too close to the tracks for it to be safe. But that did not occur to me at all. I just sat down, waited, and watched, and watched, and watched. This was a cargo train, and I was absolutely transfixed as what seemed like an endless parade of cars passed before me. Some were open, carrying automobiles and other large pieces of machinery. Countless others were of different configurations, designs, and colors, but I could only imagine the contents. And imagine I did, daydreaming about what was inside, where it was coming from, and where it was going.

I am not sure why this experience stuck in my mind the way that it has and for so long. There was something about watching the procession of train cars pass before me that felt exotic and adventurous. It made me consider, perhaps for the first time in my young life, my place in the world. I think it is fair to say that most ten-year-old boys don't typically spend a lot of time deep in existential thought. I certainly hadn't, at least. It was an unexpected event that I just happened to stumble into when left to my own devices. Being alone at the time allowed it to become a deeply personal experience of contemplation and imagination. For many reasons, ten-year-olds today are much less likely to have this same opportunity.

The transition from early to later childhood is a time of flux, instability, and conflicting forces when it comes to experiences of solitude. Parents are primarily responsible for populating younger children's social calendar, be it with family time, playdates, or organized activities. As they get older, children start to assert more autonomy and control over how they spend their time. They also mature to the point where it is more plausible, at least from a safety perspective, for them to spend time truly alone, or at least out of sight and hearing range for more extended periods of time (be it in their rooms, in the basement, or in the backyard). For these reasons, older children may have more opportunities to spend time alone, if they so choose, during their free time.

At school, the situation is somewhat different. As kids get older, the social norms and expectations change, particularly among classmates and other peers. Older children have much more highly developed social and communication skills, which allow them to sustain more prolonged social interactions than young children. The nature of friendship also starts to change. For younger children, a friend is something fairly concrete, such as someone who lives near you or whom you play with. For older children, friendship gradually becomes more abstract. A friend is someone who likes to do and play the same things as you do, who is nice to you, and whom you feel comfortable talking to.

As kids get older, the power and influence of friends and classmates rise steadily. Peer pressure also increases, mirrored by a similar rise in children's desire to be like the others and to conform to social demands. Suddenly, being different from your classmates becomes a significant source of concern. Negative attention from your peers becomes a bane to avoid at all costs.

In this dynamic and often confusing social context, solitude at school takes on a different meaning with different implications. In kindergarten, a child playing alone at recess is common, normative, and does not garner much attention, if any, from classmates. Indeed, as we have seen, young children are typically observed to be directly talking, playing, or otherwise engaging with other children less than half the time. This does not remain the same as children age.

My colleagues and I conducted one of the few observational studies of solitary play and social interaction among older children. We spent hours a day for several months watching almost three hundred children aged nine to twelve years in the schoolyard during recess and lunch over a four-week period. This was an enormous task and involved an army of student research assistants. It was a logistical nightmare to get enough eyeballs on each of the children enough times during the observational period. We learned quickly why this type of research was quite rare. But we persisted, and overall, we found that the children spent more than 90 percent of their time interacting with a friend or group of friends while in the schoolyard.

The flip side of this is that, on average, children spend less than 10 percent of their time at recess or lunch alone. Keep in mind, recess and lunch are likely their only opportunities to spend time alone all day at school. In this environment, where almost constant social interaction is expected, children who spend time alone stick out like a sore thumb, and unfortunately, they tend to attract the unwanted kind of attention from others. For children who might enjoy time alone and sometimes crave it, this age period has the potential to offer a fairly hostile environment.

This also means that solitude is a bit of a precious commodity for older children and tweens—and parents need to be mindful of that. That's why my main piece of advice for parents of older children is to make sure to give your child some time and space for solitude. There are many forces working against "me time" for older children. This can be an unacknowledged source of stress, particularly for those children who may be craving solitude. Parents may need to take an active role in helping children to regularly carve out the time and place to be alone.

With that in mind, let's talk a bit about children's extracurricular activities. Compared with years past, there are now a plethora of organized outside-of-school activities potentially available for children. These opportunities come in every size and shape, spanning the realms of sports and the arts and the entire gamut of more idiosyncratic interests. To be clear, I think this is awesome. Participating in organized extracurricular activities can be amazing for children and youth. It provides them with opportunities to connect with new social groups, discover and hone new skills and interests, expand their horizons, and become more engaged with life. Having all these different types of activities available makes it even more likely that children can find something that suits their specific tastes and needs. I am not shaking my fist at the clouds here. The world has certainly changed a lot since I was a kid, and, of course, a lot of this newfangled stuff is pretty good!

My daughter had some issues with anxiety when she was young. Meeting new people and being the center of attention were often challenging circumstances for her. In her case, participating in extracurricular activities provided a pathway to self-discovery and self-confidence. For me, it was pure joy to trace her growth over the years as she progressed from piano lessons, to tae kwon do, to competitive dance and, eventually, all the way to musical theater. My heart kvells* to see her now, a self-assured and dynamic young woman belting out songs onstage in front of a packed theater.

However, as a particularly sensitive child, my daughter also needed quiet time while growing up. She became a voracious reader who consumed books at an astonishing rate, proudly displaying her ever-growing collection, sorted by series, genre, and color on the quickly overstuffed bookshelves in her bedroom. My daughter also spent many hours playing the computer game *The Sims*, retreating into fantasy worlds of her own creation.†

So, like much of the advice around solitude, parents need to help their older children find the right personal balance for them between programmed and free time, which directly impacts their opportunities for socializing versus solitude. There is a happy medium for each child at this age that takes into account their personalities and interests. If I can stand on my soapbox for just a moment, I would implore parents not to overprogram their children's schedules. Yes, hanging out with friends is important at this age, and extracurricular activities can also be a critical and unique contributor to positive youth development. But children still have a need for solitude, and several factors in their social spheres actively conspire to frustrate that need. Parents need to

---

* Yiddish word meaning "to burst with pride."

† I must confess that it was not until years later that I learned that some of the content of *The Sims* game may not have been entirely appropriate. It turns out that there was a series of popular "challenges" that players shared with one another online, including the 100 Baby Challenge, where the goal was to give birth to one hundred babies in as few generations as possible (and there are other challenges that are even more R-rated, involving sex, divorce, and death).

be mindful of this and can help to make sure that their child's already super-busy schedule still allows for some "me time" too.

Solitude During Adolescence: Figuring Out Who I Am Alone

Haim Ginott was a child psychologist who wrote several influential books for parents in the late 1960s. His approach to parenting emphasized respecting children's feelings, while at the same time setting limits for their behaviors. I mention him here at the outset of this section because he also famously said that "adolescence can be a time of turmoil and turbulence, of stress and storm. Rebellion against authority and against convention is to be expected and tolerated for the sake of learning and growth."

As a developmental psychologist myself, I read, studied, and learned a lot about parenting before I became one myself. However, and I say this with the acquired humility of experience, you don't really know much about being a parent until you become one. I felt this at every stage of my children's development, but perhaps never more than when they were teenagers. The transformation was abrupt and jarring. Suddenly, my thirteen-year-old daughter was asking me to drop her off a block before she met her friends so that they did not see me with her. Apparently, dads become a significant source of embarrassment at this age. Suddenly, my son went from bursting to tell me everything that had happened to him at school each day to communicating solely in monosyllabic grunts. Honestly, most of the time he could not even be bothered to move his lips when responding to my questions about . . . anything. This went on for several years. In order to get news about his life, I had to rely on sporadic conversations with his teammates' parents (with whom he apparently conversed all the time) while enduring the freezing cold air and rock-hard seats of the arenas where he played for a local youth hockey team. People who have not or have not yet parented an adolescent are likely reading this and chuckling at what they perceive as my exaggerated anecdotes. In contrast, I am guessing that current and previous parents of adolescents are simply nodding along knowingly right now.

Parents of teens in my previous study on beliefs about solitude also viewed things a bit differently from how parents of younger children did. For example, mothers of teenagers were more likely to cite mental health concerns, the potential for risky behaviors, and the heightened probability of excessive or inappropriate screen time among their worries about solitude. On the flip side, they also were more apt to consider solitude as a place for restoration at this age. Again, yet more evidence—as if we needed it—that moms are wise.

As children continue down the path into teenagerhood, the pull away from the influence of family and into the gravity of peers escalates. Relationships with friends become more intense and intimate. Many teens start to navigate the complexities of romantic relationships and their emerging sexuality. Increased autonomy also brings with it a swell of new responsibilities and pressures at school, among friends, and in general life.

Across the adolescent years, teens' views about solitude also evolve. Among older adolescents, spending time alone becomes increasingly viewed as normative and simply part of being a teenager. These changing attitudes are driven by the accompanying increase in the desire for privacy that simultaneously emerges at this time. This is also a development stage where self-consciousness becomes even more prominent (particularly when it comes to the potential for your dad to embarrass you in front of your friends!). In short, adolescents can really use some "freedom from," and solitude offers them a place where they can find respite from social pressures.

For many teens, time alone also offers a critical opportunity for self-exploration. Teenagers suddenly find themselves dealing with lots of seemingly "big issues," the most daunting of which is often figuring out "Who am I?" and "Who do I want to be?" However, and importantly for parents to understand, solitude can also be a lonely and unwanted place for teens, one where they face worry, stress, and self-doubt. This is yet another compelling example of the duality of solitude in terms of its impact on well-being.

The University of Illinois Urbana-Champaign researcher Reed Larson was a pioneer in the study of solitude and one of the first to champion its potential positive effects, particularly among teenagers. In a series of extremely influential studies conducted in the late 1980s and 1990s, Larson equipped participating teenagers with pagers and beeped them at random intervals throughout the day over a one-week period. Upon receiving an alert, participants were asked to immediately complete a short questionnaire about what they were doing and whom they were with.

Among the results of one of these studies, Larson found that solitude became more voluntary in adolescence compared with later childhood, and this time alone contributed to emotional renewal. Specifically, teens tended to feel better after, but not necessarily during, time alone. Importantly, Larson's studies also concretely demonstrated evidence in support of a critical theme of this book: teens who spent an *intermediate* amount of time alone were better adjusted, overall, than those who spent relatively little or a great deal of time in solitude. Again, this bolsters the idea that finding an optimal personal balance between solitude and socializing is key for our well-being.

For parents of adolescents, understanding the important role of solitude in the lives of teenagers will go a long way toward helping them navigate this tumultuous time in their lives. As much as you can, try to respect your teens' increased need for privacy, and be mindful that there will be instances when spending time alone really is the best thing for them. Parents also need to be vigilant for signs that teens are not spending too much or too little time alone. This can be challenging, particularly when teens are primarily communicating in monosyllabic grunts. Taken together, you want your teenager to know that you respect their need for privacy and desire for solitude and, at the same time, that you love and support them and they can come to you anytime, particularly for the "big stuff."

Finally, it is important to remember that parents of children of all ages still need alone time too! It is okay to take some time to yourself. This remains true at all stages of the parenting journey, amid the constant demands and sleep deprivation often faced by parenting infants and toddlers, to being the event planner and chauffeur for older children, to struggling to help your high schooler with their math homework. Some people are also caught in the sandwich generation, caring for children and aging parents simultaneously. It may always seem like there is just not enough time in the day to do even half of what we need to do.

But our need for solitude does not suddenly vanish when we become parents. Of course our children become our priority, but it is also the case that taking some time alone will help you be a better parent. More than that, not taking enough time alone seems to have particular consequences for parents. The Indonesian psychology researcher Fitri Abidin and her colleagues found that aloneliness* was a primary contributor to parental burnout among mothers and fathers. And as we will discuss in the next chapter, solitude can also, somewhat paradoxically, improve the quality of your relationships with others—your children included.

* Reminder: the negative feelings that arise from not spending enough time alone.

User's Guide for Solitude

LEARNING TO PLAY SOLO IS AN IMPORTANT TASK FOR YOUNG CHILDREN, AND PARENTS CAN HELP THEM DEVELOP AND FLEX THEIR SOLITUDE "MUSCLES."

→ Try to build in some solitude time as part of your child's regular routine. They may resist it at first, but keep with it. Children will also benefit from choosing how they want to spend time alone, but for children under the age of five years, screen time should not be a regular solitary activity.

SOLITUDE MAY BE HARDER TO COME BY FOR OLDER CHILDREN, AND PARENTS MAY NEED TO HELP THEM CARVE OUT TIME AND SPACE TO BE ALONE.

→ Be mindful not to overprogram children's schedules. Older children are often dealing with a social environment conspiring against them getting time alone. This can be a source of stress that is not often acknowledged, particularly for children who crave solitude.

PARENTS OF ADOLESCENTS SHOULD BE MINDFUL OF A GROWING NEED FOR PRIVACY AND DESIRE FOR SOLITUDE THAT OFTEN COMES AT THIS AGE.

→ Parents should strive to grant their teenagers a reasonable amount of autonomy, privacy, and time alone. At the same time, parents should also be vigilant for signs that their teenagers' experiences of solitude are not solely fraught with loneliness and angst.

PARENTS STILL NEED THEIR SOLITUDE TOO.
→ Grant yourself permission to spend some time alone. For many people, a small investment in "me time" offers the valuable return of being a better parent and a better person.

Chapter 12

Being Single or Being Alone Together

How to Navigate Solitude in Your Relationships

My partner Christy and I first met when we were both in our twenties. Back then, circumstances didn't permit us to be more than just passing acquaintances. We fell out of touch, and each of us went on to live our respective lives. About twenty-five years later, we reconnected. Lots of life had happened in between, including busy careers, marriages, children, and divorces. We were both single again, and at this very different life stage, the time was right for both of us.

Like many couples, in some ways we are very alike, and in others we are very different. One trait that we do share is an appreciation of and need for alone time. My daily walking routine is where I get most of mine. Christy often prefers taking a drive or playing her cello. We cherish our time together, but we also value solitude. We are extremely fortunate because we understand that about each other. This is no small thing, and we are better together because of it. As the Austrian poet Rainer Maria Rilke wrote in *Letters to a Young Poet*, "I hold this to be the highest task of a bond between two people: that each should stand guard over the solitude of the other."

I have also noticed regular occasions where there is considerable blur between whether we are alone versus with each other. For example, on a typical night before bed, we will lie next to each other, propped up by our respective pillows, and do our own thing for a while. For me, this is almost always working on a crossword puzzle. Sometimes I use my phone to catch up on the day's headlines. Christy usually reads a chapter or two from whatever novel she is currently making her way through, plays a few rounds of *Candy Crush*, or scrolls through TikTok on her phone. We pass this time mostly in silence.

It is a unique kind of scenario. There is a pervasive calmness to it—I don't feel at all like I am "onstage." Instead, I am in a deeply personal, but also shared, space. In this way, it feels like I am alone, but I am also intimately connected to this person lying next to me. We are alone together. We are partners in solitude. And it is wonderful.

This shared experience of aloneness was recently described and named by the UK-based psychology researcher Netta Weinstein and her colleagues. They conducted in-depth interviews with sixty adults aged nineteen to eighty years old. During these hour-long discussions, participants were asked to define solitude, reflect on what solitude means to them, and describe some of their previous experiences of being alone. Their responses speak to many of the aspects of solitude that we have considered already in this book. For example, some individuals described solitude as a physical separation from other people, whereas others homed in more on perceived or psychological separation, which allowed them to be alone in public.

One subset of participants described a very specific type of solitude that occurred for them in the presence of someone they are close with. Some gave examples familiar to me and Christy, of two members of a couple in the same room but each engaged in their own pursuits.*

* Hearkening back to my grad school days observing similar behavior among preschoolers, I might also call this "parallel play" for adults.

Others told stories of two close friends traveling together, sharing a quiet moment while taking in a scenic vista. One participant recalled how he and his father would regularly spend early mornings on a lake, fishing for hours in comfortable silence. These experiences were frequently described as creating a "bubble"—a space shared with another person, but one in which you are also "alone in your own head" and free to engage in your own pursuits. Weinstein and her colleagues dubbed this shared solitary experience as *companionate solitude*. As we have seen, there are lots of ways to be in solitude.

Livin' la Vida Solo

At the very outset of this book, I mentioned that time spent alone has been gradually but steadily increasing for decades, with an even steeper incline over the last twenty years. At least part of this is due to the sharp growth in single-person households. According to information from the US Census Bureau, the percentage of one-person households has risen from about 8 percent in 1940 to almost 30 percent in 2020. This rising trend of people living alone is even more prevalent in Europe, with countries like Germany, Sweden, and Norway now reporting more than 40 percent solo households.

It has been argued that this sociodemographic trend has some potentially negative implications. For example, living alone may be less eco-friendly: people who live alone tend to consume more water and electricity, as well as produce more garbage. On a more personal level, the Anglo-Welsh historian Keith Snell connected what he called the "unprecedented" historical global rise in single-person households with accompanying increases in loneliness and social isolation. He was careful to note that living alone does not necessarily lead to loneliness; nevertheless, there is some evidence to suggest that people who live alone are at increased risk for experiencing social isolation, loneliness, and depression.

Most of the research in this area has focused on older adults. For example, the Swedish gerontology researcher Gerdt Sundström and his colleagues explored the links between living arrangements and loneliness in a sample of close to nine thousand Europeans aged sixty-five and older. They found some interesting differences between countries. For example, rates of loneliness were higher in southern European countries compared with northern European countries. They speculated that this may have to do with cultural differences. In southern Europe, expectations about social interactions are more intense and communal living is still the norm. In contrast, in northern Europe, living alone is more common and even seen as a desirable sign of independence. Even so, across all countries, people who lived alone consistently reported more loneliness than those living with a spouse or partner.

But of course, and not surprisingly given everything we have talked about in this book, the link between living alone and loneliness is more complicated than just that. All people who live alone are not the same. And the implications of living alone have a lot to do with the *reasons* someone is living alone. Some people are compelled to live alone by circumstances, such as divorce, widowhood, or certain professions. But others make the active and personal choice to live by themselves. As we now know, choice matters when it comes to solitude, and it matters here too. Different reasons for spending time alone, as well as for living alone, impact our well-being in different ways.

For example, the UK-based psychology researchers Kimberley Smith and Christina Victor used data from the Health Survey for England to examine the impact of living alone among more than seven thousand people over the age of fifty. They identified six subgroups of people based on their living situation, levels of loneliness, and social isolation.[*] For example, the largest group, representing just under half of the sample, comprised individuals who did not live alone and reported low levels of loneliness and social isolation. They also found two very different groups of people who lived alone. The first represented about 12 percent of the entire sample. They lived alone and reported comparatively low levels of loneliness and social isolation. In fact, their reported lack of loneliness and social isolation were at similar levels to the largest subgroup of people living with others. This particular group of people living alone were also no more prone to mental or physical health problems than individuals who did not live alone. The other subgroup of people who lived alone represented about 10 percent of the sample. They reported moderate to high levels of loneliness and social isolation and were more likely to report symptoms of depression and overall poorer health. Thinking about this another way, more than half the people living alone in this large sample seemed perfectly content to do so. Thus, as is the case with solitude in general, living alone does not necessarily equate with loneliness.

The German psychology researcher Philipp Kersten and his colleagues studied a sample of close to four hundred midlife adults aged thirty-five to sixty years, all of whom were living alone. His results showed even more differences among groups of "solo living" people. As with the UK study, many people who lived alone were doing quite well. For example, despite living alone, about one-third of the sample described a large and diverse network of family and nonfamily social contacts, reported relatively low levels of loneliness, and generally had high life satisfaction. A second, smaller group, about 10 percent, reported being in a close romantic relationship and appeared to be functioning similarly well.[†]

---

* Social isolation was measured in terms of their frequency of communication with friends and family and participation in social recreational activities, such as sports, clubs, and hobbies, as well as social community activities, such as politics and volunteering.

† As an aside, this appears to be a growing trend in Western societies, with increasing numbers of adults in romantic relationships opting for what has been dubbed "living apart together."

Kersten and his colleagues also identified two other subgroups of middle-agers living alone who seemed to be doing less well. About half of people living alone described what was labeled as "loose-knit" social networks, with only a small number of close relationships. This loose-knit group appeared to be faring the worst while living alone, particularly in terms of loneliness and life dissatisfaction. The last group was described as "restricted" and had the smallest social network and fewest daily social interactions. However, the restricted group had a mixed pattern in terms of well-being, typically falling between the seemingly more well-adjusted "diverse" and "partner-focused" groups and the least well-adjusted "loose-knit" group.

I think we can conclude from this research that people end up living alone for different reasons, have different experiences of living alone, and, as a result, may be impacted both positively and negatively in terms of their well-being and mental health. However, most adults who live alone are not married. This makes it hard to tease apart effects due to living circumstances versus relationship status. So, let's briefly consider this complex and sometimes emotionally charged issue, before moving on to discuss solitude within the context of close relationships.

Saying "I Do" to Being Single

Data made available from the US census suggests many reasons for the growing trend in people living alone. One is that more young adults are living alone because they now tend to get married and start families later. In 1960, the average age of marriage was about twenty years for women and twenty-two for men. By 2023, this age had risen to about twenty-eight years for women and thirty for men. It is also the case that an increasing number of people are choosing never to marry, with this proportion rising from about 25 percent of men and 20 percent of women in 1960 to just under 40 percent of men and 30 percent of women by 2022. As a result, the gap between married and unmarried adults in the United States has also narrowed considerably: in 1950, about two-thirds of adults were married versus unmarried;* by 2023, this difference had decreased to just over half of adults married versus unmarried. In other words, the number of married people living in the United States has almost doubled over the last seventy years, from about 74 million to almost 138 million. However, during this same time period, the number of unmarried people has more than tripled, going up over 3.5 times, from about 37 million to almost 134 million.

Are married people happier than singles? I think it is fair to say that this is a long-standing and widely held societal belief. And there is ample evidence often cited to support it. For example, in 2024, Gallup released the results of a mammoth survey exploring connections between marriage and well-being in the United States. Led by the economist Jonathan Rothwell, the survey included more than 2.5 million people who responded to questionnaires between the years 2002 and 2008. Let's just say that the results are evident in the title of the report: *Married People Are Living Their Best Lives*. The authors summarized their findings as follows: "Comparing across relationship status, adults who are married are by far the happiest, as measured by how they evaluate their current and future life."

However, and as acknowledged by the authors of this very report, surveys like this one, which compare married people with people who are not married, have a clear design problem: marital status is not randomly assigned. To really determine if marriage makes us happier, we would need to design and carry out an experiment that looked something like this: First, we would start with a large group of unmarried people and collect measures of how happy they are right now. Next, we would put all their names in a giant hat and randomly pull out

* This includes individuals who are separated, divorced, widowed, and never married.

half of them to be assigned to the "married" group. These participants would then need to immediately get married to someone. As for the remaining other half of participants, they would be the "single" group. We would need to prevent them from getting married for the duration of the experiment, which would need to last at least several years. After some predetermined period of time, let's say ten years for a nice round number, we would come back and measure happiness in all the participants. We could then assess if and how happiness had changed in the married versus single groups. In this way, we could then make the argument that, all other things being equal, any differences in happiness that were observed at this stage could be reasonably attributed to marital status.

Of course, for obvious reasons, this is not an experiment that we can conduct in real life. So, we cannot rule out alternative causal explanations for the link between happiness and marriage. Why is that the case? For one, it is easy to interpret the study's result as evidence that getting married causes people to become happier. However, the effect might just as well operate in the opposite direction.* That is, it may be that people who are generally happier in life are more likely to get married. This could be because people who are happier might be more likely to seek out marriage for themselves. Or maybe happier people are more likely to receive marriage proposals from others. Other explanations are also plausible. For example, people with certain personality traits—agreeableness for instance—could be more likely to be both happier in general and to marry. All these alternative causal pathways are equally plausible interpretations of study findings that demonstrate a link between marriage and happiness at a single point in time.

Furthermore, all unmarried people are not the same. In her review of the psychological literature on the implications of being single for

* In psychology, this is sometimes referred to as the *directionality problem*.

well-being, the Polish researcher Katarzyna Adamczyk noted many different reasons adults may be unmarried. Some people are single because of external circumstances, such as being widowed, divorced, or separated. Some simply haven't met the "right person" yet. Yet others may be single because of a perceived personal deficit (such as being too shy) or the belief that they are simply not "ready" emotionally or psychologically. And importantly, some people make the personal choice to be single as a life decision. More on this group in a bit.

The Canadian psychology researchers Shawn Grover and John Helliwell acknowledge these issues and point out that those who marry also tend to be more social, healthier, better educated, and have more engaging jobs compared with those who do not marry. Each of these characteristics is also likely to increase people's happiness with or without marriage. To try to tease apart some of these factors, Grover and Helliwell analyzed data from two large-scale studies in the UK, the British Household Panel Survey and Annual Population Survey. Both these studies tracked marital status and aspects of well-being at repeated points in time over many years in a sample of more than thirty thousand people. This allowed them to at least consider some of the causal direction issues that plague this type of research. They found, among many things, evidence to suggest that people who were happier at the outset of the study were more likely to get married at some point during the study than their less happy counterparts. However, even after accounting for these levels of premarital life satisfaction, those who went on to get married still reported being happier than those who remained single.

It has also been argued that the happiness-boosting effects of marriage are only short term. Grover and Helliwell's findings undermine this idea. They showed that although the benefits for well-being are greatest immediately after marriage, these boosts to happiness and life satisfaction persisted in the long term, albeit at a notably smaller level. The impact of marriage on well-being was also very much dependent on the quality of the marital relationship. Not surprisingly, people in happy marriages tended to be happier than those in unhappy unions.

Offering an alternative perspective, the University of California, Santa Barbara, researcher and author Bella DePaulo has passionately championed the positive aspects of being single. In a 2023 essay aptly titled "Single and Flourishing: Transcending the Deficit Narratives of Single Life," she highlighted the theories and research that describe the many people who are "single and flourishing." DePaulo makes a detailed case for the existence of what she calls the *couple norm*, a cluster of historical societal biases against people who are unmarried. This includes a series of ingrained tacit assumptions that marginalize single people, such as "everyone wants to marry, and just about everyone does," "a coupled partnership is the one truly important peer relationship," and "those who have a coupled partnership are better people—more valuable, worthy, and important, and probably happier and less lonely." She points out that even the words we use to describe single people invoke the notion of some sort of deficit, such as being "unattached," "failing to marry," or not possessing a "significant other." She also notes that in the United States, as well as many other places around the world, laws, the tax system, pensions, benefits, estate planning, and many other bureaucracies are designed to favor those who are married over those who are single.

Particularly relevant to our discussion of solitude and choice, DePaulo uses the term "single at heart" to describe people who make the conscious decision to be single and embrace their single lives. As she explains, people who are single at heart are not happy in spite of being single; they are happy *because* of it. In a series of studies, she interviewed people who described themselves as single at heart about the advantages they see in this life choice. The most common theme found in their replies was freedom. This included the autonomy to choose everything from the mundane (what should I eat today?) to life-altering decisions (where do I want to live?). Other commonly mentioned benefits included greater opportunities to pursue a rich and meaningful life and the ability to focus on close social ties with family and friends. Of particular note for our purposes, many singles responded that it was especially important for them to have time alone and that they have come to savor solitude rather than fear it.

All this complicated and conflicting data makes for an interesting debate. However, within the context of this book, it is actually somewhat moot. It may or may not be the case that overall, and on average, married people tend to be happier than singles. Moreover, even if marriage *does* make people happier on average, we should not presume from this that marriage makes *everyone* happier. It is certainly not the case that all people would be happier if they were married or, for that matter, single. As we have discussed in this book, there is no one-size-fits-all recipe for happiness and well-being. With that in mind, let's return our focus to solitude and consider an additional paradoxical aspect of spending time alone as it relates to our social relationships.

Revisiting a Paradox: How Solitude Can Improve Relationships with Others

As the old adage states, "absence makes the heart grow fonder." The earliest historical trace of this saying that I could find is attributed to the ancient Latin poet Sextus Propertius, who lived around 50 BCE in what is now Assisi, Italy. But is it true? Aalto University computer scientists led by Kunal Bhattacharya analyzed a huge database of mobile phone records over a seven-month period. They looked for connections between several different characteristics of mobile communications, including the time between calls to the same person, the length of each call, the geographical distance between people who were communicating, and who was calling whom. After lots of math, they concluded that being at a physical distance from someone with whom you share a close relationship results in a greater investment in maintaining close communication. They suggest that the greater risk posed by being at a distance from someone whose relationship you value causes people to prioritize allocating more resources toward keeping things going. It is an interesting proposition, but I have to wonder how long such a system can be maintained before it comes at too great a cost for the people involved.

Of course, this is only a small piece of the puzzle: this study did not track how people communicated or otherwise devoted time and energy toward maintaining relationships in ways that did not involve a mobile phone. As almost always, it is not that simple. The Hope College psychology researchers Patricia Roehling and Marta Bultman examined how work-related travel by one member of a couple impacted marital satisfaction. Their results were quite complex and varied depending upon which member of the couple was traveling, whether there were children in the family, and how traditional each person in the relationship was in terms of attitudes toward gender roles. Results from other studies also demonstrate a bit of a mixed bag here. Perhaps Charles Schulz, beloved creator of the *Peanuts* comic strip, said it best when he drew Charlie Brown saying, "Absence makes the heart grow fonder, but it sure makes the rest of you lonely."

A long-distance romance is also a very specific context for considering how solitude might impact our relationships with others. Setting aside that particular example, there is good reason to believe the somewhat paradoxical notion that spending time alone can be beneficial to our social lives in general. We have already discussed some of the reasons this is the case. Solitude helps to calm our more jagged emotions and stimulates us to consider new ideas and perspectives. Time alone also affords us opportunities to reconnect with ourselves and to better understand who we are, what we want, and what is important to us. When we are away from others, we also better appreciate the value of our relationships with people who are not currently in our presence. Essentially, sometimes it can be nice to have the chance to miss someone you love. In this way, solitude becomes a context for strengthening our relationships with ourselves, which in turn fosters our abilities to connect with others in healthy ways.

The University of Washington communications researcher Valerie Manusov summarizes these benefits by describing solitude as a "fertile void." She argues that the quiet, stillness, and privacy that solitude provides allow opportunities for people to focus their thoughts both inwardly and outwardly. Inward-focused thoughts are related to self-exploration, self-reflection, problem-solving, and the cultivation of inner peace. Outward-focused thoughts often turn to important others and can allow us to deepen our relationships with people, even in their absence. In this way, solitude can actually promote intimacy with others.

In collaboration with my colleague and frequent collaborator Julie Bowker, her graduate student Hope White, and the Cincinnati Children's Hospital Medical Center faculty member Ryan Adams, we set out to try to provide some of the first direct support for these ideas. In a rather labor-intensive study, we recruited a sample of more than four hundred young adults and had them complete "daily diary" reports at the end of seven consecutive days. These end-of-day reports included how much time each person spent alone and with others, as well as their emotional states. This allowed us to get some idea of participants' typical daily experiences during this time period.

We found that on days when participants spent more time alone than usual, they also reported increased enjoyment during social interactions with others. This leads to some pretty straightforward advice. A small investment in taking time for yourself on any given day can pay off in terms of improving your time with others. So maybe absence does indeed make the heart grow a bit fonder.

The Canadian psychology researcher Christiane Hoppmann and her colleagues also explored these questions in a series of recent studies. In a study led by Yoonseok Choi, they explored links between adults' time spent in solitude and the quality of their relationships with close others over a ten-day period. Similar to our results, they found that people who generally had positive relationships with others in their lives felt better after days when they had time to themselves. And not surprisingly, they also found that days with more solitude served to reduce negative emotions for people who had a close relationship with a spouse, friend, or family member that was higher in conflict.

Once again, the duality of solitude is on full display. The participants in this study who chose to spend time alone felt better about their relationships with others. However, those who escaped into solitude to relieve, at least temporarily, some of the bad feelings stemming from less healthy relationships found that their time alone did not necessarily do anything to alter these situations. As we have seen, solitude does us much better if we approach it as a desired experience instead of using it as a way to avoid social situations or specific relationships that make us unhappy.

Another recent study by Hoppmann and her colleagues, this one led by Elizabeth Zambrano Garza, focused on experiences of solitude and relationships among older adults. As we have discussed previously, time alone steadily increases as we get older. Combined with many other factors associated with aging, such as loss of mobility, health issues, and loss of a life partner, social isolation and loneliness represent major concerns among the elderly. Yet, for many older adults, solitude also remains a time to be cherished.

Hoppmann and her colleagues recruited adults in their mid-sixties to their eighties to participate in the study. Then the target participants were asked to invite one "close other" to join them in the study. Just over half of these close others were spouses, but some friends, siblings, adult children, and even some grandchildren were included in these pairs as well. Participants in this research completed daily diaries over a ten-day period. In these reports, people described what they did each day, whether they were alone or with others, how they were feeling, and, more specifically, how they were feeling about the quality of their relationship with their chosen close other. When measuring time alone, researchers also distinguished between *desired* solitude, which participants chose and viewed positively, and what they called *bothersome* solitude, which participants did not necessarily choose and viewed more negatively. Finally, thanks to a particularly interesting aspect of this study design, the researchers were able to get these reports from both members of the social pairs.

The results were striking. On days when the primary participant reported getting more desired solitude, they reported an overall better mood, and fascinatingly, their close other also reported fewer negative emotions. In contrast, on days when the primary participant reported more bothersome solitude, both members of the social pairs reported worse moods. The researchers argued that these effects can be explained by *broaden-and-build theory*, which was first proposed by the University of North Carolina at Chapel Hill psychology researcher Barbara Fredrickson. In a nutshell, this theory states that the experience of positive emotions broadens our awareness and encourages new ideas, actions, and coping strategies. Over time, this builds up our internal resources and strengthens our well-being. Relating this back to the study, the researchers explained that chosen solitude helps us recharge our batteries, which provides a boost to our positive emotions. Bolstered by these resources, we are better able to engage in higher-quality social interactions with others.

One final tidbit from this study: primary participants reported that on days when their close other had more experiences of desired solitude (and thus presumably less time devoted to the primary participant), primary participants actually reported feeling like they received *more* support from their close others. On the surface, this seems particularly paradoxical. But I think it is another example of quality being more important than quantity. Taking some time for yourself each day can be good for both you and the people you are close with. Even if you end up spending a little bit less time directly interacting with loved ones, the quality of that time will be improved enough that the people around you will feel better about their relationships with you. Following this reasoning, we should all be encouraging people who matter to us to spend time in desired solitude every day. Because when they do, not only will we both feel better, but they will end up giving us more support.

Asking for Alone Time

Many years ago, I was visiting with a psychology colleague who was a world-leading authority on the topic of parenting. During my stay, I had the opportunity to attend one of his public workshops for parents. He spoke at length about the importance of warmth, communication, and patience in building relationships with your children, and he presented numerous strategies for resolving issues without escalating things into full-blown conflicts. His presentation was informative and engaging, peppered with anecdotes from his experiences as a parent. It was impressive.

After his session, we were scheduled to go out for dinner, but he asked if it would be okay if we first went to pick up his son. I went along with him for the ride and stayed in the car as he went to go fetch his twelve-year-old boy. It was a hot day, so I rolled my window down while I waited. That is why I was able to hear them approaching the car even before I could see them. The two of them were engaged in a knock-down, drag-out screaming match. I have no idea what they were fighting over, but they were definitely not communicating well, there was certainly no warmth, and they had both clearly lost patience with each other.

The moral of this story is that it is one thing to know how you should be acting and quite another to actually behave that way in any given moment. I have been guilty of this myself many times in my life, and perhaps not surprisingly, it has often been about solitude. I think most people perceive me as a sociable person. I teach large classes of students and try my best to bring enthusiasm and energy to my lectures. At social gatherings, I am chatty and often make (very bad) puns that draw attention to myself. I play piano and sing onstage in front of crowds of people. I am not uncomfortable doing any of these things. In fact, I find them enjoyable. But I also need my solitude.

However, for much of my life, I have not acted as I knew I should; I have just not been willing or able to ask for time alone when I knew that I needed it. I can trace this pattern all the way back to my teenage years. Sometimes the reasons were related to self-consciousness and perceived peer pressure. My friends would be going out on a Friday or Saturday night. What I really wanted to do was stay home and curl up with a book or in front of the TV. But instead, worried about what others would think of me, I would head out with them for the night. Other times, I was motivated by shame and perceived responsibilities, feeling like I needed to put the needs of others ahead of my own. This is something that we all must do from time to time—maybe even most of the time when it comes to our children. But for me, and I am sure for many others, solitude is a necessary form of self-care, and if I go down, I am no good to myself or anyone around me. And sometimes I simply did not know how to tell the person I was with that I needed some alone time—and that this did not have anything to do with them.

After studying solitude for more than thirty years, and with the wisdom of hindsight from a lot of accumulated life experiences, I have finally come to a place where I am perfectly comfortable simply asking for some time alone when I need it. And I have made it a personal mission to raise awareness about this and normalize such requests as much as possible. It needs to be okay to say you want to stay in on a Friday night without having to make up excuses as to why. It needs to be okay to ask for some "me time," even when you are the parent of young children. It needs to be okay to say to someone whom you are close to, "I love you, I love spending time together with you, but right now I need a few hours by myself."

If your "close other" happens to be a raging extravert, they may not be able to easily comprehend how spending time alone could possibly be beneficial or desirable, thinking only about how much they personally would hate such an experience. "That is okay," you can tell them. "We are all different when it comes to solitude." I would also suggest to them that they should read this book for some tips on how they can build up their solitude muscles and unlock some of the benefits that solitude can offer to everyone—even extraverts. You can also tell them that science has now shown that time alone can strengthen relationships. So, not only will solitude help you be a better you, but it will also help you and them be a better us.

User's Guide for Solitude

WHEN IT COMES TO MAJOR LIFE DECISIONS THAT MAY BE RELATED TO SOLITUDE (SUCH AS LIVING ALONE OR BEING SINGLE), THERE IS NO ONE-SIZE-FITS-ALL RECIPE FOR HAPPINESS.

→ People benefit from both time alone and time with others, and they should strive to live their lives in a way that encourages a balance that works for them. Even if it were the case that marriage makes people happier overall, this does not mean that getting married will make everyone happier.

A SMALL INVESTMENT IN TAKING TIME FOR YOURSELF ON ANY GIVEN DAY CAN PAY OFF IN TERMS OF IMPROVING YOUR TIME WITH OTHERS.

→ Even if you end up spending a little bit less time directly interacting with others, the quality of that time will be improved enough that people around you will feel better about their relationships with you.

IT IS OKAY TO ASK FOR ALONE TIME.

→ Taking time for yourself is okay, even when you are the parent of young children. It should be completely normative and acceptable to say to someone whom you are close with, "I love you, I love spending time together with you, but right now I need a few hours by myself."

Chapter 13

Ending Up Alone

Some Final Thoughts About Solitude

As we near the end of this book, I find myself looking back and looking forward. I got hooked on the study of solitude more than thirty years ago, spending all those hours sitting in preschools and kindergartens watching endless groups of children at play. I could not have imagined at the time how this budding interest would become the central spine of my research career, spanning decades and branching out into countries around the world.

If you were to sit and watch young children today playing in preschool or kindergarten, you would observe many of the same behaviors that I did all those years ago. Some children look like soloists, spending most of their time happily playing alone. Other children look shy, warily hovering near where classmates play but not joining in. And others look ostracized, rebuffed in their efforts to play with others, leaving them alone and frustrated.

The difference is that we have learned much more about why these different children tend to play alone at school. Because of this, there is a raised awareness among parents, teachers, school counselors, and others about how to respond—and when not to respond—when children are spending time alone at home or at school. More broadly, we have come to understand how powerfully these different "reasons" for being alone impact experiences of solitude and their implications for our well-being across the lifespan. We have made a lot of progress. Yet, long-standing misconceptions are notoriously hard to change. I still routinely read a headline or scroll past a post on social media that makes me want to stand on a rooftop and shout for everyone to hear, "Solitude and loneliness are not the same thing!" or "It is okay to ask for time alone!"

Looking Forward to Being Alone

What does the future hold for solitude? It is safe to say that there is now more research being conducted on the topic of solitude than ever before. We are learning new things every day.* So, with an eye toward the future, here is a brief preview of the top three topics related to solitude that I think we will be hearing a lot more about over the next few years.

(1) Alone in the world. The study of solitude has historically been dominated by research in Western cultures. We are only just beginning to understand how the meaning and implications of solitude might vary around the world. For example, in a large international study with participants across ten countries, my colleagues and I found that university students in Turkey and China expressed the strongest preference for solitude. In contrast, participants in Argentina, India, and Italy reported the weakest desire for time alone, whereas students in the United States, Canada, Norway, Australia, and South Korea fell in the middle.

Preferring to spend time alone is generally viewed as a normative and acceptable behavior in Western cultures, where individual choice is highly valued. But as we saw earlier, this same characteristic is more

* Note to my publisher: In a few years, there will be more than enough new research to justify me writing a follow-up book to this one!

likely to be perceived as selfish and deviant in countries such as China, where contributing to the collective is a central tenet of cultural norms. For example, a 2024 review by a team of psychology researchers led by Na Hu found that Chinese children and adolescents who express a preference for spending time alone tend to be rejected, excluded, and victimized by their peers and classmates. But with the proliferation of cross-cultural research related to solitude, I am confident that we will be learning a lot more about the differences—and similarities—in people's experiences of solitude across the globe.

(2) Alone in your head. Along with uncovering these *macro*-level differences in solitude across cultures, researchers are also digging deeper into the *micro*-level processes that might help us better understand what is going on in our brains when we experience different types of solitude. For example, Elisa Baek and her colleagues at the University of California, Los Angeles, used functional magnetic resonance imaging (fMRI) to take detailed scans of university students' brains while they watched a series of videos. The results showed that patterns of neural responses among lonely participants were much more diverse than those of the "non-lonely" participants. The researchers suggest that these idiosyncratic responses in the brains of lonely people may contribute to making them feel more disconnected from others.

At the opposite end of the spectrum, the UK-based psychologist Chengli Huang and her colleagues used new techniques in electroencephalography (EEG) to see how motivations for solitude might connect with different patterns of electrical activity in the brain.* They found at least some evidence to suggest differences in the brains of "soloists" compared with those of people who do not prefer or enjoy spending time alone. As these technologies continue to advance, I

* These included frontal alpha asymmetry, beta power, and posterior versus frontal theta activity.

suspect we will uncover even more nuanced ways that our individualized brains impact our unique experiences of solitude.

(3) Alone with your bots. Continuing advances in technology are not just limited to brain imaging techniques. One of the hottest topics around is how new advances in artificial intelligence are already changing almost every aspect of our lives. How could this relate to solitude? For one, we know that unwanted solitude often leads to loneliness, and as we have seen, loneliness sucks. Can chatbots, who are increasingly able to mimic sophisticated human communication, potentially reduce loneliness? The very preliminary evidence is somewhat mixed. For example, Tianling Xie and other researchers at the University of Toledo conducted a series of studies exploring the implications of repeated interactions with the social chatbot Replika. Many participants reported that they developed a strong attachment to the chatbot and felt that this relationship helped to ease their loneliness. However, they also found evidence to suggest that frequent interactions with chatbots can trigger psychological over-dependence, which may undermine benefits for well-being.

Similar results were reported in a sample of adults aged sixty and above by the researchers Karima Al Mazroui and Mohammed Alzyoudi in the United Arab Emirates. Participants engaged in conversational sessions with the chatbot ChatGPT three times over a two-week period. Participants reported that ChatGPT was convenient and easy to use, that it was empathetic and emotionally supportive, and that they felt an emotional connection. They also felt less lonely following these interactions.

As we have seen, older adults are at particular risk for loneliness. This issue will be of increasing significance in the years ahead. In 2020, the United Nations estimated the worldwide population of adults aged sixty-five or older at more than 700 million—and this number is expected to more than double in the next twenty-five years. Although these results are preliminary in nature, they illustrate the potential of chatbots as alleviators of loneliness. However, it also seems clear that chatbots should be considered complements to, rather than replacements for, human social contact.

You Can Help Solitude Keep Its Promise

At the very outset of this book, I asked you to sit alone with your thoughts for fifteen minutes. Take a moment and recall that experience. Do you remember how it felt? Did you cheat and look at your phone? Did you abandon the exercise before fifteen minutes was up? Were you mostly just bored? Or did you quietly revel in peaceful silence? As we reach the end of this book, I invite you to repeat the exercise. Recall that in one experiment, people who read a short blurb about the potential benefits of solitude had a more positive experience sitting alone for fifteen minutes than those who read about an unrelated topic. Now that you've read an entire book about this topic, you should be more than ready to dive in.

Solitude remains a paradox. Like the tarot card of the Hermit drawn upside down, it can be a harbinger of loneliness and depression. But like the Hermit card drawn right side up, it also offers the promise of serenity and bliss. As we all strive to find our right balance between our social and solitary lives, remember that although you may sometimes feel all alone, we are *all* alone sometimes . . . and that is a good thing.

User's Guide for Solitude

KNOWLEDGE ABOUT SOLITUDE IS POWER.

→ Keep a solitude diary where you track your time alone, solitary activities, and mood every day for a week. Afterward, examine it for patterns, make some tweaks, and see if you can improve your mood.

WHEN IT COMES TO SOLITUDE, YOU DO YOU.

→ Everyone needs to find their personal "just right" amount of solitude and to personalize their alone time with their preferred solitary activities.

IF YOU DON'T ENJOY SOLITUDE, FAKE IT TILL YOU MAKE IT.

→ Just thinking positive thoughts while alone can improve experiences of solitude, and being reminded of the benefits of solitude can improve the strength of those effects.

ENGAGE IN MICRODOSES OF SOLITUDE.

→ Spending as little as fifteen minutes alone a day can have measurable and lasting positive effects. And remember, "practice makes better" applies to alone time as well. Make a plan for how you can integrate a little bit of solitude into your routine on most days—and stick to it!

WHEN ALONE, DON'T WORRY, BE HAPPY.

→ If you find yourself ruminating while alone, try to distract yourself with another activity, write out your thoughts to get them out of your head and onto paper, or make some concrete plans to address your worries. If you still struggle with these negative thoughts, consider seeing a therapist. There is really good help available, and it can make a huge difference.

WHEN YOU ARE ALONE, LOOK FORWARD TO LETTING YOUR MIND WANDER.

→ Use time alone as an opportunity to let your mind wander. But be mindful that your daydreams do not deteriorate into daymares. Although this can be challenging, thinking happy thoughts and focusing on positive feelings can help.

TO HELP GET UNSTUCK, INCUBATE AND SWITCH.

→ To boost creative solutions to stubborn problems, take a solitude break and switch to a different activity. Ideally, this activity should not be too engaging, not too boring, but "just right." Take some time and experiment with different approaches to find your own optimal activity for this.

FIND YOUR BALANCE BETWEEN SOLITUDE AND SOCIALIZING.

→ To help with the creative process, and to generally boost your mood and well-being, alternate between episodes of being alone and time with others. Again, this balance will require some time to figure out, and it will look different for different people.

SOLITUDE IS AN OPPORTUNITY TO GO WITH THE FLOW.

→ Time alone can also be an opportunity to achieve a state of flow. Find an activity that you enjoy, find challenging, and feel motivated to pursue. Dive in, immerse yourself in the experience, and let it lead you to wherever it goes.

IF YOU ENJOY SPENDING TIME ALONE, CONSIDER TURNING OFF YOUR PHONE FOR A WHILE.

→ For soloists and introverts, optimal alone time likely entails no or minimal use of technology. Too much tech can interfere and distract from positive experiences of solitude.

IF YOU FIND SOLITUDE ANXIETY-PROVOKING, BORING, OR AVERSIVE, YOUR PHONE CAN BE HELPFUL IN TERMS OF MAKING YOUR TIME ALONE MORE PLEASANT.
→ Be mindful of using your alone time exclusively to interact virtually with others. You are likely missing out on a lot of "freedoms" that solitude has to offer. Consider at least turning off your notifications and refraining from the more "social" uses of your phone.

WE SHOULD ALL ASPIRE TO FEEL SOME JOMO.
→ Try to reframe each solitary "time-out" from technology as a joyful respite from your phone's constant demands for your attention. Relish and revel in all the stuff you are (temporarily) missing out on.

WHEN ALONE, TRY TO USE TECHNOLOGY FOR "GOOD" INSTEAD OF FOR "EVIL."
→ Aim to reduce obsessive monitoring of social media timelines or doomscrolling through anxiety-provoking news headlines and be mindful of how such activities impact your mood. Instead, focus on activities that reduce your stress, such as reading, listening to music, engaging in hobbies, or playing mindless games that facilitate mind wandering.

SPENDING TOO MUCH TIME SCROLLING THROUGH SOCIAL MEDIA CAN RUIN YOUR TIME ALONE—AND LIKELY MAKE YOU FEEL BAD ABOUT YOURSELF UNDER ALMOST ANY CIRCUMSTANCES.
→ This advice is presented without caveat!

LEARNING TO PLAY SOLO IS AN IMPORTANT TASK FOR YOUNG CHILDREN, AND PARENTS CAN HELP THEM DEVELOP AND FLEX THEIR SOLITUDE "MUSCLES."

→ Try to build in some solitude time as part of your child's regular routine. They may resist it at first, but keep with it. Children will also benefit from choosing how they want to spend time alone, but for children under the age of five years, screen time should not be a regular solitary activity.

SOLITUDE MAY BE HARDER TO COME BY FOR OLDER CHILDREN, AND PARENTS MAY NEED TO HELP THEM CARVE OUT TIME AND SPACE TO BE ALONE.

→ Be mindful not to overprogram children's schedules. Older children are often dealing with a social environment conspiring against them getting time alone. This can be a source of stress that is not often acknowledged, particularly for children who crave solitude.

PARENTS OF ADOLESCENTS SHOULD BE MINDFUL OF A GROWING NEED FOR PRIVACY AND DESIRE FOR SOLITUDE THAT OFTEN COMES AT THIS AGE.

→ Parents should strive to grant their teenagers a reasonable amount of autonomy, privacy, and time alone. At the same time, parents should also be vigilant for signs that their teenagers' experiences of solitude are not solely fraught with loneliness and angst.

PARENTS STILL NEED THEIR SOLITUDE TOO.

→ Grant yourself permission to spend some time alone. For many people, a small investment in "me time" offers the valuable return of being a better parent and a better person.

WHEN IT COMES TO MAJOR LIFE DECISIONS THAT MAY BE RELATED TO SOLITUDE (SUCH AS LIVING ALONE OR BEING SINGLE), THERE IS NO ONE-SIZE-FITS-ALL RECIPE FOR HAPPINESS.

→ People benefit from both time alone and time with others, and they should strive to live their lives in a way that encourages a balance that works for them. Even if it were the case that marriage makes people happier overall, this does not mean that getting married will make everyone happier.

A SMALL INVESTMENT IN TAKING TIME FOR YOURSELF ON ANY GIVEN DAY CAN PAY OFF IN TERMS OF IMPROVING YOUR TIME WITH OTHERS.

→ Even if you end up spending a little bit less time directly interacting with others, the quality of that time will be improved enough that people around you will feel better about their relationships with you.

IT IS OKAY TO ASK FOR ALONE TIME.

→ Taking time for yourself is okay, even when you are the parent of young children. It should be completely normative and acceptable to say to someone whom you are close with, "I love you, I love spending time with you, but right now I need a few hours by myself."

Acknowledgments

It is not at all lost on me that although I wrote this book mostly sitting alone at my computer, it was very much the culmination of a group effort.

On the professional side, I owe a debt of profound gratitude to my agent, Jennifer Weis, who introduced me to the world of publishing outside of academics, gently nudged and prodded me as we shaped the central spine of this book, shepherded me through all the stages of this complex process, and supported and encouraged me as I stumbled along the way to finding my narrative voice. The raw clay of this book was also sculpted with virtuosity by my editor, Ian Straus, at Simon & Schuster. From the big ideas to the minutiae, Ian's guidance was invaluable: he talked me through all the hard stuff, and this book is inestimably better as a result. Thank you also to the rest of the incredible team at Simon & Schuster, who expertly and seamlessly navigated me through all the different stages of turning my text into a book.

I also had lots of help in crafting that text. My profound gratitude to Tiffany Cheng, Alyssa Nolan, Jaimie Coplan, and Christy Lenhardt for providing detailed feedback on earlier drafts. You made this book so much better in ways that I could not have envisioned. And thank you to Marwa Ibrahim for helping to research quotations, stories, and "fun facts" to include in the book.

On the academic side, this book does not exist without my longtime mentor and friend, Ken Rubin, who started me on my academic journey and continues to inspire me more than thirty-five years later. I have also had the immense honor and pleasure to collaborate with brilliant scholars. I have learned so much from these colleagues, and we have done such good work together. But most wonderfully, they have become friends. In particular, I would like to acknowledge the contributions of previous and ongoing collaborators: Julie Bowker, Linda Rose-Krasnor, Barry Schneider, Xinyin Chen, Junsheng Liu, Stefania Sette, Yan Li, Xuechen Ding, Dan Li, Mona Bekkhus, Sandra Bosacki, Larry Nelson, Geir Nyborg, Fitri Abidin, Ray Crozier, Liv Mjelve, and Evalill Bølstad.

And, of course, my collaborators also include my incredible students, who are the lifeblood of my career. They bring me pride and joy, and I learn from them every day. My apologies for the long list, but the contributions of my previous and current graduate students cannot go unacknowledged: Alicia McVarnock, Tiffany Cheng, Anna Stone, Megan DeGroot, Alyssa Nolan, Will Hipson, Kristen Archbell, Bowen Xiao, Laura Ooi, Amanda Bullock, Mila Kingsbury, Kathleen Hughes, Kathleen Wood, Murray Weeks, Kimberly Arbeau, Mandy Armer, Adrienne Matheson, Leanne Findlay, Kavita Prakash, Daniel Seguin, Morgan Dufour, Lori Watanabe, Danielle Baldwin, Noelle Strickland, Gabriella Nocita, Alison Kirkpatrick, Amy Epstein, Jessica Paul, Daniel Totten, Adam Kingsbury, Claire Rowsell, Allison Graham, Alberta Girardi, Julie Desjardins, Dana Stimpson, Marie-Helene Gavinski-Molina, Kim O'Neil, Catherine Mills, and Caryn Moulton.

To my parents, Barbara and Stephen, and siblings, Ellen, Janet, and Jeff, thank you for your endless love and support. Joe, I really appreciated our long talks as I muddled my way through various parts of this process. Adam and Jai, my love for you knows no bounds—and you fill me with pride and amazement every day. And I appreciate you allowing me to share a few stories about you in here. Gabby and Angie, thank you for letting me be a part of your lives. And, of course, Christy, who understands my need for solitude but shows me every day how it can also be better together.

Bibliography

Chapter 1
I Am Alone: Introducing Solitude

Buttrick, N., H. Choi, T. D. Wilson, et al. "Cross-cultural consistency and relativity in the enjoyment of thinking versus doing." *Journal of Personality and Social Psychology* 117, no. 5 (2019): e71–e83. https://doi.org/10.1037/pspp0000198.

Coplan, R. J., and K. H. Rubin. "Exploring and assessing nonsocial play in the preschool: The development and validation of the Preschool Play Behavior Scale." *Social Development* 7, no. 1 (1998): 72–91. https://doi.org/10.1111/1467-9507.00052.

Coplan, R. J., K. H. Rubin, N. A. Fox, S. D. Calkins, and S. Stewart. "Being alone, playing alone, and acting alone: Distinguishing among reticence and passive and active solitude in young children." *Child Development* 65, no. 1 (1994): 129–37. https://doi.org/10.1111/j.1467-8624.1994.tb00739.x.

Coplan, R. J., M. H. Gavinski-Molina, D. G. Lagacé-Séguin, and C. Wichmann. "When girls versus boys play alone: Nonsocial play and adjustment in kindergarten." *Developmental Psychology* 37, no. 4 (2001): 464–74. https://doi.org/10.1037/0012-1649.37.4.464.

Wilson, T. D., D. A. Reinhard, E. C. Westgate, et al. "Just think: The challenges of the disengaged mind." *Science* 345, no. 6192 (2014): 75–77. http://dx.doi.org/10.1126/science.1250830.

Chapter 2
I Think I'm Alone Now: What Solitude Is (and Is Not)

Bowker, J. C., L. L. Ooi, R. J. Coplan, and R. G. Etkin. "When is it okay to be alone? Gender differences in normative beliefs about social withdrawal in emerging adulthood." *Sex Roles* 82 (2020): 482–92. https://doi.org/10.1007/s11199-019-01065-5.

Campbell, S. W., and M. Q. Ross. "Re-conceptualizing solitude in the digital era: From 'being alone' to 'noncommunication.'" *Communication Theory* 32, no. 3 (2022): 387–406. https://doi.org/10.1093/ct/qtab021.

Dadds, M. R., and L. A. Tully. "What is it to discipline a child: What should it be? A reanalysis of time-out from the perspective of child mental health, attachment, and trauma." *American Psychologist* 74, no. 7 (2019): 794–808. https://doi.org/10.1037/amp0000449.

Hipson, W. E., S. Kiritchenko, S. M. Mohammad, and R. J. Coplan. "Examining the language of solitude versus loneliness in tweets." *Journal of Social and Personal Relationships* 38, no. 5 (2021): 1596–1610. https://doi.org/10.1177/0265407521998460.

Kretzler, B., H. H. König, and A. Hajek. "Pet ownership, loneliness, and social isolation: A systematic review." *Social Psychiatry and Psychiatric Epidemiology* 57 (2022): 1935–57. https://doi.org/10.1007/s00127-022-02332-9.

Muris, P., and T. H. Ollendick. "Contemporary hermits: A developmental psychopathology account of extreme social withdrawal (hikikomori) in young people." *Clinical Child and Family Psychology Review* 26 (2023): 459–81. https://doi.org/10.1007/s10567-023-00425-8.

Ratner, R. K., and R. W. Hamilton. "Inhibited from bowling alone." *Journal of Consumer Research* 42, no. 2 (2015): 266–83. https://doi.org/10.1093/jcr/ucv012.

Wood, K. R., R. J. Coplan, W. E. Hipson, and J. C. Bowker. "Normative beliefs about social withdrawal in adolescence." *Journal of Research on Adolescence* 32, no. 1 (2022): 372–81. https://doi.org/10.1111/jora.12617.

Chapter 3
Why Solitude Gets a Bad Rap: I've Got a Theory

Allen, K.-A., D. L. Gray, R. F. Baumeister, and M. R. Leary. "The need to belong: A deep dive into the origins, implications, and future of a foundational construct." *Educational Psychology Review* 34 (2022): 1133–56. https://doi.org/10.1007/s10648-021-09633-6.

Baumeister, R. F., and M. R. Leary. "The need to belong: Desire for interpersonal attachments as a fundamental human motivation." *Psychological Bulletin* 117, no. 3 (1995): 497–529. https://doi.org/10.1037/0033-2909.117.3.497.

Boyce, W. T., P. O'Neill-Wagner, C. S. Price, M. Haines, and S. J. Suomi. "Crowding stress and violent injuries among behaviorally inhibited rhesus macaques." *Health Psychology* 17, no. 3 (1998): 285–89. https://doi.org/10.1037/0278-6133.17.3.285.

Brown, G. E., M. C. O. Ferrari, P. H. Malka, L. Kayello, and D. P. Chivers. "Retention of acquired predator recognition among shy versus bold juvenile rainbow trout." *Behavioral Ecology and Sociobiology* 67 (2013): 43–51. https://doi.org/10.1007/s00265-012-1422-4.

Chen, X. "Culture, temperament, and social and psychological adjustment." *Developmental Review* 50a (2018): 42–53. https://doi.org/10.1016/j.dr.2018.03.004.

Epley, N., and J. Schroeder. "Mistakenly seeking solitude." *Journal of Experimental Psychology: General* 143, no. 5 (2014): 1980–99. https://doi.org/10.1037/a0037323.

Reis, H. T., S. D. O'Keefe, and R. D. Lane. "Fun is more fun when others are involved." *Journal of Positive Psychology* 12, no. 6 (2017): 547–57. https://doi.org/10.1080/17439760.2016.1221123.

Stavrova, O., and D. Ren. "Is more always better? Examining the nonlinear association of social contact frequency with physical health and longevity." *Social Psychological and Personality Science* 12, no. 6 (2021): 1058–70. https://doi.org/10.1177/1948550620961589.

Triplett, N. "The dynamogenic factors in pacemaking and competition." *American Journal of Psychology* 9, no. 4 (1898): 507–533. https://doi.org/10.2307/1412188.

Chapter 4
Not Only the Lonely: Confronting the Very Worst of Solitude

Cacioppo, J. T., S. Cacioppo, and D. I. Boomsma. "Evolutionary mechanisms for loneliness." *Cognition and Emotion* 28, no. 1 (2014): 3–21. https://doi.org/10.1080/02699931.2013.837379.

Chotpitayasunondh, V., and K. M. Douglas. "The effects of 'phubbing' on social interaction." *Journal of Applied Social Psychology* 48, no. 6 (2018): 304–316. https://doi.org/10.1111/jasp.12506.

Eisenberger, N. I., M. D. Lieberman, and K. D. Williams. "Does rejection hurt? An fMRI study of social exclusion." *Science* 302, no. 5643 (2003): 290–92. https://doi.org/10.1126/science.1089134.

Fox, N. A., K. H. Rubin, S. D. Calkins, et al. "Frontal activation asymmetry and social competence at four years of age." *Child Development* 66, no. 6 (1995): 1770–84. https://doi.org/10.2307/1131909.

Hawkley, L. C., S. Buecker, T. Kaiser, and M. Luhmann. "Loneliness from young adulthood to old age: Explaining age differences in loneliness." *International Journal of Behavioral Development* 46, no. 1 (2022): 39–49. https://doi.org/10.1177/0165025420971048.

Howard, M. C., J. E. Cogswell, and M. B. Smith. "The antecedents and outcomes of workplace ostracism: A meta-analysis." *Journal of Applied Psychology* 105, no. 6 (2020): 577–96. https://doi.org/10.1037/apl0000453.

Lemay, E. P., J. Cutri Jr., and N. Teneva. "How loneliness undermines close relationships and persists over time: The role of perceived regard and care." *Journal of Personality and Social Psychology* 127, no. 3 (2024): 609–637. https://doi.org/10.1037/pspi0000451.

Poon, K.-T., Y. Jiang, and F. Teng. "Putting oneself in someone's shoes: The effect of observing ostracism on physical pain, social pain, negative emotion, and self-regulation." *Personality and Individual Differences* 166, no. 110217 (2020). https://doi.org/10.1016/j.paid.2020.110217.

Stavrova, O., and D. Ren. "Alone in a crowd: Is social contact associated with less psychological pain of loneliness in everyday life?" *Journal of Happiness Studies* 24 (2023): 1841–60. https://doi.org/10.1007/s10902-023-00661-3.

Wade, M., J. Parson, K. L. Humphreys, et al. "The Bucharest Early Intervention Project: Adolescent mental health and adaptation following early deprivation." *Child Development Perspectives* 16, no. 3 (2022): 157–64. https://doi.org/10.1111/cdep.12462.

Wang, F., Y. Gao, Z. Han, et al. "A systematic review and meta-analysis of 90 cohort studies of social isolation, loneliness and mortality." *Nature Human Behavior* 7 (2023): 1307–1319. https://doi.org/10.1038/s41562-023-01617-6.

Wang, P., L. Yin, M. Ouyang, et al. "Parental phubbing, loneliness, and adolescent materialism: A cross-lagged panel study." *Mobile Media & Communication* 13, no. 1 (2025): 255–75. https://doi.org/10.1177/20501579241297941.

Williams, K. D., and B. Jarvis. "Cyberball: A program for use in research on interpersonal ostracism and acceptance." *Behavior Research Methods* 38 (2006): 174–80. https://doi.org/10.3758/BF03192765.

Williams, K. D., C. K. T. Cheung, and W. Choi. "Cyberostracism: Effects of being ignored over the internet." *Journal of Personality and Social Psychology* 79, no. 5 (2000): 748–62. https://doi.org/10.1037/0022-3514.79.5.748.

Xiao, B., N. Parent, J. Shapka, and R. J. Coplan. "How do young adults feel about receiving 'likes' on social media? The moderating roles of shyness and cyber-victimization." *Emerging Adulthood* (2025).

Zeanah, C. H., C. A. Nelson, N. A. Fox, et al. "Designing research to study the effects of institutionalization on brain and behavioral development: The Bucharest Early Intervention Project." *Development and Psychopathology* 15, no. 4 (2003): 885–907. https://doi.org/10.1017/s0954579403000452.

Chapter 5
Well Enough Alone? I've Got a Theory

Berman, M. G., J. Jonides, and S. Kaplan. "The cognitive benefits of interacting with nature." *Psychological Science* 19, no. 12 (2008): 1207–212. https://doi.org/10.1111/j.1467-9280.2008.02225.x.

Hanley, A. W., V. Dehili, D. Krzanowski, et al. "Effects of video-guided group vs. solitary meditation on mindfulness and social connectivity: A pilot study." *Clinical Social Work Journal* 50 (2022): 316–24. https://doi.org/10.1007/s10615-021-00812-0.

Jo, H., C. Song, and Y. Miyazaki. "Physiological benefits of viewing nature: A systematic review of indoor experiments." *International Journal of Environmental Research and Public Health* 16, no. 23 (2019): 4739. https://doi.org/10.3390/ijerph16234739.

Kaplan, R., and S. Kaplan. *The Experience of Nature: A Psychological Perspective*. Cambridge University Press, 1989.

Kaplan, S. "The restorative benefits of nature: Toward an integrative framework." *Journal of Environmental Psychology* 15, no. 3 (1995): 169–82. https://doi.org/10.1016/0272-4944(95)90001-2.

Long, C. R., and J. R. Averill. "Solitude: An exploration of benefits of being alone." *Journal for the Theory of Social Behavior* 33, no. 1 (2003): 21–44. https://doi.org/10.1111/1468-5914.00204.

Maslow, A. H. "A theory of human motivation." *Psychological Review* 50, no. 4 (1943): 370–96. https://doi.org/10.1037/h0054346.

McVarnock, A., R. J. Coplan, B. De Zoysa Siriwardene, and A. Stone. "Is solitude in our nature? Emerging adults' anticipated affective responses to spending time alone vs. with others in natural vs. indoor environments." Paper presented at the Biennial Meeting of the International Society for the Study of Behavioural Development, Lisbon, Portugal, June 18, 2024.

Nguyen, T. T., R. M. Ryan, and E. L. Deci. "Solitude as an approach to affective self-regulation." *Personality and Social Psychology Bulletin* 44, no. 1 (2018): 92–106. https://doi.org/10.1177/0146167217733073.

Nikitin, J., F. S. Rupprecht, and C. Ristl. "Experiences of solitude in adulthood and old age: The role of autonomy." *International Journal of Behavioral Development* 46, no. 6 (2022): 510–19. https://doi.org/10.1177/01650254221117498.

Ryan, R. M., and E. L. Deci. "Self-determination theory and the facilitation of intrinsic motivation, social development, and well-being." *American Psychologist* 55, no. 1 (2000): 68–78. https://doi.org/10.1037/0003-066X.55.1.68.

Thomas, V., and M. Azmitia. "Motivation matters: Development and validation of the Motivation for Solitude Scale—Short Form (MSS-SF)." *Journal of Adolescence* 70, no. 1 (2019): 33–42. https://doi.org/10.1016/j.adolescence.2018.11.004.

Weinstein, N., M. Vuorre, M. Adams, and T.-V. Nguyen. "Balance between solitude and socializing: Everyday solitude time both benefits and harms well-being." *Scientific Reports* 13 (2023): e21160. https://doi.org/10.1038/s41598-023-44507-7.

Chapter 6
When Solitude Is "Just Right": Aloneliness and the Goldilocks Principle

Abidin, F. A., G. N. Sunardy, W. Yudiana, Y. Alverina, and R. J. Coplan. "Assessment and correlates of aloneliness among Indonesian adolescents." *Heliyon* 10, no. 7 (2024): e28862. https://doi.org/10.1016/j.heliyon.2024.e28862.

Brunetti, M., S. Sette, E. Longobardi, F. Laghi, and R. J. Coplan. "Loneliness and aloneliness as mediators of the associations between social withdrawal and internalizing problems in late childhood and early adolescence." *Journal of Early Adolescence* 44, no. 6 (2024): 790–814. https://doi.org/10.1177/02724316231207282.

Coplan, R. J., W. E. Hipson, and J. C. Bowker. "Social withdrawal and aloneliness in adolescence: Examining the implications of too much and not enough solitude." *Journal of Youth and Adolescence* 50, no. 6 (2021): 1219–33. https://doi.org/10.1007/s10964-020-01365-0.

Coplan, R. J., W. E. Hipson, K. A. Archbell, et al. "Seeking more solitude: Conceptualization, assessment, and implications of aloneliness." *Personality and Individual Differences* 148 (2019): 17–26. https://doi.org/10.1016/j.paid.2019.05.020.

Luo, M., T. Pauly, C. Röcke, and G. Hülür. "Alternating time spent on social interactions and solitude in healthy older adults." *British Journal of Psychology* 113, no. 4 (2022): 987–1008. https://doi.org/10.1111/bjop.12586.

McVarnock, A., R. J. Coplan, H. I. White, and J. C. Bowker. "Looking beyond time alone: An examination of solitary activities in emerging adulthood." *Journal of Personality* 93, no 1 (2025): 81–100. https://doi.org/10.1111/jopy.12905.

"On the Uses of Solitude." In *The Voice of Experience*. Grosset & Dunlap, 1933.

Przybylski, A. K., and N. Weinstein. "A large-scale test of the Goldilocks hypothesis: Quantifying the relations between digital-screen use and the mental well-being of adolescents." *Psychological Science* 28, no. 2 (2017): 204–215. https://doi.org/10.1177/0956797616678438.

Swets, J. A., and C. R. Cox. "Aloneliness predicts relational anger and aggression toward romantic partners." *Aggressive Behavior* 48, no. 5 (2022): 512–23. https://doi.org/10.1002/ab.22044.

Uziel, L., and T. Schmidt-Barad. "Choice matters more with others: Choosing to be with other people is more consequential to well-being than choosing to be alone." *Journal of Happiness Studies* 23 (2022): 2469–89. https://doi.org/10.1007/s10902-022-00506-5.

Yang, P., R. J. Coplan, Y. Zhang, X. Ding, and Z. Zhu. "Assessment and implications of aloneliness in Chinese children and early adolescents." *Journal of Applied Developmental Psychology* 85 (2023): 101514. https://doi.org/10.1016/j.appdev.2023.101514.

Chapter 7
Loners & Homebodies & Introverts, Oh My!
The Memes Versus Realities of Preferring Solitude

Anglim, J., and S. Horwood. "Effect of the COVID-19 pandemic and Big Five personality on subjective and psychological well-being." *Social Psychological and Personality Science* 12, no. 8 (2021): 1527–37. https://doi.org/10.1177/1948550620983047.

Buecker, S., M. Maes, J. J. A. Denissen, and M. Luhmann. "Loneliness and the Big Five personality traits: A meta-analysis." *European Journal of Personality* 34, no. 1 (2020): 8–28. https://doi.org/10.1002/per.2229.

Cain, S. *Quiet: The Power of Introverts in a World That Can't Stop Talking*. Crown Publishers, 2012.

Cheng, T., A. McVarnock, A. Stone, and R. J. Coplan. "Let's run a vibe check! Automatically coding qualitative responses about attitudes towards solitude with natural language processing techniques." Poster presented at the Biennial Meeting of the International Society for the Study of Behavioral Development, Lisbon, Portugal, June 17, 2024.

Coplan, R. J., L. L. Ooi, and G. Nocita. "When one is company and two is a crowd: Why some children prefer solitude." *Child Development Perspectives* 9, no. 3 (2015): 133–37. https://doi.org/10.1111/cdep.12131.

Eysenck, H. J., and M. W. Eysenck. *Personality and Individual Differences: A Natural Science Approach*. Plenum Press, 1985.

Hatano, A., C. Ogulmus, H. Shigemasu, and K. Murayama. "Thinking about thinking: People underestimate how enjoyable and engaging just waiting is." *Journal of Experimental Psychology: General* 151, no. 12 (2022): 3213–29. https://doi.org/10.1037/xge0001255.

Jacques-Hamilton, R., J. Sun, and L. D. Smillie. "Costs and benefits of acting extraverted: A randomized controlled trial." *Journal of Experimental Psychology: General* 148, no. 9 (2019): 1538–56. https://doi.org/10.1037/xge0000516.

Jung, C. G. *The Collected Works of C. G. Jung*. Edited by R. F. C. Hull, translated by H. G. Baynes. Vol. 6, *Psychological Types*. Bollingen Series 20. Princeton University Press, 1971.

Kroencke, L., S. Humberg, S. M. Breil, et al. "Extraversion, social interactions, and well-being during the COVID-19 pandemic: Did extraverts really suffer more than introverts?" *Journal of Personality and Social Psychology* 125, no. 3 (2023): 649–79. https://doi.org/10.1037/pspp0000468.

Margolis, S., and S. Lyubomirsky. "Experimental manipulation of extraverted and introverted behavior and its effects on well-being." *Journal of Experimental Psychology: General* 149, no. 4 (2020): 719–31. https://doi.org/10.1037/xge0000668.

Ren, D., and O. Stavrova. "Does a pandemic context attenuate people's negative perception and meta-perception of solitude?" *International Journal of Psychology* 58, no. 2 (2023): 134–42. https://doi.org/10.1002/ijop.12885.

Ren, D., O. Stavrova, and A. M. Evans. "Does dispositional preference for solitude predict better psychological outcomes during times of social distancing? Beliefs and reality." *Journal of Personality* 91, no. 6 (2023): 1442–60. https://doi.org/10.1111/jopy.12821.

Ren, D., W. W. Loh, J. M. Chung, and M. J. Brandt. "Person-specific priorities in solitude." *Journal of Personality* 93, no 1 (2025): 12–30. https://doi.org/10.1111/jopy.12916.

Zelenski, J. M., M. S. Santoro, and D. C. Whelan. "Would introverts be better off if they acted more like extraverts? Exploring emotional and cognitive consequences of counterdispositional behavior." *Emotion* 12, no. 2 (2012): 290–303. https://doi.org/10.1037/a0025169.

Chapter 8
Learning to Play Solo: How to Do Solitude Better

Fredrick, J. W., K. Nagle, J. M. Langberg, et al. "Rumination as a mechanism of the longitudinal association between COVID-19-related stress and internalizing symptoms in adolescents." *Child Psychiatry and Human Development* 55 (2024): 531–40. https://doi.org/10.1007/s10578-022-01435-3.

Hipson, W. E., R. J. Coplan, M. Dufour, et al. "Time alone well spent? A person-centered analysis of adolescents' solitary activities." *Social Development* 30, no. 4 (2021): 1114–30. https://doi.org/10.1111/sode.12518.

Jamieson, J. P., W. B. Mendes, E. Blackstock, and T. Schmader. "Turning the knots in your stomach into bows: Reappraising arousal improves performance on the GRE." *Journal of Experimental Social Psychology* 46, no. 1 (2010): 208–12. https://doi.org/10.1016/j.jesp.2009.08.015.

Kwapil, T. R., P. J. Silvia, I. Myin-Germeys, et al. "The social world of the socially anhedonic: Exploring the daily ecology of asociality." *Journal of Research in Personality* 43, no. 1 (2009): 103–106. https://doi.org/10.1016/j.jrp.2008.10.008.

Rodriguez, M., B. W. Bellet, and R. J. McNally. "Reframing time spent alone: Reappraisal buffers the emotional effects of isolation." *Cognitive Therapy and Research* 44 (2020): 1052–67. https://doi.org/10.1007/s10608-020-10128-x.

Rodriguez, M., S. Pratt, B. W. Bellet, and R. J. McNally. "Solitude can be good—if you see it as such: Reappraisal helps lonely people experience solitude more positively." *Journal of Personality* 93, no 1 (2025): 118–35. https://doi.org/10.1111/jopy.12887.

Watkins, E. R., and H. Roberts. "Reflecting on rumination: Consequences, causes, mechanisms and treatment of rumination." *Behaviour Research and Therapy* 127 (2020): e103573. https://doi.org/10.1016/j.brat.2020.103573.

Yan, K. S., and R. Dando. "A crossmodal role for audition in taste perception." *Journal of Experimental Psychology: Human Perception and Performance* 41, no. 3 (2015): 590–96. http://dx.doi.org/10.1037/xhp0000044.

Chapter 9
Making It Alone: How Solitude Can Enhance Your Creative Side

Baird, B., J. Smallwood, M. D. Mrazek, et al. "Inspired by distraction: Mind wandering facilitates creative incubation." *Psychological Science* 23, no. 10 (2012): 1117–22. https://doi.org/10.1177/0956797612446024.

Baldwin, C. L., D. M. Roberts, D. Barragan, et al. "Detecting and quantifying mind wandering during simulated driving." *Frontiers in Human Neuroscience* 11 (2017): 406. https://doi.org/10.3389/fnhum.2017.00406.

Bowker, J. C., M. T. Stotsky, and R. G. Etkin. "How BIS/BAS and psycho-behavioral variables distinguish between social withdrawal subtypes during emerging adulthood." *Personality and Individual Differences* 119 (2017): 283–88. https://doi.org/10.1016/j.paid.2017.07.043.

Cai, X., J. Cebollada, and M. Cortiñas. "Self-report measure of dispositional flow experience in the video game context: Conceptualisation and scale development." *International Journal of Human-Computer Studies* 159 (2022): e102746. https://doi.org/10.1016/j.ijhcs.2021.102746.

Csikszentmihalyi, M. *Flow: The Psychology of Optimal Experience*. Harper & Row, 1990.

Gable, S. L., E. A. Hopper, and J. W. Schooler. "When the Muses strike: Creative ideas of physicists and writers routinely occur during mind wandering." *Psychological Science* 30, no. 3 (2019): 396–404. https://doi.org/10.1177/0956797618820626.

Galanaki, E. P., and K. D. Malafantis. "Loneliness and solitude in gifted writers: The legacies of childhood." *Journal of Psychosocial Studies* 17, no. 1 (2024): 77–97. http://dx.doi.org/10.1332/14786737Y2024D000000012.

Gilhooly, K. J., G. Georgiou, and U. Devery. "Incubation and creativity: Do something different." *Thinking & Reasoning* 19, no. 2 (2013): 137–49. https://doi.org/10.1080/13546783.2012.749812.

Irving, Z. C., C. McGrath, L. Flynn, A. Glasser, and C. Mills. "The shower effect: Mind wandering facilitates creative incubation during moderately engaging activities." *Psychology of Aesthetics, Creativity, and the Arts* 18, no 6 (2024): 1096–1107. https://doi.org/10.1037/aca0000516.

Korde, R., and P. B. Paulus. "Alternating individual and group idea generation: Finding the elusive synergy." *Journal of Experimental Social Psychology* 70 (2017): 177–90. https://doi.org/10.1016/j.jesp.2016.11.002.

Kyaga, S., M. Landén, M. Boman, et al. "Mental illness, suicide and creativity: 40-year prospective total population study." *Journal of Psychiatric Research* 47, no. 1 (2013): 83–90. https://doi.org/10.1016/j.jpsychires.2012.09.010.

Liu, T., and M. Csikszentmihalyi. "Flow among introverts and extraverts in solitary and social activities." *Personality and Individual Differences* 167 (2020): e110197. https://doi.org/10.1016/j.paid.2020.110197.

Ovington, L. A., A. J. Saliba, C. C. Moran, J. Goldring, and J. B. MacDonald. "Do people really have insights in the shower? The when, where and who of the aha! moment." *Journal of Creative Behavior* 52, no. 1 (2018): 21–34. https://doi.org/10.1002/jocb.126.

Paulus, P. B., J. B. Kenworthy, and L. R. Marusich. "Alone Versus Together: Finding the Right Balance for Creativity." In *The Handbook of Solitude: Psychological Perspectives on Social Isolation, Social Withdrawal, and Being Alone*. 2nd ed. Edited by R. J. Coplan, J. C. Bowker, and L. J. Nelson. Wiley Blackwell, 2021.

Ruby, F. J. M., J. Smallwood, H. Engen, and T. Singer. "How self-generated thought shapes mood—the relation between mind-wandering and mood depends on the socio-temporal content of thoughts." *PLOS ONE* 8, no. 10 (2013): e77554. https://doi.org/10.1371/journal.pone.0077554.

Simonton, D. K. "Creativity and psychopathology: The tenacious mad-genius controversy updated." *Current Opinion in Behavioral Sciences* 27 (2019): 17–21. https://doi.org/10.1016/j.cobeha.2018.07.006.

Smallwood, J., and J. W. Schooler. "The science of mind wandering: Empirically navigating the stream of consciousness." *Annual Review of Psychology* 66 (2015): 487–518. https://doi.org/10.1146/annurev-psych-010814-015331.

Spreng, R. N., E. Dimas, L. Mwilambwe-Tshilobo, et al. "The default network of the human brain is associated with perceived social isolation." *Nature Communications* 11 (2020): e6393. https://doi.org/10.1038/s41467-020-20039-w.

Wallas, G. *The Art of Thought*. Jonathan Cape, 1926.

Wallimann, M., S. Peleg, and T. Pauly. "Time-savoring moderates associations of solitude with depressive mood, loneliness, and somatic symptoms in older adults' daily life." *Applied Psychology: Health and Well-Being* 16, no. 3 (2024): 1497–1515. https://doi.org/10.1111/aphw.12538.

Chapter 10
Me, Myself, and AI: How to Be Alone with Your Phone

Barry, C. T., E. E. Smith, M. B. Murphy, B. M. Halter, and J. Briggs. "JOMO: Joy of missing out and its association with social media use, self-perception, and mental health." *Telematics and Informatics Reports* 10 (2023): e100054. https://doi.org/10.1016/j.teler.2023.100054.

Burnell, K., M. J. George, and M. K. Underwood. "New Media and Solitude: Implications for Peer Relations." In *The Handbook of Solitude: Psychological Perspectives on Social Isolation, Social Withdrawal, and Being Alone*. 2nd ed. Edited by R. J. Coplan, J. C. Bowker, and L. J. Nelson. Wiley Blackwell, 2021.

Campbell, S. W., and M. Q. Ross. "Re-conceptualizing solitude in the digital era: From 'being alone' to 'noncommunication.'" *Communication Theory* 32, no. 3 (2022): 387–406. https://doi.org/10.1093/ct/qtab021.

Coplan, R. J., A. McVarnock, W. E. Hipson, and J. C. Bowker. "Alone with my phone? Examining beliefs about solitude and technology use in adolescence." *International Journal of Behavioral Development* 46, no. 6 (2022): 481–89. https://doi.org/10.1177/01650254221113460.

Coyne, S. M., L. A. Stockdale, W. Warburton, et al. "Pathological video game symptoms from adolescence to emerging adulthood: A 6-year longitudinal study of trajectories, predictors, and outcomes." *Developmental Psychology* 56, no. 7 (2020): 1385–96. https://doi.org/10.1037/dev0000939.

Diefenbach, S., and K. Borrmann. "The smartphone as a pacifier and its consequences: Young adults' smartphone usage in moments of solitude and correlations to self-reflection." Paper presented at the Proceedings of the 2019 CHI Conference on Human Factors in Computing Systems, Glasgow, Scotland, May 2019. https://doi.org/10.1145/3290605.3300536.

Hygen, B. W., V. Skalicka, R. J. Coplan, et al. "Norwegian adolescents in the initial stages of COVID-19 restrictions: Links between interactions, digital media use, loneliness, and mental health problems." *Journal of Media Psychology* 36, no. 5 (2024): 317–29. https://doi.org/10.1027/1864-1105/a000401.

Jerz, D. G. "Somewhere nearby is colossal cave: Examining Will Crowther's original 'Adventure' in code and in Kentucky." *Digital Humanities Quarterly* 1, no. 2 (2007). https://www.digitalhumanities.org/dhq/vol/1/2/000009/000009.html.

Kraut, R., M. Patterson, V. Lundmark, et al. "Internet paradox: A social technology that reduces social involvement and psychological well-being?" *American Psychologist* 53, no. 9 (1998): 1017–31. https://doi.org/10.1037/0003-066X.53.9.1017.

Przybylski, A. K., K. Murayama, C. R. DeHaan, and V. Gladwell. "Motivational, emotional, and behavioral correlates of fear of missing out." *Computers in Human Behavior* 29, no. 4 (2013): 1841–48. https://doi.org/10.1016/j.chb.2013.02.014.

Radtke, T., T. Apel, K. Schenkel, J. Keller, and E. von Lindern. "Digital detox: An effective solution in the smartphone era? A systematic literature review." *Mobile*

Media & Communication 10, no. 2 (2022): 190–215. https://doi.org/10.1177/20501579211028647.

Rodríguez-García, A.-M., A.-J. Moreno-Guerrero, and J. López Belmonte. "Nomophobia: An individual's growing fear of being without a smartphone—a systematic literature review. *International Journal of Environmental Research and Public Health* 17, no. 2 (2020): 580. https://doi.org/10.3390/ijerph17020580.

Stevic, A., K. Koban, A. Binder, and J. Matthes. "You are not alone: Smartphone use, friendship satisfaction, and anxiety during the COVID-19 crisis." *Mobile Media & Communication* 10, no. 2 (2022): 294–315. https://doi.org/10.1177/20501579211051820.

Thomas, V., B. Balzer Carr, M. Azmitia, and S. Whittaker. "Alone and online: Understanding the relationships between social media, solitude, and psychological adjustment." *Psychology of Popular Media* 10, no. 2 (2021): 201–11. https://doi.org/10.1037/ppm0000287.

World Health Organization. "Addictive Behaviours: Gaming Disorder." October 22, 2020. http://www.who.int/features/qa/gaming-disorder/en/.

Chapter 11
Growing Up Alone: How to Promote Healthy Solitude in Children

Abidin, F. A., E. Fitriana, V. Anindhita, et al. "Parental burnout assessment: Validation in Indonesian parents." *Mental Health & Prevention 36* (2024): 200372. https://doi.org/10.1016/j.mhp.2024.200372

Archbell, K. A., R. J. Coplan, and L. Rose-Krasnor. "What did your child do today? Describing young children's daily activities outside of school." *Journal of Early Childhood Research* 18, no. 2 (2020): 189–99. https://doi.org/10.1177/1476718X19898724.

Coplan, R. J., J. P. Weingarten, J. C. Bowker, L. L. Ooi, and K. Archbell. "Maternal beliefs about the costs and benefits of solitude in childhood and adolescence." *Journal of Child and Family Studies* 33 (2024): 1517–30. https://doi.org/10.1007/s10826-023-02713-x.

Coplan, R. J., L. L. Ooi, and D. Baldwin. "Does it matter when we want to be alone? Exploring developmental timing effects in the implications of unsociability." In "Personality Development from Multiple Perspectives and Contexts," ed. L. A. Schmidt. Special issue, *New Ideas in Psychology* 53 (2019): 47–57. https://doi.org/10.1016/j.newideapsych.2018.01.001.

Coplan, R. J., L. L. Ooi, and L. Rose-Krasnor. "Naturalistic observations of schoolyard social participation: Marker variables for socio-emotional functioning in early adolescence." *Journal of Early Adolescence* 35, no. 5–6 (2015): 628–50. https://doi.org/10.1177/0272431614523134.

Coplan, R. J., M. H. Gavinski-Molina, D. G. Lagacé-Séguin, and C. Wichmann. "When girls versus boys play alone: Nonsocial play and adjustment in kindergarten." *Developmental Psychology* 37, no. 4 (2001): 464–74. https://doi.org/10.1037/0012-1649.37.4.464.

Ginott, H. G. *Between Parent and Teenager.* Macmillan, 1969.

Hill, D., N. Ameenuddin, Y. Reid Chassiakos, et al. "Media and young minds." *Pediatrics* 138, no. 5 (2016): e20162591. https://doi.org/10.1542/peds.2016-2591.

Katz, J. C., and E. S. Buchholz. "'I did it myself': The necessity of solo play for preschoolers." *Early Child Development and Care* 155 (1999): 39–50. https://doi.org/10.1080/0030443991550104.

Larson, R. W. "The emergence of solitude as a constructive domain of experience in early adolescence." *Child Development* 68, no. 1 (1997): 80–93. https://doi.org/10.2307/1131927.

Larson, R. W. "The solitary side of life: An examination of the time people spend alone from childhood to old age." *Developmental Review* 10, no. 2 (1990): 155–83. https://doi.org/10.1016/0273-2297(90)90008-R.

Winnicott, D. W. "The Capacity to Be Alone (1958)." In *The Maturational Processes and the Facilitating Environment.* International Universities Press, 1965.

Chapter 12
Being Single or Being Alone Together: How to Navigate Solitude in Your Relationships

Adamczyk, K. "Current and Future Paths in Research on Singlehood." In *The Handbook of Solitude: Psychological Perspectives on Social Isolation, Social Withdrawal, and Being Alone.* 2nd ed. Edited by R. J. Coplan, J. C. Bowker, and L. J. Nelson. Wiley Blackwell, 2021.

Bhattacharya, K., A. Ghosh, D. Monsivais, R. Dunbar, and K. Kaski. "Absence makes the heart grow fonder: Social compensation when failure to interact risks weakening a relationship." *EPJ Data Science* 6 (2017): e1. https://doi.org/10.1140/epjds/s13688-016-0097-x.

Choi, Y., T. Pauly, E. Zambrano Garza, et al. "Having time to oneself in times of extended togetherness: Solitude experiences during the COVID-19 pandemic." *Applied Psychology: Health and Well-Being* 15, no. 1 (2023): 217–37. https://doi.org/10.1111/aphw.12401.

DePaulo, B. "Single and flourishing: Transcending the deficit narratives of single life." In "Theorizing Singlehood." Special issue, *Journal of Family Theory & Review* 15, no. 3 (2023): 389–411. https://doi.org/10.1111/jftr.12525.

Fredrickson, B. L. "The broaden-and-build theory of positive emotions." *Philosophical Transactions of the Royal Society B: Biological Sciences* 359, no. 1449 (2004): 1367–77. https://doi.org/10.1098/rstb.2004.1512.

Grover, S., and J. F. Helliwell. "How's life at home? New evidence on marriage and the set point for happiness." *Journal of Happiness Studies* 20 (2019): 373–90. https://doi.org/10.1007/s10902-017-9941-3.

Kersten, P., M. Mund, and F. J. Neyer. "Does living alone mean being alone? Personal networks of solo-living adults in midlife." *International Journal of Behavioral Development* 48, no. 1 (2024): 12–24. https://doi.org/10.1177/01650254231206329.

Long, H., S. Shi, Z. Tang, and S. Zhang. "Does living alone increase the consumption of social resources?" *Environmental Science and Pollution Research* 29 (2022): 71911–22. https://doi.org/10.1007/s11356-022-20892-w.

Manusov, V. "In praise of voluntary solitude: The 'fertile void' and its role in communication and relationships." *Atlantic Journal of Communication* 28, no. 1 (2020): 68–83. https://doi.org/10.1080/15456870.2020.1684158.

Roehling, P. V., and M. Bultman. "Does absence make the heart grow fonder? Work-related travel and marital satisfaction." *Sex Roles* 46 (2002): 279–93. https://doi.org/10.1023/A:1020272428817.

Rothwell, J. *Married People Are Living Their Best Lives*. Institute for Family Studies and Gallup, 2024. https://ifstudies.org/ifs-admin/resources/briefs/ifs-gallup-marriagewellbeingbrief-feb9.pdf.

Smith, K. J., and C. Victor. "Typologies of loneliness, living alone and social isolation, and their associations with physical and mental health." *Ageing & Society* 39, no. 8 (2019): 1709–730. https://doi.org/10.1017/S0144686X18000132.

Snell, K. D. M. "The rise of living alone and loneliness in history." *Social History* 42, no. 1 (2017): 2–28. https://doi.org/10.1080/03071022.2017.1256093.

Sundström, G., E. Fransson, B. Malmberg, and A. Davey. "Loneliness among older Europeans." *European Journal of Ageing* 6 (2009): 267–75. https://doi.org/10.1007/s10433-009-0134-8.

Weinstein, N., H. Hansen, and T. Nguyen. "Definitions of solitude in everyday life." *Personality and Social Psychology Bulletin* 49, no. 12 (2023): 1663–78. https://doi.org/10.1177/01461672221115941.

White, H. I., J. C. Bowker, R. E. Adams, and R. J. Coplan. "Solitude and affect during emerging adulthood: When, and for whom, spending time alone is related to positive and negative affect during social interactions." *International Journal of Behavioral Development* 46, no. 6 (2022): 490–99. https://doi.org/10.1177/01650254221133296.

Zambrano Garza, E., T. Pauly, Y. Choi, et al. "Daily solitude and well-being associations in older dyads: Evidence from daily life assessments." *Applied Psychology: Health and Well-Being*, 16, no. 1 (2024): 356–75. https://doi.org/10.1111/aphw.12494.

Chapter 13
Ending Up Alone: Some Final Thoughts About Solitude

Baek, E. C., R. Hyon, K. López, et al. "Lonely individuals process the world in idiosyncratic ways." *Psychological Science* 34, no. 6 (2023): 683–95. https://doi.org/10.1177/09567976221145316.

Bowker, J. C., S. Sette, L. L. Ooi, et al. "Cross-cultural measurement of social withdrawal motivations across 10 countries using multiple-group factor analysis alignment." *International Journal of Behavioral Development* 47, no. 2 (2023): 190–98. https://doi.org/10.1177/01650254221132774.

Hu, N., W. Zhang, A. Haidabieke, et al. "Associations between unsociability and peer problems in Chinese children and adolescents: A meta-analysis." *Behavioral Sciences* 14, no. 7 (2024): 590. https://doi.org/10.3390/bs14070590.

Huang, C., J. W. Butterworth, A. J. Finley, et al. "There is a party in my head and no one is invited: Resting-state electrocortical activity and solitude." *Journal of Personality*, 93, no 1 (2025): 155–73. https://doi.org/10.1111/jopy.12876.

Mazroui, K. Al, and M. Alzyoudi. "The role of ChatGPT in mitigating loneliness among older adults: An exploratory study." *Online Journal of Communication and Media Technologies* 14, no. 4 (2024): e202444. https://doi.org/10.30935/ojcmt/14777.

Xie, T., I. Pentina, and T. Hancock. "Friend, mentor, lover: does chatbot engagement lead to psychological dependence?" *Journal of Service Management* 34, no 4 (2023): 806–28.

World Population Ageing 2020 Highlights: Living Arrangements of Older Persons. United Nations Department of Economic and Social Affairs, 2020. https://www.un.org/development/desa/pd/sites/www.un.org.development.desa.pd/files/undesa_pd-2020_world_population_ageing_highlights.pdf.

Index

Index

About the Author

Robert J. Coplan, PhD, is a psychologist, researcher, teacher, and author who has been studying solitude for more than thirty years. He is a Chancellor's Professor in the Department of Psychology at Carleton University (Ottawa, Canada). Over the course of his career, he has authored more than two hundred academic papers and published five academic books, including *The Handbook of Solitude* and *Quiet at School: An Educator's Guide to Shy Children.* His research has been featured by *The New York Times, The Washington Post, Psychology Today, WebMD*, and National Public Radio. In his spare time, Robert plays piano and sings with a local band, drinks too much coffee, takes daily long walks along the water, and tries to find the right balance between enjoying the company of cherished others and basking in the calm of solitude.